ALSO PUBLISHED BY

Days in the Lives of Social Workers:
41 Professionals Tell Real-Life Stories from Social Work Practice

The New Social Worker:
The Magazine for Social Work Students and Recent Graduates

The Non-Profit Handbook: National Edition

The Non-Profit Internet Handbook

The Pennsylvania Non-Profit Handbook

THE SOCIAL WORKER'S INTERNET HANDBOOK

THE SOCIAL WORKER'S INTERNET HANDBOOK

Gary B. Grant
and
Linda May Grobman

Harrisburg, Pennsylvania

THE SOCIAL WORKER'S INTERNET HANDBOOK

Gary B. Grant and Linda May Grobman

Published by

White Hat Communications

222 Pine Street
P.O. Box 5390
Harrisburg, PA 17110-0390
717-238-3787

http://www.socialworker.com

ISBN: 0-9653653-5-2
Library of Congress Catalog Card Number: 98-90255

TABLE OF CONTENTS

Preface

Technology is, for many of us, a scary new "frontier." The new terms, jargon, and lingo are overwhelming. The culture is new. The very concepts and ways of thinking that arise are unfamiliar at first and may generate a certain fear of the unknown. Perhaps some people find this exciting and leap in with no discomfort, but for most, we doubt that this is the case.

While we hope this book will make the transition from unfamiliarity with cyberspace to a solid understanding of the Internet as easy as possible, you must also trust your own ability to grasp (eventually) all of the intricacies and facets of this new technology. For now, we can at least say that if we were able to learn it, so can you.

Do not be too put off by the terminology. Words that are unfamiliar in one place will become more familiar as you go on. It is not possible to define all the terms right up front, and much of it must be learned in context and through experience and practice. Do not get stuck wrestling with understanding any particular section, but rather forge forward and trust that your familiarity and understanding will come about soon enough.

This book is designed for all social workers, those who are using the Internet for the first time, as well as those who have already seriously begun to tap the richness of information and the variety of Internet tools in their work or personal lives. The first section of this book will provide an understanding of the Internet and the landscape described metaphorically as "cyberspace." The majority of the book, however, is intended as a "user's guide." We detail the ways the Internet can be incorporated into the activities performed by social workers every day.

It would be a monumental task to define all social work activities and to detail all the Internet resources applicable to those activities. Instead, look to this book for examples of the range of such activities. Our intent is to provide information about resources available on the Internet, free for the most part, that will help you accomplish your tasks more easily, better, or faster. If you find that your daily work is not adequately described in any of the sections, then we hope you will at least find valuable leads in thinking about how the Internet fits into your work.

There are several ways to use this manual. First, it can be reviewed as a whole. It is our hope that social workers will read this manual as a way to gain a practical understanding of what is and what is not available on the Internet—of what can be done, as well as what cannot—and why. In this regard, use this manual to:

1. *Determine if you would benefit from having access to the Internet and to what degree.*

2. *Make more informed choices about the cost effectiveness of newer computer purchases for yourself or your agency.*

3. *Determine specific ways to integrate the Internet into your existing work.* You will be able to find examples of the work social workers do and, we hope, find ways to utilize the Internet to reshape this work for the purpose of improving efficiency, becoming more effective, or having a broader impact on your clients.

4. *Determine if there are new activities to explore.* It is wise to distinguish between using the Internet for improving upon your existing responsibilities and for creating new ones. You will almost certainly find exciting new opportunities through the Internet, but be sure that these are undertaken only if they are truly a higher priority, or if they can be added thanks to the improved efficiency and time saved in other areas of responsibility.

A second way to use this book is as a desktop resource. Even with the most careful planning of your work, there will likely be times when your work finds you considering whether the best solution is to be found either the old way, whatever that may be, or online. In order to avoid a fruitless search, this book should help you in determining quickly and easily which route to take. In this regard, use this manual to:

1. *Have a ready reference manual at your fingertips for information about issues relating to the Internet.* Among these issues discussed in this book are Netiquette, trademark and copyright law, cryptography, virus transmission, and other general issues.

2. *Find information about how social workers are using the Internet.* What is working and what is not? We've interviewed social workers who are using the Internet every day, and we share their experiences with you.

3. *Locate specific sites with the information you need.* Start with the index, and find out whether the information you seek is listed here. Opening the book will be far less time-consuming than aimlessly surfing through the Internet.

A third use of this manual is as a tutorial for building your own Web site and planning its content and value to the rest of the Internet community. Once the Internet is demystified for you (and you may be surprised at how quickly this comes), you may find yourself assessing the value of contributing to its content. This book will not only offer a few tips on how to get started with this, but will help to ensure that what you do does not duplicate already existing Internet resources.

New Internet resources are developing every day, and existing ones frequently change or move to new locations. If you find that this book contains any errors or outdated information, or omits valuable sites or substantive areas that you would like to see included in future editions, please contact us with your suggestions or comments at:

linda.grobman@paonline.com
or
g-grant@uchicago.edu

Or write to us c/o the publisher, White Hat Communications, 222 Pine Street, P.O. Box 5390, Harrisburg, PA 17110-0390. We also invite you to visit the companion site to this book online at *http://www.socialworker.com/swintbk.htm.*

Gary B. Grant
Linda May Grobman
Spring 1998

Acknowledgments

The authors gratefully acknowledge their families for their assistance and support during the writing of this book. Our spouses, Kerry Baronnette Grant and Gary Grobman, encouraged us to complete this project and made it possible to devote the time and effort necessary to achieve the vision we had for it. We also thank "our" children, daughter Alyann Grant and son Adam Grobman, for their patience.

For contributions, and other forms of assistance and guidance, we want to thank Arlene Alpert and the University of Chicago School of Social Service Administration's (SSA) Continuing Education Committee, which sponsored the first programs that helped Gary Grant develop some of the original material. In particular, we thank Anna Senkevitch, Robert Tell, Steve Roller, John Aravosis, David Grotke, Sheila Peck, Jennifer Luna-Idunate, Robert Canon, Tobi Ann Shane, Andrew Davis, and Carolyn Biondi. Each gave us permission to incorporate materials they wrote into this book. Sheila Peck and Tobi Shane, in addition to other contributions, wrote some of the Web site reviews, for which we are thankful. We also wish to thank Jennifer Yang and Mika Nagamine for their assistance. We are forever indebted to those who read various drafts of the book and provided comments to us, especially social workers Gretchen Waltman and Susan Mankita, who contributed hours of their valuable time to help us make this book useful to both novice and experienced Internet users.

We especially thank Jeanne Marsh, Dean of the University of Chicago School of Social Service Administration, for encouraging us to pursue the project and for supporting the work at SSA toward preparing human services workers for using Internet technology in their work. Thank you also to the scores of people we talked to, and those we formally interviewed for this book—we appreciate your taking time from your busy schedules to share your ideas with us. During the preparation of the technical material in this book, we consulted other books to see how complicated concepts were simplified, and we adapted many of the innovative explanations. So, we thank those authors who have come before us, helping us in our own understanding, and paving the way for making the Internet understandable and accessible to the general public.

Similarly, the Internet itself has been a primary source of information and background material for us. We are especially appreciative of the thousands of Webmasters who, with no expectation of financial gain, have posted information of high quality and value for the public to learn from, their only reward being the satisfaction of knowing that they have improved society by their efforts. We acknowledge the many colleagues we have met, had discussions with, and learned from on the SOCWORK, BPD, HSWEB, SOCIALWEB, and other Internet mailing lists. They have been wonderful mentors and friends, and they make the Internet a great place for social workers.

We thank all of those who gave us permission to use descriptions and screen shots of their Web sites, and to reproduce material we believe will be useful to our readers. Almost everyone we contacted for these permissions was enthusiastic in accommodating our needs, and we are grateful.

We thank our very talented editor John Hope for his insights and for organizing the material so that it made sense to our readers. He was able to see our work from a fresh perspective, and he did a great job.

Finally, we wish to thank Gary Grobman for his many contributions to this book. Gary served with Gary Grant as co-author of *The Non-Profit Internet Handbook*, from which much of the general information in this book was adapted. Gary served as an editor and proofreader for this book, spent many hours staring at his computer while double-checking URLs, and wrote many of the Web site reviews. Without his vision and substantive contributions, this book would never have been possible.

PART I:

Introduction to the Internet

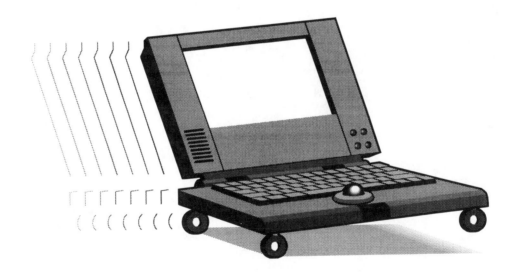

Chapter 1

Why Should *Social Workers* Care About the Internet?

Everywhere we look these days, the Internet is there. We see e-mail addresses on business cards, brochures and billboards. Television commercials for everything from the latest movie to toys for your children to the newest brand of toothpaste shout, "Visit our Web site!" But the Internet is not just showing up in the general media, and it's not just in technical circles that one hears talk about URLs and ISPs. Professionals in all fields, organizations, associations, and groups of every kind are creating their own online presence or, in many cases, such groups are actually forming online.

At the Web sites of professional associations and organizations, one can find, fill out, and submit membership forms, job applications, and other documents used to interact with them. Many of these offer the ability to contribute online, to learn more about their mission, and to participate in many different ways from education to advocacy. Individual social workers are finding in the Internet a new and exciting way to meet one another, share information, and network. In fact, the authors of this book first met one another through such professional interactions online.

There are many questions and concerns we hear from those who have not yet explored the Internet (and from some who have). There is ambivalence about its value compared to its costs. There are fears of the unknown it represents and the technological expertise necessary to get online or the time it will take to learn one's way around. Many wonder whether the Internet is a fad—the pet rock of the '90s. Others are concerned that the people online and the content they offer represent not the mainstream of the profession or of society, but rather a fringe element.

Above all, people feel that getting online represents a major leap, which bears some risks. Furthermore, while the risks (in cost and time spent) are easy to imagine, the gains are uncertain and often anecdotal. Probably all of us have had friends and colleagues who, like the old cereal commercial, implore us to "try it—you'll like it!" But without a concrete understanding about what we are getting into and why, it is a hard choice to make.

A major goal of this book is to help address these concerns and to provide answers that will help make the Internet more valuable more quickly for social work professionals and will demystify this resource for anyone involved in the field.

The Internet has become increasingly mainstream. A survey by Intelliquest Information Group in February 1998 found that 62 million people in the United States over the age of 16—representing 30 percent of the total U.S. population—were online. The study predicted that this number could rise to 70 million by the end of 1998. The number of Internet users worldwide in February 1998, according to NUA's "How Many Online" report, was 112.75 million. How many of these are social workers is impossible to say, but social work sites are recording astounding site visit statistics. (*The*

New Social Worker magazine had 51,000 visitors from July 1997 to April 1998. The Social Work Café records as many as 1,000 visitors each week. The Social Work Access Network (SWAN) saw about 36,000 visitors last year.)

Thus, it is clear that social workers are already online and their numbers are growing every day.

Consider this. In January 1997, when the National Association of Social Workers' new Code of Ethics went into effect, that organization's national office in Washington, DC was flooded with calls from members requesting copies of the document. When told that they could download and print it from NASW's World Wide Web site, 90% said they had the ability to do this through access to the Internet either at home, at work, or through a friend!

Imagine the implications, including the savings in printing and mailing costs, for this and other organizations, as social workers continue to gain access to the Internet.

In September 1997, the Illinois Department of Children and Family Services received its first e-mailed report of child abuse. The department uses its site to make child welfare information widely available to the public, such as providing brochures online for prospective foster parents. The department is carefully evaluating the benefits and risks of both anticipated and unanticipated ways its site can help people interface with the agency. Meanwhile, it is clear that the Internet creates a unique and multi-faceted opportunity that can positively serve the public and the clients of social workers.

Individually, social workers in every area of practice are finding innovative ways to use this technology in their work. Sheila Peck, a social worker in private practice on Long Island, NY, e-mails clients between sessions rather than play telephone tag when an appointment needs to be changed. She even gives clients e-mail assignments to work on between sessions.

Susan Mankita, a hospital social work director in Miami, FL, networks with other social workers through the weekly social work chats she moderates on America Online and has found new employees through online resources.

Barbara Nielsen, a pediatric social worker in Canada, facilitates an e-mail support group for parents of children with a rare bladder condition.

These are just a few of the many examples of how practitioners and social work agencies and organizations can apply the Internet to social work. The many resources that are now available to be used on behalf of clients already make the Internet an essential tool for social workers. Moreover, the Internet is a partnership between those creating resources and those who use them. As social workers connect to the Internet and use it on behalf of those they serve, the resources will certainly continue to expand and new ones will be created to fill almost any need.

Connecting to the Internet, finding the tools that are helpful, and learning how to apply them are steps that this book can help you with. Both of this book's authors discovered the Internet and its applications to social work in similar ways. Linda was introduced to the Internet in the early 1990s when she and her husband first subscribed to an online service. Their son had just been born prematurely, and the service offered numerous "message boards," some of which related to parenting. Through these, they were able to "connect" with others who had infants on apnea monitors and, as their son grew, they found forums for parents of 6-month olds, 1-year olds, potty training forums, and so on.

She eventually learned of e-mail "mailing lists," and the benefits of the Internet to the online social worker quickly became apparent to her. She subscribed to the SOCWORK list, where she could connect with hundreds of social workers in one e-mail message. She could find social workers who shared her professional interests. She could "hear" what other social workers around the country and the world were "talking" about, and she could contribute to these discussions of social work ethics and other important issues.

Gary was introduced to the Internet through his work at the University of Chicago School of Social Service Administration. Here he began to explore the Internet with alumni and students, so they could teach one another its relevance to the field. His daughter was born with food allergies. Immediately after learning this, he found Web sites where parents discussed the issues this raised and shared experiences, knowledge, and even elimination recipes, which he uses daily.

In 1996, Gary found a Web site where he could play chess by e-mail, helping him to re-discover a favorite pastime. One of his first games was with a retired man who had Parkinson's Disease. Several times during the game, the man was hospitalized, but was able to continue playing by using the hospital's e-mail. He reported frequently that the ability to do this helped substantially to ease the burdens of his hospitalization. An example like this can only make one imagine the benefits the Internet offers for addressing the need for human contact for anyone in similar isolated circumstances.

Linda and Gary continue to expand their professional and personal uses of the Internet. E-mail and other discussion forums allow them to stay up-to-the-minute on news in their fields and bring them into contact with numerous others who share ideas and perspectives from all parts of the world. It has been as if they could transport themselves into a social work conference at any time of day in which doing so was convenient. It was (and is) the ultimate in networking.

Over the last few years, the World Wide Web has become a vast knowledge base, and it is growing into the encyclopedia of the world. Who could not enjoy a resource that enables us to find the answer (or at least some information, a reference, or an appropriate person that could be asked) on almost any question one could conceive?

And yet, the Internet has its shortcomings. It takes practice and patience to find what is needed. It can be frustrating to follow links to sites that provide only more links and no content. In addition, one has to be particularly cautious of the accuracy of facts presented. Sometimes too much information can be a curse rather than a blessing. There are few roadmaps or guides and no real user's manual. The purpose of this book, however, is to provide such a reference—one that will lead the way for social workers, in particular, as they try to sort out all that the Internet has to offer them and their clients.

For both authors, the Internet is now a part of everyday life, as it is for thousands of social workers. Some use it as frequently as the telephone or postal mail. We use it for everyday needs, as well as for professional applications. We are expanding upon and improving the work we do and are finding new and exciting activities that we think make us better in our fields. We hope that by sharing what we have learned, we can help others to achieve these benefits more quickly and effectively. And we look forward to our readers' feedback so that we can continue growing in this way.

As the Internet becomes more and more a part of everyday culture, social workers who are not familiar with it may find themselves unprepared. They may have difficulty when their clients who use it talk about "surfing" on the "Web," or ask whether they can benefit from a site that addresses their needs. Social workers need to understand enough about this environment to know the risks and benefits it offers to clients who are online.

Social workers should not let themselves miss out on the opportunities the Internet offers. These include accessing (and sharing) knowledge about effective programs, interventions, and practices. They include being able to research information on any disorder, rare diagnosis, or treatment without having to leave the office. Social workers can become part of local, national and global networks of other practitioners as well as connecting to online communities organized around specific topics within the field of social work.

The Internet is not a panacea. Electronic communication will not and should not take the place of real human interaction. Practicing psychotherapy by computer may or may not be a good thing, and there are varying opinions on this controversial topic. The benefits of face-to-face contact over indirect communication are well documented. However, such contact is not always possible or practical, and in the past, this limitation was one that could not be surmounted. The Internet makes simple and convenient a level of research, communication, interactions, networking, and dialogue that was once unimagined. We feel confident that as you explore the Internet, a world can literally be opened for you.

We hope that this book will be valuable initially and along the way as you open that world and all its possibilities. In it you will find many (though by no means all) the tools and resources that are relevant to social workers. You will find suggestions and examples of how these can be applied. You will see how other social workers have used and benefited from such resources. We hope many will be inspired enough by this richness to contribute their own valuable resources for others to share online.

We will start with general information about the Internet, how it works, and what it has to offer in Part I. In Part II, we will look at the various ways social workers are using (and can use) the Internet in professional practice. Finally, Part III provides reviews of over 350 existing Web sites that may be of interest to you as a social worker.

So, put on your seatbelt, get your surf board, and hold on tight. We're going on a ride through cyberspace!

Chapter 2

The Internet

What is the Internet?

"The Internet" is a term that refers to linked networks of computers all over the world that communicate with each other using a standardized connection protocol called TCP/IP (Transmission Control Protocol/Internet Protocol). For the typical Internet user, all of the technical details are totally transparent; communicating from an Apple computer or an IBM on the Internet makes no difference, provided each computer is running the same protocol. Cyberspace is not a geographical place. There is no mega-computer that holds all of the Internet's information. Instead, the term "cyberspace" defines many thousands of computers all connected to one another.

What this means for you, in practical terms, is that—assuming you have the necessary equipment and an Internet connection (the ability to link your desktop computer to any in this network)—you can correspond electronically with anyone in the world who also has an Internet connection. And you can access the vast (and ever-growing) array of information available in cyberspace.

In one sense, computers have always been connected. It has always been possible to copy any file to a disk, whether it was a software program, a letter or document, a poster or picture. The disk could be given to others who could presumably use it on their computers (providing the computers were compatible, or could read the same software program).

The transfer of information through disks was (and is) a great convenience. Documents did not have to be retyped or recreated. Instead, they could be printed, revised, or copied to another computer. Other than saving time, however, transferring the disk was as much a physical act as transferring a document or letter.

The goal of the Internet, and its great achievement, has been to facilitate the transfer of information through phone lines rather than by disk.

How It All Started

The Internet evolved from a Department of Defense initiative designed to provide for communication among the armed services in order to survive a nuclear attack. It traces its origins back to 1969, with the establishment of ARPANet (after the Advanced Research Projects Agency, which administered the first program), a highly restricted electronic bulletin board that linked four mainframe computers. The theory was that in the event of such an attack, a centralized system might be destroyed. By creating a decentralized system that would automatically reroute messages around

5

servers that were damaged or destroyed, the messages could still get through to their destinations. During the next decade, this network was joined by the scientific and academic community's National Science Foundation Network (NSFNET), and public access remained restricted. One application was to permit supercomputer centers of NSF to be utilized without actually having to be at the Center. The bulk of communications on this network were related to government and academic research. Commercial applications were strictly taboo.

The vast majority of computers connected to this network ran on UNIX, a clumsy, arcane operating system that didn't encourage user-friendliness (and the vestiges of which we are still stuck with for some Internet applications).

Only since the early 1990s has the Internet become a part of the popular culture and available to the masses. New communications software, commercial providers that market to the general public, the emergence of the World Wide Web, advances in technology such as high speed modems, and competition in the industry have made Internet access popular. Even millions without their own personal computers have access to the Internet through public libraries, educational institutions, and the workplace. It was not until the 1990s that one million host computer servers were connected to the Internet. As of this writing, the number is perhaps five million and growing rapidly.

How the Internet Works

But the Internet is even more ambitious than this. The Internet makes communication possible and information available at any time of day or night to any part of the world, without using long distance phone charges in most localities. To do this, the Internet is comprised of thousands of specially designed and programmed computers, called servers. A server is, on one hand, just a computer, but it functions in such a way that it overcomes problems of compatibility between computers. Connecting to the Internet means connecting to a server.

Through any server, your computer may reach and interact with similar servers anywhere in the world for no more than the local telephone connection to your host server. By interact, we mean primarily the ability to view documents (Web pages) stored on these servers. In addition, we mean the ability to send a message to a person who uses any other server in the world to send and receive messages.

Your host server will know how to route either of these activities so that all you need to have is the destination address (a person's e-mail address or a Web page location/address). Keep in mind that merely linking to your server does NOT mean that anyone can view what is on your computer or affect your files in any way. Servers provide content for public use and consumption. Your computer, merely by using a server, is not exposed.

Thus, you begin to get a sense for what servers are doing. Each resource on the Web has its own unique Web address. We also call this a location, or more specifically, a URL (uniform resource locator). The URL has a standardized format that (as we will see later) is useful for identifying its source. For now, it is helpful to know that the address gives you a server name, a file path, and a file name for every document online.

In terms of e-mail, think of a server as analogous to a post office. When a friend addresses a letter to you, from any part of the world, the local post office has one responsibility—to get the letter to your local post office. And it is your post office that is charged with the duty to get the letter into your mailbox.

This is how the Internet provides for electronic mail (e-mail) communication. Each server has its own name, and each e-mail address includes the name of the recipient's server. Let's say you want to send a message to Gary Grant, co-author of this book. His e-mail address is: g-grant@uchicago.edu. Your server sees that the name of his server is "uchicago.edu." Your server sends your message to that server and it is the duty of the server to put it in a file (mailbox) established for him, called "g-grant," to which only he has access.

Gary's computer does not have to be turned on when you send the message, as long as his service provider's server is operating. When he turns on his computer and connects to his server using an appropriate e-mail program, he will be sent your message. He can read and respond to it at his convenience.

How about the World Wide Web (WWW)? What is happening when you look at a Web site? Servers are quite versatile. In addition to acting as a post office for e-mail, they can also serve as the repository for information that is made available to the Internet world at large. In these cases, readers must connect to a server, but having done so, they can then connect through it to others in order to see documents (or other files) that have been made available through "pages" on the Web.

For example, if you visit the University of Chicago School of Social Service Administration's Web page *(http://www.chas.uchicago.edu/ssa/index.html)*, you will see a textual and graphical gateway to other pages which together comprise SSA's "Web site." Web page addresses have "http://" at the beginning, which tells the server to use a universal language that allows you (with the appropriate software, called a browser) to view that site's home page. (However, most newer browsers now allow you to access a site without typing in "http://".) Everything between "http://" and ".edu/" represents the domain name of the site you are visiting—the server containing the file you are reading on your computer. Everything after ".edu/" represents the name of the file on the server and the path where it can be found.

Another great accomplishment of the Internet and the language used to make Web sites is the ability to create "hypertext links." This merely means that the address of another site can be "clicked to" right on the page you are reading, sending you to any other page, either on that server or some other server anywhere else in the world. The ability to move from file to file, from Web page to Web page, from server to server, as easily as turning the pages in a book, though admittedly, not as fast, is what makes it seem very much like a Web.

E-mail and the WWW are two of the most popular applications of the Internet. We will discuss these and others in more detail later.

Who Runs the Internet?

No one really officially runs the Internet. But the policies relating to it are established by a volunteer board called the Internet Society (ISOC). Committees and *ad hoc* working groups report to this Society. One influential committee is the Internet Architecture Board, which sets standards for many of the protocols and technical standards that make universal interconnection possible. There is no court to put those who abuse the Internet on trial, although some proposals have been made to create one. Generally, enforcement is through peer pressure—those who violate the written or unwritten rules are either shunned or "flamed" (publicly or privately harshly criticized by use of an electronic message).

Internet Demographics

In the early 1990s, men comprised as much as 90% of the population of Internet users. As cultural barriers fell and the World Wide Web became popular, the gender imbalance changed. A 1997 study by NetSmart-Research predicted that women would make up 60% of Intenet users by the year 2005, and a FIND/SVP report in 1997 revealed that almost 10 million children are online. A few years ago, Internet users were reported to have higher incomes and education levels than the general population, but that is also changing. A report by Intelliquest Information Group in February 1998 showed that 25% of Internet users had gone online for the first time in 1997, and that this new group of Internet users represented "middle America." They were, in general, less educated and had less disposable income than those who had gone online sooner.

As the Internet develops, the demographics change and more surveys are being performed. Among the Web sites that have demographic information about Internet users are:

YAHOO!'s Internet Statistics Section
http://www.Yahoo.com/Computers_and_Internet/Internet/Statistics_and_Demographics/

The Internet Index
http://www.openmarket.com/intindex/

NUA Internet Surveys
http://www.nua.ie/surveys/

Internet Applications

When we speak of the Internet's most useful resources for social workers in this book, we will be primarily referring to the following major tools:

> 1) People-to-People Applications—e-mail, mailing lists, USENET newsgroups, and chat
> 2) Applications to Access Data—FTP, gopher, and telnet
> 3) Applications that Combine the Two—the World Wide Web (or WWW for short)

We will describe each briefly here.

People-to-People Applications

E-mail refers to a communication system in which you can use your computer to electronically send a written message to a specific person or group. As such, e-mail is one of the easier concepts to grasp, since it is similar to writing a letter. E-mail is described in more detail in Chapter 4.

Mailing lists (LISTSERV® is the name of the software used to maintain many of them) are e-mail discussion lists organized around a specific topic or interest group. Any person in the world may "subscribe" by simply sending a message to the list's administration address. Once you join, you will begin to receive e-mail whenever any other subscriber writes to the list. If you wish, you can respond to it, sending your response to the whole list or to an individual, or you may just decide to "lurk" (listen in without responding) for a while. Mailing lists are described in more detail in Chapter 5.

USENET newsgroups (or just Usenet) are bulletin boards where discussion takes place, also around a particular topic. Usenet groups can be visited at your convenience, to either read or to participate in the discussion. Readers tend to follow discussion "threads," where someone replies to a question, and others reply to the reply. Some of these threads consist of hundreds of individual messages. Others fizzle out after just a response or two. Messages posted on Usenet are not sent to individuals as e-mail. Users instead select the messages they want to see, based on their titles and where they have been posted. Usenet groups are described in more detail in Chapter 5.

Internet Relay Chat (IRC)

Also known as "chat," IRC—the Internet equivalent of ham radio—first appeared in Finland in 1988. Using IRC, you can have a "conversation" with someone by using the computer keyboard, all in real time. What you type and the response of the other participant(s) appears on your screen

Up Close: Social Work Chat Rooms

Several chat rooms have been designed specifically for online discussion of social work topics. Listed below is the name of the chat room and the location where the chat room can be accessed. Some chat rooms have regularly scheduled chat times, which are subject to change. Check the sites for current schedules.

AOL Social Work Chat
for America Online subscribers only
keyword: sssocial work
click on Academic Quad
Thursday nights, 9-10:30 p.m. EST

***The New Social Worker's* Social Work Careers Chat**
http://www.socialworker.com

Tom Cleereman's Social Work Chat
http://www.sparknet.net/~tjcleer

The Social Work Cafe Chat Room
http://www.geocities.com/Heartland/4862/swcchat.html

For a listing of social work chat rooms, see Michael McMurray's page at *http://129.82.209.104/chatrooms.htm.*

immediately. It is possible to have an agency board or committee meeting entirely by IRC, although you will need to decide for yourself whether this is the best way to conduct such a meeting. There is a lack of social and nonverbal cues—some consider this a drawback, while others see it as an advantage. Most commercial providers can provide for privacy among those who participate. More popular, however, are informal chats among those who just happen to frequent an IRC channel. More and more, these channels are becoming specialized, so that participants have something in common.

When you enter an IRC channel, your screen name appears to everyone on the channel. While there are over 100 IRC commands, you can reasonably participate by knowing a few of the important ones, such as:

/HELP (gives you a list of available commands)
/BYE (exits the IRC)
/JOIN (insert channel#here) (joins an IRC channel)
/LEAVE (leaves the IRC channel you are on)
/WHO (lists those who are on the IRC channel)

Consult your Internet Service Provider for details on how to log onto an IRC channel.

Web-Based and Other Chat Applications

Besides IRC, there are other ways to chat with other Internet users. Most commercial online services have "chat rooms" where their subscribers can talk to each other, sending messages and getting an immediate response from others in the room. Many of these services have regularly scheduled topics on various topics, such as America Online's weekly social work chat (see above and page 66 for more information). These chat rooms do not require the user to know the commands necessary for IRC chat. One only needs to know how to get to the room. For example, to get to the America Online Social Work Chat, an AOL subscriber would go to the keyword for the Social Work Forum (sssocial work) and then click on "Academic Quad Chat" at the scheduled day and time. Once that was done, the subscriber would be able to see what others in the room are "saying" and would be able to join in the conversation by typing a response and clicking "send." When in the AOL chat room, the user can see a list of the screen names (AOL e-mail addresses) of the others in the room.

Many Web sites also have their own chat rooms. In general, there will be a link on a Web page that the user clicks to get into the chat room. Then, the user enters a nickname (or "handle") and other information in order to log into the room. Once in, the user can participate in the discussion, similarly to the above description of AOL chat rooms.

Web site chat rooms are being used to conduct support groups on a variety of topics. There are several chat rooms for social work professionals and students, as well. (See page 9 for a listing.)

Applications to Access Data

FTP, or file transfer protocol, is the tool used to connect to a computer and transfer files from one computer to another. Using FTP, you can "upload" (or put on a host server) your Web site's pages to a remote server. Or you can "download" (or get from one computer and put on your own computer) Michael McMurray's list of social work-related Web sites. You may need to become familiar with FTP procedures if you develop your own Web site and don't have your own server.

Gopher is a menu-based tool that allows access to network resources of a variety of types, including telnet and Web sites. It was originally developed at the University of Minnesota (the name is a multiple pun — the mascot of the campus is the "golden gopher," a gopher is a burrowing animal, which is what the gopher does, and it is also a "go fer"). Before the World Wide Web was developed, the gopher tool was the most popular for logging on to remote computer sites. There are still thousands of useful gopher-compatible sites around the world, but the gopher is fast becoming an extinct virtual animal on the Internet because of the explosion of the Web, which offers graphical abilities gophers cannot.

Telnet is the protocol for connecting with a computer in a remote location and interacting with it in real time, as if you are directly operating that computer on site. Using Telnet, you can use software that is locally unavailable or play games or engage in simulations with others who are also logged in. Telnet is an older, text-based software program. It allows you to find much of the same information as you can on Web pages and some things that are only available through Telnet.

Applications that Combine the Two

The World Wide Web refers to individual pages and sites containing information you can access, complete with text and pictures (graphics), and often accompanied with sound and video. These are created by people and organizations as a way to promote their interests or provide you with information you may find helpful. In short, the Web is a new way to communicate—a form of "publishing" for the world to see. It is egalitarian in the sense that each entity that publishes on the Internet can create an equally appealing site, whether that entity is a precocious sixth grader with some Internet "street smarts," a computer whiz, a social service agency, or a corporate giant. The Web is described in more detail in Chapter 6.

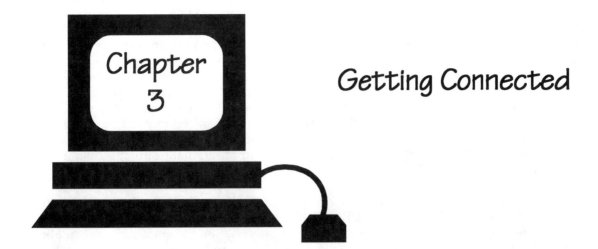

Chapter 3

Getting Connected

The first step toward taking advantage of all the Internet has to offer is getting connected to it. In order to do this, you will need five things:

1. A sufficiently advanced computer and monitor
2. A modem (or ISDN terminal adapter)
3. A telephone line (or an ISDN line)
4. Access to an Internet Service Provider (ISP)
5. Appropriate software

Computer and Monitor

The computer holds the communications software, provides the mechanism to download and store data from the Internet, provides a convenient way to dial into the Internet, and takes advantage of many new technological wonders, such as using the Internet to have real time audio conversations. Although a printer is optional, you may find it useful to print out some of what you find on the Internet. Almost any new computer you purchase will be advanced enough to access the Internet, but older machines might not be. In particular, older computers may not have the graphical capabilities to view Web sites as they are intended to be viewed, or the memory to support the software typically used for Internet communication. Whether you use an IBM-PC or an Apple (or their "clones") is irrelevant, but you will need to have certain minimum memory and storage requirements for the software you will be using.

Almost every computer can be connected to the Internet, although some older or less powerful computers may only allow you to view text and not graphics. For personal computers, four megabytes of Random Access Memory (RAM) is a minimum standard for access to the Internet. RAM refers to the computer memory that temporarily holds programs and data, and that can be erased and replaced with new content (unlike ROM, read-only memory). Most browsers that support graphics require a minimum of eight megabytes of RAM; however, if you have only the minimum amount of RAM, you should expect graphics to load slowly. Typical computers being sold today come with 32 MB (megabytes, or million bytes) of RAM.

The storage space available for data and programs on the hard drive is also measured in megabytes. Typical computers being sold today come with at least 1 and up to 6 GB (gigabytes, where 1 GB is a thousand megabytes) of disk space. It is useful to have sufficient capacity to upgrade your computer's hard disk space. Just a few years ago, a 40MB hard drive was sufficient for most personal computer applications. Now, many individual computer programs require more than that.

You will probably need about 100 megabytes of disk space for your browser, communications software, newsgroup readers, e-mail program, e-mail storage, cache file (a file that stores data received by your browser via the modem), and related Internet programs. You can get by with less than that, but you will need to monitor your disk space usage carefully and empty your cache file often (see page 31).

 Be sure to ask if and how your computer is capable of accessing the Internet when you purchase it. The computer is clearly the most significant investment you will make to get Internet access. In most cases, the computer you purchase will already have a high-speed modem, communications software, an Internet browser, and several "free trial" membership offers from commercial services or Internet Service Providers (ISPs). When you set up your computer, make sure it is near a working telephone jack.

Monitors also make a difference in how you view the Internet. Among the main parameters of interest are screen size (14" is standard; 15" and 17" are common, but more expensive), viewing area (which is directly proportional to screen size), dot pitch (.28mm is common, and smaller dot pitches, which increase screen resolution, are more expensive), and the frequency, in Megahertz, of the refresh rate (the higher the frequency, the less screen "flicker").

Modem/ISDN Line

Unless your employer uses an ethernet substitute (a technology that uses a Local Area Network to transmit data between computers at 10-100 million bits per second), you will need a modem. The purpose of the modem is to take the digital output from your computer, and change it to analog output (and vice-versa) so that information can be exchanged from your computer to another through telephone lines.

Virtually all new personal computers sold today (1998) have a built-in (internal) modem, typically 28,800 or 33,600 baud. The higher the baud rate, the faster data can be transferred over the telephone line. A 2,400 baud modem is sufficient for the transfer of text, although large files take proportionately longer than smaller files. With the advent of the World Wide Web, which takes advantage of graphics, sounds, animations, videos, and other byte-intensive files, the modem speed becomes critical. The World Wide Web is almost inaccessible using a 2,400 baud modem. Modems are relatively inexpensive, ranging from about $30 to several hundred dollars. A baud rate of 33.6k (33.6 kilobytes) should make using the Internet particularly enjoyable.

Many Internet users find that even a 33.6k baud modem is not fast enough, and there are technological breakthroughs that use special digital cable modems to provide data transfers several times faster than the conventional analog modems of most personal computers.

ISDN (Integrated Services Digital Network) lines are an increasingly popular choice for those who spend a lot of time downloading files from the Internet or "surfing" the Web. As more and more Web sites become sophisticated with flashy graphics, video-multi-media presentations, animations, and even virtual reality, it takes longer and longer to download data through a modem. While technology is improving and 57.6k modems are now available, there is no reason to believe that the modem speed technology will improve forever. There are limitations with telephone line technology resulting from a transformation of tones back and forth between analog signals and digital signals; after a certain point, data transmission through a modem would likely become unreliable, unless there are unanticipated technological breakthroughs, although cable connections may promise faster communication in the future. With ISDN lines, there is no conversion between digital and analog. A typical ISDN line is equivalent to five times the speed of the fastest modem available.

Installation of an ISDN line can run several hundred dollars, and a typical monthly service fee is about $65. Lines are ordered through the local telephone company and most apply a modest charge for each minute the line is in use. The ISDN service must also be compatible with the Internet Service Provider. As you might expect, specialized hardware and software are required to connect using an ISDN line.

Telephone Line

The Internet transfers information from a host computer to your computer by sending packets of data over a telephone line. You can purchase a dedicated telephone line to use only for computer communication. More typically, you will use an existing line if online time is minimal. Many social service agencies now use a separate line dedicated to the fax machine, which can be diverted to online use. Obviously, when online communication is occurring on the dedicated fax line, no faxes may be received or sent on that line.

Internet Service Provider

While it is possible to make a direct connection to the Internet and become, in effect, your own service provider, doing so is expensive, time-consuming, and technically difficult. The choice for almost all individual social workers and social service agencies has become to purchase an account with an Internet Service Provider (ISP). Among the commercial service providers are Delphi/MCI (1-800-695-4005), America Online (1-800-827-6364), Prodigy (1-800-776-3449), and The Microsoft® Network (1-800-386-5550). Hundreds of national and local Internet Service Providers have sprung up to compete, and many charge less than the commercial companies. The commercial online services provide their own content, in addition to Internet access. The local companies typically offer Internet access only. Typical costs for a service are $10- $20/month. Most offer access for a limited number of hours each month with an additional charge for each hour online above that threshold. Unlimited access accounts are also widely available.

Internet Service Providers (ISPs) provide direct access to all the features of the Internet. Some may provide their own content, but most do not. For the most part locally based, they provide an alternative to the national commercial online services. Look in the business section of your local newspaper or the "Internet" section of the telephone book to find local ISPs.

The table on the following page compares the advantages of commercial service providers, national Internet Service Providers, and local Internet Service Providers. As this table demonstrates, local or national ISPs are generally better choices if you want to be assured that the costs will be minimal and you want the freedom to use any kind of software. If you think you will use the Internet only very infrequently, want to practice in a more easy-to-learn environment, at least to start with, or want to take advantage of being part of a "community" of other Internet users, then a commercial service provider might be preferable.

Note that the choice need not be a permanent one. Nothing prevents you from changing your mind later, or even from trying out more than one provider at the same time and canceling the one you don't like as much. However, changing providers has its inconveniences. You may have printed your e-mail address on your organization's stationery and business cards. Hundreds of people may have your old address. Forwarding your e-mail to a new address can be, at best, a significant inconvenience, and, at worst, cannot always be done. In most cases, when a person sends e-mail to an address that no longer exists, the mail is returned with an automated message saying that it is undeliverable.

Communications and Other Software

Basic communications software is included in virtually every personal computer sold, in the form of the Terminal program included in Microsoft® Windows® or HyperTerminal included with Windows

Internet Service Providers
Comparison Chart

	Commercial Service Provider	National Internet Service Provider	Local Internet Service Provider
Examples	America Online, Microsoft Network	Netcom, Pipeline, AT&T	Pennsylvania Online, Epix, Ezonline
Online Content	Proprietary content (access to publications, services, and forums) provided in quantity.	Limited or none.	Generally none.
Relative Costs	May be most costly; charged by hourly or monthly usage time. May offer flat rate monthly fee.	Charged by usage by the hour or month. May offer flat rate monthly fee.	May be least costly; charged by hourly or monthly usage fee. May offer flat rate monthly fee.
Local Access Numbers	Yes; may offer toll-free number when local service is not available, but may impose an hourly charge for use of that number.	Yes; may offer toll-free number when local service is not available, but may impose an hourly charge for use of that number.	Yes, restricted to the limited geographical area served by the company.
Community	Members are part of an online community.	Members are generally not part of an online community.	Members are generally not part of an online community.
Special Events	Yes; such as celebrities available in a chat room.	No special events.	No special events.
Connection and Browser Software	Easy-to-load software is provided by the company, and usually cannot be modified.	Basic software is provided by the company, but consumer can usually upgrade or modify it.	Basic software is provided by the company, but consumer can usually use own software.

95. There is an equivalent for MAC-based systems as well. Many personal computers also include demonstration or full versions of communications software designed to connect to the Internet, an e-mail manager, a Web browser, File Transfer Protocol (FTP) software, and a newsgroup reader. Some examples are: Internet Office!, The Instant Internet Kit, Quarterdeck InternetSuite, and Internet In a Box. Many of the programs included in these packages may be obtained in some version for free from various sources. In order to use these packages, you will need to pay a fee to an Internet Service Provider.

Over time, you may find yourself needing a variety of different software applications to do various things, such as sending files to your server or viewing video clips online. You may obtain many of these software programs for free over the Internet. For our current purposes, we will focus on four kinds of applications:

(1) one that connects you to your server;
(2) one that allows you to view Web pages on the Internet;
(3) one that allows you to send and receive e-mail; and
(4) one that allows you to read newsgroups.

Each of these should be available from your Internet provider, who can also help you install and set them up properly. You may also need (or want) software that allows you to use the Internet to conduct telephone conversations or to transfer files (FTP, or file transfer protocol, software) across the Internet.

Internet Telephone

With the right equipment and software, it is relatively easy and not very expensive to use the Internet for voice communication. The equipment includes a computer sound card that supports duplex transmission (or else only one person can speak at a time, as with a walkie-talkie), a microphone, external speakers (although they are not required), and a high quality Internet connection. Your modem should be at least 14,400 baud. Much of the software required can be downloaded free from the Internet, or is included with Web browsers. For most applications, the person you are talking to must have a similar software configuration.

Internet telephone is one strategy social workers or their employing agencies may consider using to cut long distance telephone costs, particularly when many calls are made to the same number. The thought of saving thousands of dollars makes it a tempting option. For more information about using Internet telephone, visit the Internet Telephony Consortium at *http://itel.mit.edu/*.

E-Mail

E-mail is electronic mail, and it allows you to send a message from your computer to that of a friend or colleague who also has an e-mail account. Each Internet user has an address for sending and receiving these messages. E-mail is relatively simple to use, and although it does not replace the many other ways we have to communicate (phones, letters, faxes), it adds a new way—one that is sometimes appropriate and better.

How E-mail Works

It is possible to "mail" a message from most computers, and there is a variety of software available for this purpose. Computers use a standard form called "simple mail transfer protocol" (SMTP) to transmit these messages. In writing and sending mail, though, you do not need to know about SMTP—instead, you use software such as Microsoft Mail, NuPop, Eudora, Z-Term, or customized software provided by your Internet Service Provider, all of which do the work for you to transmit the message in the proper protocol.

A message sent from the other side of the world will use computers along the way like stepping stones along a path. The message eventually (in seconds or minutes) arrives at the computer in your local area network (LAN), which acts as a repository for mail. Messages "addressed" to you are "dropped off" in your "mailbox" at regular intervals and stay there until you collect them. Mail can not only be "read," but it can also be "saved" to your hard drive, or you can "forward" it to another person (but be sure to get the original sender's permission, if necessary), or "reply" to the sender. You can also get rid of it by "deleting" it.

The notable distinction between e-mail and "snail mail" (paper documents that travel at a snail's pace compared to e-mail), other than speed of conveyance, is one of cost. With the U.S. Postal System, picking mail up is free to us, but sending costs are relative to the distance between the originating post office and the destination. With e-mail, you often pay a monthly fee for your "mailbox" (to an Internet Service Provider) and another, nominal fee for getting yourself to that mailbox (a local phone call). But you pay nothing additional for sending mail to Michigan, Monterey, or Malaysia.

One of the most convenient uses of e-mail is to get a single message out to a lot of people who have e-mail addresses. You can type a message once, put several e-mail addresses on it (or create a "mailing list," which serves as a proxy for all those e-mail addresses), and the message will be sent to everyone on the list.

Benefits of Using E-Mail

E-mail features the following benefits:

(1) *Low cost.* The total cost is the local call to your server, even if the message is sent internationally.

(2) *Speed.* Messages arrive at their destinations almost instantly, although they are not read until the recipient checks his or her e-mail. (A 1997 study reported in the *Washington Post* showed that 86% of e-mail messages arrive in less than five minutes; less than two percent take over an hour.)

(3) *No busy signal.* Unless a computer or server is down, the message gets there regardless of whether the recipient is online or offline. There is no game of "telephone tag."

(4) *Broadcast capability.* A single message can be sent to multiple recipients simultaneously.

(5) *Attachments.* Documents and files from your computer can be attached and sent to the recipient's computer.

(6) *Indexed content.* Most e-mail programs allow the recipient to prioritize reading of messages based on the subject line.

(7) *Saving/Printing.* The text of a message can be saved for documenting a conversation or to be used in other documents, can be filed electronically, and can be printed out immediately or later.

(8) *Forwarding capability.* E-mail messages can be forwarded to a third person.

Some of these benefits are also drawbacks. You might not, for example, want the recipient to have your written word on his or her computer. There are also confidentiality issues involved, since e-mail can potentially be intercepted and read by others in transit. This is not likely to happen, given the increasingly large quantity of e-mail traffic and automation of the process, but it is technically possible.

E-mail's convenience can also result in your becoming overwhelmed with communication. E-mail becomes much less effective when you receive 100 or more messages a day. The president has an e-mail address at president@whitehouse.gov, but one wonders how effective it can be, given the volume of mail sent to this address. On the other hand, this medium does provide a way for more people to respond to issues and for opinions to be tallied, even if messages are not carefully read.

You will likely find that e-mail enhances your communication in a variety of ways. E-mail has made it possible for us to communicate with more people and more frequently than before. For example, the authors of this book met through the Internet. The idea for our collaboration on this book came as a result of a series of e-mail exchanges. The bulk of this book was written collaboratively even before we met face-to-face for the first time. Various drafts were exchanged over the Internet as e-mail and attached files.

To be sure, all essential communications happened before e-mail, but now we can communicate with a number of people we did not have the time to communicate with in the past. We might be in touch with distant friends with whom we had previously lost contact. We can correspond more broadly and regularly with colleagues.

But there are many stories of those who clicked on the wrong Internet address from an e-mail "address book" and inadvertently sent the right communication to the wrong person. Or of people who hit the "send" button too hastily and later regretted something they wrote. The consequences of doing so have ranged from simple embarrassment to family breakup or job loss.

Sometimes it is to your advantage to send a letter or fax, or to pick up the telephone and make a call. Other times, e-mail is the communication method of choice. Those who master each of the options have a powerful advantage.

Deciphering an E-Mail Address

All e-mail addresses follow the same format: the person's userid (read "user I.D."), the "at" sign or "@," and the name of the computer, or "domain name." Here is an example:

> tljones@uchicago.edu
> [userid@domain]

First, how does one say this address, for example, to someone over the phone? Typically, one would follow this convention: "T L Jones at U chicago dot e d u."

where the "tl," the "U," and the "edu" are spoken as letters, and the last name, "at" sign and domain are spoken as words.

We know several pieces of information immediately from inspecting this address. The address holder is university affiliated (".edu"), and more specifically connected to the University of Chicago ("uchicago"). Further, we might guess that the user's last name is Jones (from "tljones"), though this is not necessarily certain.

By looking at the end of an e-mail address, we can tell what sort of entity an individual has e-mail access through, if in the United States, or what country he or she hails from, if not. In the U.S., the endings can be:

.edu   educational institution
.com   commercial
.gov   federal or state government
.mil   military
.net   a connection provider
.org   a non-profit organization

A public process was initiated to add to this list of "top level" domain names, motivated in part by the fact that the catch-all suffix ".com" is considered to be too limited, considering the millions of business organizations that have or will seek their own domain names. Seven of these new top level domains were approved in 1997: .firm for businesses, .shop for businesses offering goods for purchase, .web for entities focusing on activities related to the World Wide Web, .arts for cultural and entertainment-oriented entities, .rec for recreation/entertainment organizations, .info for those providing information services, and .nom for people who want a personal domain name. As this book went to press, it was expected that these new domains would be in use sometime in 1998.

Outside of the U.S., these codes are replaced by a country code, regardless of the type of institution providing the access. Examples of these are:

.au   Australia
.ca   Canada
.fr   France
.ke   Kenya
.uk   United Kingdom
.de   Germany
.mx   Mexico

An interesting development is the use of conventions similar to those used in the U.S., such as the use of *.ac.uk* for academic institutions in the United Kingdom.

Finding an E-mail Address

A number of Web sites exist that can help you find addresses, phone numbers, and e-mail addresses or locate businesses and other organizations. BigBook *(http://www.bigbook.com/)* is an example of a comprehensive and well-designed business listing site—an online "yellow pages"—allowing you to locate businesses by name, type, or location/address. You can even view two-dimensional maps that enhance the amount of information you can obtain in looking for needed services, resources, and products.

In searching for people, there are numerous "white pages" options. One example of these is Lookup *(http://www.four11.com)*, a site that allows you to find a person's e-mail address by searching the domain name, among other methods. For example, if you are looking for Gary Grant's e-mail address, and you know he is at uchicago.edu, you can look up that domain and find Gary's address. Another site, Switchboard *(http://www.switchboard.com/)*, finds people by name and, if desired, by city and state. National in scope, sites like Switchboard expand your ability to find people in regions beyond your local printed white pages, and using it is free, unlike using the telephone company's directory assistance. While Switchboard typically provides information such as that found in telephone directories, it may provide the person's e-mail address, in some cases. You can update your own listing to either give more detail, correct errors, or make yourself unlisted. In creating these white pages, companies have used publicly accessible resources.

Even with the online directories, it is often still necessary to use old technology to find someone's e-mail address. Call on the telephone and ask for it, and add it to your e-mail program's address book.

Signatures

It is possible for those who use e-mail to attach a signature file to the end of every e-mail message. The signature provides information about the sender (such as his or her real name, address, telephone and fax number), and may contain an inspirational message, famous quotation, ASCII art (sketches made from standard computer keyboard-generated characters), or witticisms. Remember that if you do include your address and/or telephone number, you are more vulnerable to uninvited communications. Here is a fictitious example:

```
***************************************************************
John Jones, LCSW, ACSW
Specializing in family and marital therapy
123 Anywhere Lane, Hometown, USA
(321) 555-1234  jjones@hometown.com  http://www.jjones.com
***************************************************************
```

Emoticons

One of the disadvantages of e-mail is that it is totally text-based. It does not communicate body language, irony, or sarcasm, and this can completely change how the recipient perceives the meaning of the message. One system for conveying emotion is known as "emoticons," pictures made from keyboard characters. Among the most popular are (be sure to look at these with your head tilted to the left):

:-) smiling
:-(frowning
:'-(crying
;-) winking
8) person with glasses smiling

There are many more of these symbols. There is also a short-hand that has evolved for cliche phrases. Among them are:

4U (for you)
BBL (be back later)
BRB (be right back)
BTW (by the way)
CUL8R (see you later)
FYI (for your information)
ROFL (rolling on the floor laughing)
TTYL (talk to you later)
RTM (read the manual)
IMHO (in my humble opinion)
LOL (laughing out loud)
OTOH (on the other hand)

Security and Confidentiality

Since social workers routinely handle confidential information, and since confidentiality of client-related information is one of the ethical principles on which the profession is based, social workers need to take precautions to prevent revealing such information through e-mail and other electronic communication.

One way to safeguard against leaking confidential information is simply not to include such information in e-mail messages to clients, other professionals, or anyone else. Another is to consider using software such as PGP Mail, which encrypts messages, so that the only person who can see the message is the intended user. Encryption scrambles the message when it is sent, and the recipient deciphers it. The message looks like gobbledygook to any third party without the "key" to unscramble it.

We will discuss confidentiality in further detail in Chapter 15.

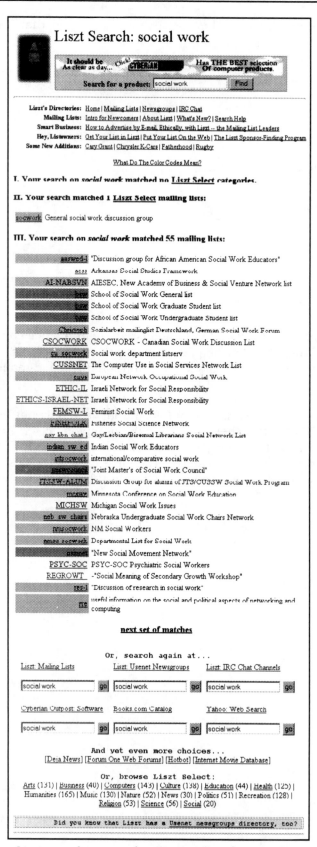

Liszt Search: social work

It should be
As clear as day... *Click!* **CYBERIAN** Has THE BEST selection
Of computer products.

Search for a product: [social work] [Find]

Liszt's Directories: Home | Mailing Lists | Newsgroups | IRC Chat
Mailing Lists: Intro for Newcomers | About Liszt | What's New? | Search Help
Smart Business: How to Advertise by E-mail, Ethically, with Liszt -- the Mailing List Leaders
Hey, Listowners: Get Your List in Liszt | Put Your List On the Web | The Liszt Sponsor-Finding Program
Some New Additions: Cary Grant | Chrysler K-Cars | Fatherhood | Rugby

What Do The Color Codes Mean?

I. Your search on *social work* matched no Liszt Select categories.

II. Your search matched 1 Liszt Select mailing lists:

socwork General social work discussion group

III. Your search on *social work* matched 55 mailing lists:

aaswed-l	"Discussion group for African American Social Work Educators"
acss	Arkansas Social Studies Framework
AI-NABSVN	AIESEC, New Academy of Business & Social Venture Network list
bssw	School of Social Work General list
bssw	School of Social Work Graduate Student list
bssw	School of Social Work Undergraduate Student list
Christoph	Sozialarbeit mailingliet Deutschland, German Social Work Forum
CSOCWORK	CSOCWORK - Canadian Social Work Discussion List
cu socwork	Social work department listserv
CUSSNET	The Computer Use in Social Services Network List
enwk	European Network Occupational Social Work
ETHIC-IL	Israeli Network for Social Responsibility
ETHICS-ISRAEL-NET	Israeli Network for Social Responsibility
FEMSW-L	Feminist Social Work
FISHFOLK	Fisheries Social Science Network
gay lbn chat l	Gay/Lesbian/Bisexual Librarians Social Network List
indian sw ed	Indian Social Work Educators
intsocwork	international/comparative social work
jmswcouncil	"Joint Master's of Social Work Council"
JTSSW-ALUM	Discussion Group for alumni of JTS/CUSSW Social Work Program
mcswe	Minnesota Conference on Social Work Education
MICHSW	Michigan Social Work Issues
neb sw chairs	Nebraska Undergraduate Social Work Chairs Network
nmsocwork	NM Social Workers
nmsu socwork	Departmental List for Social Work
nsmnet	"New Social Movement Network"
PSYC-SOC	PSYC-SOC Psychiatric Social Workers
REGROWT	-"Social Meaning of Secondary Growth Workshop"
res-l	"Discussion of research in social work"
rc	usefil information on the social and political aspects of networking and computing

next set of matches

Or, search again at...

Liszt: Mailing Lists   Liszt: Usenet Newsgroups   Liszt: IRC Chat Channels

[social work] [go]   [social work] [go]   [social work] [go]

Cyberian Outpost: Software   Books.com Catalog   Yahoo: Web Search

[social work] [go]   [social work] [go]   [social work] [go]

And yet even more choices...
[Deja News] [Forum One Web Forums] [Hotbot] [Internet Movie Database]

Or, browse Liszt Select:
Arts (151) | Business (40) | Computers (145) | Culture (158) | Education (44) | Health (125) |
Humanities (165) | Music (130) | Nature (52) | News (30) | Politics (51) | Recreation (128) |
Religion (53) | Science (56) | Social (20)

Did you know that Liszt has a Usenet newsgroups directory, too?

Liszt search screen showing results of a search on the term "social work." Reprinted with permission.

Mailing Lists and Usenet Newsgroups

Mailing lists and newsgroups provide ways to connect with people on the Internet who have similar interests, concerns, or needs. Mailing lists are a form of e-mail that is delivered to your mailbox, while newsgroups are like bulletin boards in a supermarket, where you go to see what others have posted.

Mailing Lists

One of the most useful features of e-mail is the ability to subscribe to a mailing list, which some people refer to as a LISTSERV® after the software that manages many of these lists. A mailing list allows subscribers to send messages to, and receive messages from, a whole group of people at one time. The list is maintained by a server and set up by an individual or organization wishing to generate discussion on a particular topic or among people with something in common.

This is a very helpful and convenient way to participate in a discussion on a topic of interest and to keep up with what is happening related to that topic. Some lists are very active and generate hundreds of e-mail messages a day. Others may only generate four or five. If you are someone who enjoys getting a large amount of e-mail (especially on a topic of great interest to you) and who has the time available to read (and respond to) a lot of messages, an active list may be very useful to you. Some people, though, have a hard time keeping up with the volume of an active list and may easily get overwhelmed.

One way to address these concerns is to create a separate e-mail address for "list" mail. (Check with your ISP to see if you can have more than one address within one account.) Another is to subscribe to the "digest" version that is available with some lists, meaning that you get all messages for that list in one combined message periodically—once a day, for example.

To subscribe to a mailing list, the subscriber generally sends an e-mail message to a central address in a standard format that automatically processes the request. The command (the text of the e-mail message) to subscribe is usually: subscribe listname <your name>, where <yourname> is replaced by your actual name, not your e-mail address or screen name. (Some mailing list software, such as Majordomo, does not require <yourname>.) The command is e-mailed, without any other message, to the administrative address for the list, such as: Listserv@listserv.net. The administrative address is different from the address to which messages are sent that are intended for the entire distribution list.

Up Close: SOCWORK

SOCWORK (officially pronounced *sock-work*, although pronunciations vary) is the Internet's oldest general discussion list for social workers. It was started in 1988 by Simon Mielniczuk as a way for students in Professor Don Bellamy's social planning practice course at the University of Toronto to interact with each other and learn about computer technology. The list was open, however, and anyone could join. A few people from the University of Maryland at Baltimore and other places found out about it, got on board, and an international network of social workers was born.

At that time, there were 45 people on the list, according to Ogden W. Rogers, Ph.D., ACSW, director of the social work program at the University of Wisconsin-River Falls, and current SOCWORK "listowner." But three moves (SOCWORK has since been "housed" on servers at University of Maryland at Baltimore, University of Arkansas, and currently at University of Wisconsin-River Falls) and over a decade later, it numbers in the hundreds. At its height, there were 1,002 subscribers.

According to the "welcome message" new subscribers receive, its purpose is "to enable broad discussion of information and issues of concern to the social work community. You will find that there are other, more directed lists elsewhere for more defined social work discussion; SOCWORK tends to be 'wide-open,' and high traffic."

Indeed, discussions on this mailing list run the gamut from serious discussions of social work ethical issues like dual relationships to debates on religion in social work to ongoing discussions of pizza recipes and beer. Its members range from social work students to professors to practitioners to non-social workers who are interested in what social workers have to say.

SOCWORK is a great place to go if you have specific social work-related questions or if you have information you would like to get out to a lot of social workers. Many liken it to a conference where one can network with social workers from all over the world—except the SOCWORK

For example, if you want to subscribe to SOCWORK, a discussion list for social workers, you send the message

Subscribe SOCWORK

to majordomo@uwrf.edu (this is the administrative address for the list) without any topic, heading, or signature.

You will receive an e-mail response stating that you have successfully subscribed to the list. This message often includes useful information that you should save for future use. Once subscribed, if you want to send a message to every subscriber on the list, you will send your e-mail message to an address different from the mailing list administration address. (For SOCWORK, it is socwork@uwrf.edu.) You will immediately begin to receive e-mail messages sent by others to the mailing list.

To unsubscribe, you send a message to the list administration address, saying:

unsubscribe SOCWORK

To find a list of current mailing lists, point your Web browser to *http://tile.net/listserv* or use the Liszt directory *(http://www.liszt.com).*

conference is one that continues indefinitely, at all hours of the day or night. "I've always thought of it as a very large cafeteria filled with a lot of social workers," says Rogers. "It's a list about talking about social work and a list of social workers talking." And it's not always social work they're talking about, he adds.

SOCWORK has its flame wars like any mailing list. Social workers are not immune to rude behavior and, at times, its members question how others on the list can act that way toward each other. After all, they're "helping professionals." Some say that the mask of perceived ano-nymity can lead social workers to behave badly on the list. But as some list members have come to realize, they are not so anonymous, and they may find themselves sitting across from another list member at a job interview someday. So, it is suggested that members act as they would at any meeting of social workers—online or face-to-face. And these flame wars have led to some interesting discussions of ethics and how social work professionals *should* treat each other.

"Something that's worth reflection for anyone who's going to be interfacing with computer tech-nology is the idea that all relationships have both process and content," says Rogers. "A good reflective practitioner thinks about how his or her interaction with a keyboard rather than a human being affects the process of their relationship. I'm often reminding people in the middle of flame wars that there are human beings behind those screens."

He explains in his periodic note to subscribers, "SOCWORK has always been wild and woolly, tender and sublime, and very unmoderated. Use it well."

To subscribe to SOCWORK, send a message to majordomo@uwrf.edu that reads:
subscribe SOCWORK

To send a message to the entire SOCWORK list once you have subscribed, send it to socwork@uwrf.edu.

Some resources for finding social work-related lists include Michael McMurray's Lists of Interest for Social Workers at *http://129.82.209.104/lists.htm* (updated weekly) and SWAN's Listserv Directory at *http://theusc.csd.sc.edu/swan/listserv.html*.

There are procedures for starting your own list, and some Web hosting companies offer this as an option to their customers. For information, contact:

listserv@bitnic.educom.edu and *listserv@uottawa.bitnet*

Usenet Newsgroups

A Usenet newsgroup is a form of Internet communication that provides for group discussion of a narrow topic. Unlike mailing lists, it doesn't come to you in your e-mail box. It is like a bulletin board in the supermarket, where you have to take action to see it and read messages posted there, with an opportunity to post a reply for others to see. Sending a message to a newsgroup results in each subscriber to the newsgroup having the capability of seeing the message without receiving it as e-mail. Typically, someone makes a comment on a newsgroup, another person responds to the comment, and so on until there is a string of related messages on a topic. Simultaneously, others will start another string of messages. All of the messages are stored, often chronologically, and given a title. Viewers can pick and choose using a newsgroup reader (specialized software to facilitate reviewing newsgroups) to decide which messages to look at.

Newsgroups have a prefix, which gives an indication of their content. These prefixes are:

alt—alternative
biz—business
comp—computers
misc—miscellaneous
rec—recreation and hobbies
sci—science
soc—sociology

Most newsgroups have a posting called the FAQ (for "frequently asked questions"). It is good policy to read this before posting to a newsgroup. If you don't, and you ask a question that is covered in the FAQ (and has been raised many times before), you risk getting flame messages.

Some examples of newsgroups that may be of interest to social workers are:

alt.society.mental-health
alt.support.cancer
alt.support.depression
alt.support.divorce
misc.health.aids
misc.kids.health

To see a more complete listing of newsgroups related to social work, see SWAN's Newsgroup Directory at *http://theusc.csd.sc.edu/swan/usenet.html.*

How to Participate in a Newsgroup

To participate in a newsgroup, you will need a newsgroup reader, such as Microsoft® News. When you open the newsgroup reader and connect to your ISP's news server, a list of newsgroups will appear. You can then subscribe to those that interest you by clicking on them and clicking a button that says "subscribe." (Check your software's instructions if there is not such a button.) Once subscribed, you can read messages from others and post your own messages. If you wish to unsubscribe, just click on the name of the newsgroup again and click "unsubscribe."

How New Newsgroups Are Started

It's not as difficult as you might think to establish your own newsgroup, if you think that the existing 20,000 or so are insufficient to be a forum for one of your favorite topics. Rather than provide all of the details here, we suggest you visit one or all of the following Web sites for more information:

http://www.cis.ohio-state.edu/~barr/alt-creation-guide.html
http://www4.ncsu.edu/~asdamick/www/news/create.html
http://www.cs.ubc.ca/spider/edmonds/usenet/good-newgroup.html

Also, check out the newsgroup: *news.announce.newsgroups*

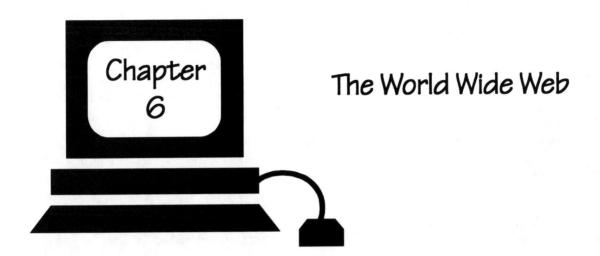

Chapter 6

The World Wide Web

"The World Wide Web" is probably the term most commonly thrown around in discussions of the Internet. You might see it abbreviated "WWW" or "W3." The Web was "invented" by physicists at the European Laboratory for Particle Physics (CERN). Their basic problem was that they wanted to find an easy way to cross reference a document with its end notes and bibliography which, at that time, often required leaving the first document and searching for the second. The objective was to code the link to the second document at the same time one was viewing the first document. The Web you see now—with graphics that can be clicked on, flashy colors, and eye-catching backgrounds—turned the WWW from what was a sterile, 1850s newspaper style to what looks more like a television or movie screen with an attitude.

The World Wide Web is exactly what its name suggests: a Web of interconnecting sites that span the world. Each "Web site" or "home page" belongs to and is operated by an organization or individual. Sometimes the terms "Web site" and "home page" are treated as synonymous, but there is a subtle difference. "Web site" refers to a collection of pages, while "home page" is the main "gateway," "index," or table of contents to the rest of the Web site.

Each document on the Web is called a "page," and Web pages contain only that information that the person or organization wants to make available to the larger Internet public. For an individual, it might include a self-description or a list of interests and links to favorite Web sites. For an organization, it might be a description or advertisement of its services, or it could be information relating to its mission. No one is in charge of maintaining or organizing the Web, so what you see is only what someone else saw fit to make available. The Web is free, and it is not directly a money maker in most cases (although that is likely to change in the next few years), so information made available on the Web is usually there because someone wants you to see or know something. It is not necessarily there just because you want it.

Thus, one way to think about navigating the Web's information is to consider whether the information you want is likely to be there. Ask yourself whether anyone has anything to gain by making the information you want available. If you are seeking to purchase something, you are likely to find what you need. If you want information from a government agency, then there is a decent chance it will be out there. But if you want to know a business's trade secrets, you are not likely to find that they advertise these on the Web.

So imagine now, a global newsstand or television network in which each and every person has the ability to create his or her own "home page show." Some people use this ability to entertain, sell goods and services, share news, ideas, or stories. Some home page shows are good, and some are pretty awful. Some are self-serving only and some altruistically offer the world some useful infor-·mation and communication contacts.

Up Close: Netscape's Web Browser

Viewing Web pages requires an Internet browser, such as Netscape® Navigator or Microsoft® Internet Explorer, the two leading and most fully featured browsers. Updated versions of Navigator are often available free on the Internet (at *http://www.netscape.com*) or from your ISP free of charge or for minimal costs.

As with all of the browsers and online services mentioned here, Netscape is "graphical," meaning that a user can "point-and-click" his or her mouse at an image on the screen to execute a function rather than typing in a command word. Netscape comes with a variety of features, some of which include:

Title Bar: At the top of the document, the name of the current home page.
Menu Bar: The pull-down menus at the very top of the screen, including:

File: Functions for printing and saving. **Edit:** Provides the Windows® traditional cut, copy and paste functions. **View:** Includes the "refresh" and "reload" commands that update a currently selected Web page. **Go:** Function for returning to sites recently visited. **Bookmarks:** Marks a URL by name for revisiting later. **Options:** Offers choices for settings, or configurations, for your Netscape software, such as what your default (starting when you first turn on Netscape) home page will be. **Directory:** Lists Netscape "services," also featured in some of the buttons below the Menu Bar, such as compiled lists of "cool" and new sites, a handbook for using Netscape, search engines, and newsgroups.

Tool Bar: Buttons that speed the completion of certain Netscape functions, including these most frequently used:

Back & Forward: Allows for moving one page back or forward. **Home:** Returns you to the default home page. **Open:** Lets you type in the address of the Internet site you wish to visit (and transports you there when you hit the "return" key). **Print:** Prints the page you are viewing. **Stop:** Aborts the transmission of the page you are moving to, or another function in process.

Location/Go to Window: Shows the address of the page you are currently viewing or, by typing in another URL address, sends you to that page.

Anyone with a Web browser can view home pages. Just as any name brand television shows the same program on the same channels, browsers show the same home pages, even if the tint, contrast, and general layout may vary from browser to browser.

A key feature of the Web, with its millions of home pages, is the ability for each page to lead you to other pages. On almost any home page, you will see some text (or pictures) underlined (or outlined) and/or in colorful boldface. These are the "hypertext links" that, when clicked on with the mouse, trigger your browser to move along to another Web page.

Sometimes one of the links will lead not to another Web site when clicked, but instead will link to an individual's e-mail address. A message form will appear, allowing you to write a message to the designated person. These are called "mailto" links.

The ability to create links is the "magic" of which the World Wide Web is formed, and is one way in which the Internet is different from television shows or newspapers. TV show producers generally

Scroll Bar: As with many other software applications, the scroll bar allows you to move up and down the page with your mouse to view text above or below the area you are viewing.

The Little Hand, and the Status Bar: When you place the pointer (the arrow) either on a "hyperlink"—the bold-faced underlined text in a home page—or in many instances a graphic— an image of a small gloved hand appears. This lets you know (since it is sometimes not obvious) that you have encountered a link to another Web site. By clicking once, the browser transports you to that link. Before this step, you can identify the URL of the new site by examining the status bar at the bottom of the document. The status bar also includes an indicator of the progression for a page transmitted to you, so that you know when it is finished receiving the page.

As a final note, you can utilize Netscape commands by clicking on any part of the screen you are viewing and holding the right mouse button down for a second without releasing it. This will make a menu appear, and the commands listed can be executed by releasing the button while highlighting the desired command. If you do this over a picture on the page you are viewing, your choices will include the ability to copy the image to your computer for use on or off of the Internet.

The Netscape browser supports e-mail and newsgroups.

The Netscape browser screen and home page. Copyright 1998 Netscape Communications Corp. Used with permission. All rights reserved. This electronic file or page may not be reprinted or copied without the express written permission of Netscape.

want you to keep viewing their shows and not move elsewhere, and written publications are intended to be read in sequential order. The Internet is often referred to as "thinking in parallel," since it allows and encourages you to explore more in depth whatever diversionary routes you wish to take. If TV were like the WWW, you could be watching "Murder, She Wrote," then move on at will to a PBS Agatha Christie special or an Alfred Hitchcock film (since these links are related as mystery shows), and then return to continue where you were in the original episode you were watching.

Anatomy of a URL

A URL ("uniform resource locator") is the address for a Web page. Each page has a unique address that you type into your browser (or link to from another page) to access it. For example, a home page might have the URL:

http://www.organization.org/

The home page might have a link to "press releases" with the URL:

http://www.organization.org/pressrel.htm

The September 18, 1997, press release on the organization's Legislator of the Year award might have the URL:

http://www.organization.org/pressrel/091897.htm

This is an important point to understand. Perhaps you are given the URL for a document and your browser gives you a "404" error message (which indicates that there is nothing available at that URL). Instead of giving up, you can try finding the page you are looking for by using the URL one directory higher, or two or three directories higher, as may be necessary. There are many times when you can find the information you are looking for even when you are given an incorrect URL.

Let's quickly deconstruct a Web address. The Web site address for the Colorado State University Department of Social Work is:

http://www.ColoState.edu/Depts/SocWork/overview.html

No spaces are allowed in a URL, so words are often separated by symbols such as dashes ("-"), tildes ("~"), and underlines ("_"). Other symbols you will find in URLs are dots (".") and slashes ("/").

Starting from the end, in the above address, the suffix ".html" indicates that the document is a Web page using HTML (hypertext markup language) codes. This is the code used to create Web pages, and these files usually end in ".html" or ".htm."

Next, each single slash mark ("/") lets you know that you are descending into further file directories in the person's server, just as you do in your own computer to find particular files or documents. This is useful to know, because there are times when you might know an address for a site that is likely to be in the ascending files. For example, suppose you wanted to find the main page for Colorado State University. Knowing the social work department's URL, you could guess that the university would be at *http://www.ColoState.edu/*. Entering this or cutting off the remaining portion of the address will, in fact, get you to the main page for the institution.

How to Open, Bookmark, and Print Web Pages

To "surf," "browse," or "navigate" the Web (these are all equivalent terms), you simply open your browser (after you have dialed in and logged on to your ISP) and type in the URL of a page, and from there explore various links. Be sure to type the URL exactly as it appears in the source where you find it. If even one character is entered incorrectly, the browser will not be able to find the site. Some parts of a URL are case-sensitive, so pay attention to which letters are capitalized and which are lower case. Also, be sure to put dashes (-), tildes (~), and other symbols in the right places. One common mistake is to type the number "1" instead of the letter "l" (a lower case "L") or vice versa—they look very similar.

You can fully access the Internet's resources even if you hardly ever enter a URL by hand. Your browser will start you off at a default home page (usually the browser company's Web site), but you can set it to start at any site you wish—your own, a favorite organization's, or a favorite navigation launching point, such as the Yahoo! directory *(http://www.yahoo.com)*. One browser feature you will come to rely on is the "back" button. Suppose you start to jump from page to page during your navigation, and realize that you have gone well off-track. The back button will retrace your steps as far back as you wish before going forward in a new direction. For a quick return to the beginning, you can always click the "home" button and begin anew.

Most browsers have a "bookmark" function that automatically records a favorite link for future use. Thus, in order to return to that page at a future time, you need only to click on the stored reference in the bookmark, rather than having to type in the entire address. For example, if you are in the Netscape browser and you find a page you like and want to return to, you simply click on the "Bookmark" menu while still on the desired page, and then click "Add bookmark."

If you find a Web page you want to print out for future reference, just go to the "File" menu while still on the page, and click "Print."

Frames

A popular Web page development is the use of frames, a device that allows more than one HTML document to be displayed on your monitor at the same time. Usually, one frame will contain a "Table of Contents" consisting of links. When you click on one of the links, the referenced document appears in another frame, while the first frame remains on the screen. In essence, you are then viewing two Web pages in one. The page that is displayed in the second frame may be another page in the same Web site as the first, or it may be a page from another site.

A significant disadvantage of using frames is that not every Web browser is compatible with them. If you are using a browser that is not, and you try to access a page with frames, you will typically get an error message such as, "Your browser does not support frames. You cannot access this site." Some of these messages may have a link to a site that permits you to download, at no charge, a browser that supports frames. Your only recourse at this point is to download (or buy) a browser that supports frames. Some sites have a frames and a non-frames version, and we recommend that you provide both if you plan to build a site using frames, so you will not alienate (or lose as visitors) those who do not have a frames-compatible browser.

The Cache File

When you visit a Web page, your computer automatically saves the HTML file and graphics files associated with it in a "cache" file on your hard drive. This file can quickly take up a large amount of space on your computer. Although some browsers may delete it automatically, we recommend that you delete it manually from time to time, especially if you notice that you are running out of memory or disk space. If you are not sure how to do this, read the documentation that came with the browser software, or ask your Internet Service Provider. Your documentation may also tell you how to set the software for automatic deletion of the cache.

Savvy Searching

Searching the Web is a process used to find particular information or otherwise explore the Web's content. It is true that the Internet is disorganized. It has been likened to a library with no librarian, no index or card catalogue system, just piles of books in random stacks throughout. But fortunately, some individuals and companies have undertaken the enormous task of indexing for the rest of us. Some people have dedicated all or part of their individual sites to creating lists of other Web sites that have some topic in common. If you are looking for resources of interest to social workers, you might want to start your search at some of the popular lists of sites created for social workers, such as SWAN (Social Work Access Network), BPD (the site of the Association of Baccalaureate Social Work Program Directors), *The New Social Worker* Online, or Gary Holden's Web Resources for Social Workers. (See the Reviews section of this book for URLs of these sites.)

Up Close: Microsoft® Internet Explorer

Microsoft® Internet Explorer, available free for download from Microsoft®'s Web site *(http://www.microsoft.com/ie)*, is gaining in use and popularity. Internet Explorer 4.0 requires a minimum of 16 MB of RAM and 30 MB of hard disk space, and operates using Windows® 95 or Windows® NT 4.0.

Besides a Web browser, this software also has components for e-mail, newsgroups, and online conferencing. We will look at the Web browser component here.

Title Bar: At the top of the document, the name of the current home page.

Menu Bar: The pull-down menus at the very top of the screen, including:

File: Functions for opening, printing and saving. **Edit:** Provides the Windows® traditional cut, copy, and paste functions **View:** Controls what is displayed on the screen. Also includes an Options menu, which offers various settings to customize your session. **Go:** Function for returning to sites recently visited. **Favorites:** Marks a URL by name for revisiting later.

Tool Bar: Buttons that speed the completion of certain Internet Explorer functions, including these most frequently used:

Back & Forward: Allows for moving one page back or forward. **Refresh:** Reloads the current page in its most up-to-date form. **Home:** Returns you to the default home page. **Search:** Loads a page that allows you to search the Internet. **Favorites:** Lists your favorite sites, allowing you to click on a site's name to go to that site. **Print:** Prints the page you are viewing. **Font:** Allows you to increase or decrease the print size of text on the pages you are viewing. **Mail:** Allows you to check and send e-mail using Internet Mail, or read and send Usenet newsgroup messages using Internet News. **Stop:** Aborts the transmission of the page you are moving to, or another function in progress.

Address Bar: Shows the address of the page you are currently viewing, or by typing in another URL address, sends you to that page.

Links: Buttons that allow you to jump to other sites. You can customize these buttons.

Scroll Bar: As with many other software applications, the scroll bar allows you to move up and down the page with your mouse to view text above or below the area you are viewing.

Status Bar: Indicates the progression for a page transmitted to you, so that you know when the browser is finished receiving the page.

Perhaps the first large scale directory, and likely the most complete topical directory is Yahoo! *(http://www.yahoo.com/)*. Here you can start with a set of about a dozen general themes (e.g. business, education, entertainment, health, social science, society and culture, and so on). From these, you begin to narrow your search to more specific topics within each category, until you find sites relating to what you want. In addition, there are companies that have created search engines, allowing you to receive a list of Web sites related to any term you enter.

None of these is perfect, complete, or comprehensive, but they give you an excellent start, and usually produce more information than you want. If you have your own Web page and you want to be noticed, then registering with the more popular directories and search engines will help. You can register your own site simply and at no cost, although there are companies that will, for a fee, register your site with many search engines at one time.

Search Engine or Directory?

How do you know whether to use a search engine or a directory? With practice, you will develop a sense for when to use each. Here are a few hints and tips to ask yourself when selecting a search option:

1. *Are you looking for a specific organization's site, and are you relatively certain it exists?* If so, the directory may be the best option, since it avoids having to look through unrelated sites. Suppose, for example, you wanted to find the University of Chicago's Web site. Searching with the term "University of Chicago" will find any page that references the University of Chicago, and may bog you down. But you can be sure that most directories would lead you easily and smoothly through education to various regions, and then to this institution's home page.

   If, on the other hand, you are researching a topic and want to access discussion and literature on it, then a search engine becomes the obvious choice, since it will automatically stack up sites relating to that topic for you.

2) *Based on what you are seeking, do you think the topic categories will be obvious?* A directory is only a good idea if you are looking for something that is easy to categorize. For example, universities may be logically connected to education and only education, but "social work" may be harder to categorize and may be listed in one directory under social sciences, another under health and welfare, and another under some other category.

   If what you are looking for doesn't fit into a clear category, a search engine may be a better starting point.

3) *How narrow or specific is your targeted information?* If your information is very specific or narrow, it may take a long time to dig it out of a directory, since you will have to go through many categories first. In such cases, a search term might get you there more quickly, especially if using an engine that prioritizes or "scores" sites. If, on the other hand, you just want to do a self "tour" through a general category of information to explore what sorts of things are available, the directory might be a better option. For example, if you are looking for information about a city you will be visiting, the directory will keep you focused on relevant regional information and avoid sites about the region that are unrelated to traveling there, such as articles, histories, or individual home pages of residents.

Search Engines

One of the complaints about the Internet in its early years was that people could find a plethora of fascinating data bases, files, and information, but it was almost impossible to find something they were actually looking for. Commercial companies offered services to assist researchers in finding Internet resources, and often charged handsomely. Recently, that has changed dramatically, with the development of powerful search tools, all of which can be accessed free of charge. Among the more popular search engines are Yahoo! *(http://www.yahoo.com)*, Lycos *(http://www.lycos.com)*, and Alta Vista *(http://altavista.digital.com)*. Users access the search engine by connecting to its address and then filling out an online form with the term or terms to search. For example, typing the term "social worker " in the Yahoo search engine generates within a second or two a list of links to more than 100 Web sites. Changing the search term to "social work" increases that number to over 600. Clicking on any one of these links transports you to the referenced page.

Up Close: Yahoo!
http://www.yahoo.com

Yahoo! is, by almost any account, the most popular search engine and directory on the 'Net. The site has grown to include numerous features, in an effort to be one of the most comprehensive available.

Yahoo!'s main directory is enormous, and well organized—an important combination for the Internet—resulting in a valuable but easy-to-access way to find what you need. Sites are added to the directory both by the staff of Yahoo!, who proactively look for sites, and by people who want their sites placed in the appropriate categories.

The Yahoo! Search Engine accomplishes two goals. First, it allows you to search by words for material that is included in the Yahoo! directory. Second, it gives you results from Alta Vista's search engine, which specializes in broad searches of the larger Internet. A search of just Yahoo!'s directory using the term "domestic violence" gives 6 directory category matches and 179 Web site matches. By contrast, the same search on Alta Vista yields 1,705,717 matching documents.

Yahoo! has also put together an impressive list of specialized subdirectories including:

Social Science: Social Work
Social Science: Communicating: Writing: Research Papers
Social Science: Sociology: Institutes: College and University Departments
Yahoo!ligans: A directory of sites created for (or by) children
National Yahoo!s: Directories for several other countries, in other languages (including Canada, France, Germany, Japan and the UK at the time of this writing
Yahoo! Metros: Directories of sites relevant to large cities, including Boston; Chicago; Washington, DC; Los Angeles; New York; and San Francisco at the time of this writing.
My Yahoo!: A feature which allows you to customize a directory for your own personal news and information, and create a default page.

Yahoo! also serves as a guide to the latest news items, from sports events to stock quotes to world events, and connects you conveniently to other news services and stories. Some of Yahoo!'s other features include tools for finding a map of any address in the U.S., and links to various search engines for finding people, their addresses, phone numbers, and e-mail addresses, as well as businesses and organizations. There is even a magazine called *Yahoo! Internet Life*, which is quite useful for finding new and practical Internet sites.

Most directories, including Yahoo, offer search engines. Not all search engines are the same. Each uses a different program (or algorithm) to search the Web for the word or words you enter. They also differ in appearances and how the information is presented to you. So, which search engine is the "best?" There is no right or wrong answer here. Any search engine will get you started in your research. You can try several in the process of finding what you need.

Yahoo! Pager
instant messaging

Hot Anti Virus
Get It Now

[   ] Search options

Yahoo! Online - $14.95 a month Internet access - sign up today

Yellow Pages - People Search - Maps - Classifieds - Personals - Chat - **Email**
Shopping - My Yahoo! - News - Sports - Weather - Stock Quotes - **more...**

- **Arts and Humanities**
  Architecture, Photography, Literature...

- **Business and Economy** [Xtra!]
  Companies, Finance, Employment...

- **Computers and Internet** [Xtra!]
  Internet, WWW, Software, Multimedia...

- **Education**
  Universities, K-12, College Entrance...

- **Entertainment** [Xtra!]
  Cool Links, Movies, Music, Humor...

- **Government**
  Military, Politics [Xtra!], Law, Taxes...

- **Health** [Xtra!]
  Medicine, Drugs, Diseases, Fitness...

- **News and Media** [Xtra!]
  Current Events, Magazines, TV, Newspapers...

- **Recreation and Sports** [Xtra!]
  Sports, Games, Travel, Autos, Outdoors...

- **Reference**
  Libraries, Dictionaries, Phone Numbers...

- **Regional**
  Countries, Regions, U.S. States...

- **Science**
  CS, Biology, Astronomy, Engineering...

- **Social Science**
  Anthropology, Sociology, Economics...

- **Society and Culture**
  People, Environment, Religion...

What's New - Weekly Picks - Today's Web Events - Yahoo! Internet Life - Message Boards
Yahooligans! - Seniors' Guide - Apply for a Yahoo! Visa Card - Yahoo! Gear - 3D Stock Viewer

World Yahoos   Australia & NZ - Canada - Denmark - France - Germany - Japan - Korea
Norway - SE Asia - Sweden - UK & Ireland

Yahoo! Metros   Atlanta - Austin - Boston - Chicago - Dallas / Fort Worth - Los Angeles
Get Local   Miami - Minneapolis / St. Paul - New York - S.F. Bay - Seattle - Wash D.C.

Smart Shopping with [VISA]

How to Suggest a Site - Company Info - Privacy Policy - Contributors - Yahoo! How-To

Yahoo! home page. Text and artwork copyright © 1998 by YAHOO! Inc. All rights reserved. YAHOO! and the YAHOO! logo are trademarks of YAHOO! Inc. Reprinted with permission.

Some search engines focus on giving you the most sites possible. These may expand your search using variations on the terms you enter. Others attempt to weed out unwanted material, giving you sites that list your terms the most frequently or evaluating them in other ways to eliminate those you are less likely to want. Some include a count of the number of documents found, and others do not. Some give just the links to the sites found, while others include a portion of the text from each site to help give you an idea of what it contains. Some allow case sensitive searching (recognizing capitalization of words) and others do not. Some engines do a better job than others at eliminating sites that no longer exist from their listings. These are just a some of the differences.

You can access a variety of search engines from Netscape (at *http://home.netscape.com/home/*) or by hitting the "Net Search" button on a Netscape browser.

Web Rings

If you are hoping to find a number of related sites on a particular topic, you might try searching the *WebRing* site *(http://www.webring.org)*. Web Rings are linked groups of sites on a related topic. When you go to a site that is associated with a Web Ring, you will find an area, usually at the bottom of the site's home page, where you can click to go to the next site in the ring, the previous site, a random site in the ring, or a list of all sites in the ring. Web Rings have been developed on mental health, domestic violence, AIDS, homelessness, disabilities, premature babies, cancer, and numerous other topics. In late 1997, Thomas Cleereman started the *Social Work Web Ring (http://www.webring.org/cgi-bin/webring?ring=800290;list)*, which by the end of the year already included several interesting sites. The Web Ring site itself also provides information on starting a Web Ring.

Chapter 7

Ethical, Legal, and Personal Issues

There are no Web police or Internet police, but some concerned cybercitizens have taken it upon themselves to develop some ethical guidelines for themselves and their fellow travelers in cyberspace.

One such group is the Health on the Net (HON) Foundation, based in Geneva, Switzerland. This group has developed the Health on the Net Code of Conduct (HONCode), which is "an initiative to help unify the quality of medical and health information available on the WWW." The Code provides guidelines for those developing Web sites containing health-related information, as well as for those visiting these sites. The principles that qualify a site to display the HONCode logo are as follows (reprinted with permission):

1. Any medical advice provided and hosted on this site will only be given by medically trained and qualified professionals, unless a clear statement is made that a piece of advice offered is from a non-medically qualified individual/organization.
2. The information provided on this site is designed to support, not replace, the relationship that exists between a patient/site visitor and his/her existing physician.
3. Confidentiality of data relating to individual patients and visitors to a medical Web site, including their identity, is respected by this Web site. The Web site owners undertake to honour or exceed the legal requirements of medical information privacy that apply in the country and state where the Web site and mirror sites are located.
4. Where appropriate, information contained on this site will be supported by clear references to source data and, where possible, have specific HTML links to that data.
5. Any claims relating to the benefits/performance of a specific treatment, commercial product or service will be supported by appropriate, balanced evidence in the manner outlined in principle 4, above.
6. The designers of this Web site will seek to provide information in the clearest possible manner and provide contact addresses for visitors that seek further information or support. The Web master will display his/her e-mail address clearly throughout the Web site.

Web sites that display the HONCode logo agree to abide by these principles. If they are in violation, they can be reported to the HON Foundation.

Another group, the Computer Ethics Institute in Washington, DC, has developed the Ten Commandments of Computer Ethics. They are as follows (reprinted with permission):

1. Thou shalt not use a computer to harm other people.
2. Thou shalt not interfere with other people's computer work.
3. Thou shalt not snoop around in other people's computer files.

4. Thou shalt not use a computer to steal.
5. Thou shalt not use a computer to bear false witness.
6. Thou shalt not copy or use proprietary software for which you have not paid.
7. Thou shalt not use other people's computer resources without authorization or proper compensation.
8. Thou shalt not appropriate other people's intellectual output.
9. Thou shalt think about the social consequences of the program you are writing or the system you are designing.
10. Thou shalt always use a computer in ways that insure consideration and respect for your fellow humans.

Netiquette

The culture of the Internet has developed over a short period of time and has changed as millions of new users have joined. Most providers have written rules about proper use of their services. There are general written and unwritten rules regarding the Internet. Among the more useful rules are:

1. Don't put a message on a newsgroup, mailing list, or even personal e-mail that you would be embarrassed to have circulated to thousands of people or to see on the front page of *The New York Times*.

2. Don't send copyrighted material to a newsgroup or mailing list, to an individual, or post it to a Web site without permission from the copyright holder.

3. Spend time "lurking" (the equivalent of listening quietly) on a newsgroup or mailing list before diving in by posting messages. Many groups and lists have a file called an FAQ (Frequently Asked Questions). Read it before posting your first message.

4. Don't post clearly commercial messages on a newsgroup or mailing list. Announcements about new products are fine; sales pitches are strictly verboten and may result in flame messages.

5. Don't, even jokingly, use the Internet to make threats, slander (or libel) others, spread rumors, or use in a manner that violates the law.

6. Do not use obscene, abusive, or threatening language in your e-mail messages and other postings.

7. Do not send chain messages without checking their legitimacy.

8. Do not broadcast an e-mail message to hundreds of people who are not likely to appreciate receiving it.

9. Don't post the work of others (including their personal e-mail messages) without obtaining their permission, or obtaining a license to do so.

10. Don't post a response to a question to an entire mailing list when a message to the poser of the question is more appropriate.

11. Do not "flame" (send insulting and/or abusive messages) on the Internet or respond to those that do.

12. If you are on vacation or otherwise offline for an extended period of time, unsubscribe from your mailing lists, unless you have sufficient space in your mailbox for messages to accumulate and the time to read the messages when you get back.

13. If you are unsubscribing or subscribing, make sure you are doing so to the correct address rather than to the list itself. Save the instructions on how to unsubscribe, and follow them.

14. Never send e-mail under someone else's name/account without their knowledge and authorization.

15. Use sarcasm and humor sparingly; it doesn't usually translate in a text-only environment.

16. Don't use your business e-mail account for personal use. (Note: There are free e-mail sources that offer you a second address for personal at-home use.)

17. If you send out broadcast e-mail to your own personal list and someone asks to be deleted from your list, honor that request and don't take it personally.

18. Keep messages to mailing lists or newsgroups short and to the point.

19.   Focus on one subject per message.
20.   Cite quotes, references, and sources when applicable/appropriate.
21.   Include your signature (a text block that contains your name and other identifying information that you wish to include) with e-mail messages.
22.   When replying to a message, only include the necessary parts of the original message.
23.   Do not "shout." (Writing in ALL CAPS is considered shouting in e-mail.)
24.   Do not attach a file to an e-mail message sent to a mailing list, unless it's of MAJOR importance to the majority of list members.
25.   Check out stories or requests for action before posting them to a list or newsgroup, or sending them to friends or colleagues. There are many stories, "urban legends," that circulate in cyberspace, some containing some kernel of truth, some not. Social workers are especially vulnerable to such urban legends as the Craig Shergold plea, which asks people to send get well cards to a boy with a brain tumor. Yes, there is a real Craig Shergold, and he wished (through the Children's Wish Foundation) to be in the *Guinness Book of World Records* for receiving the most get well cards. His wish was fulfilled in 1990, but cards continue to pour in, largely because Craig's story continues to be circulated on the Internet. As a result, the Children's Wish Foundation now has rooms filled with cards, and relies on a staff of volunteers to handle the mail and recycle the cards. (For more about Craig Shergold, see the Children's Wish Foundation Web site at *http://www.childrenswish.org.*) Other Internet hoaxes or legends are the Neiman-Marcus cookie recipe story, and more recently, the Kurt Vonnegut "sunscreen" commencement speech.

Legal Issues

Copyright

Social workers who use the Internet need to be aware of copyright laws so they can understand how materials they find on the Internet (or post there) may be legally used.

Copyright law changes all of the time, based on how individual cases are decided by the courts. Nothing in this section is intended to be legal advice; even if the information here is correct at the time of publication, the information can change. And some of this material is an interpretation of statutes and case law that many legal scholars would feel comfortable refuting. When in doubt, consult a qualified attorney.

Several Web sites keep up with Internet controversies involving what has been labeled "intellectual property" —patents, trademarks, and copyrights. Among the better sites are:

U.S. Copyright Office:
http://lcweb.loc.gov/copyright/

The ILTguide to Copyright
http://www.ilt.columbia.edu/gen/ref/ILTcopy.html

A Short Course on Copyright Issues

Copyright owners are granted the exclusive rights to reproduce a work, to modify it (such as by creating what is termed a "derivative" work), to distribute it, and to perform or otherwise show it to the public. A copyright is a government-sanctioned legal right (referenced in the U.S. Constitution in Article I, Section 8) for the creator of a work to maintain the exclusive right to copies and/or publication of that work. It is federal law, and thus the rights associated with copyrights do not vary among the states. The work must be something tangible and creative. Thus, it can't be an idea, nor can it be a collection of facts (although if the way a collection of facts is put together is itself creative, then this compilation can be eligible for copyright protection). It can be a photograph, a Usenet posting, a piece of art, or parts of this book. No special registration is required for a work to be copyrighted. You can't legally take photographs or cartoons or articles from magazines without prior permission and scan them for use in your organization's Web page or newsletter.

This legal protection is bestowed automatically on every work created in the United States after April 1, 1989. This means that even if you see a document on a Web site (or anywhere else) that lacks the copyright symbol, it is still copyright-protected, unless the creator explicitly states that the work is intended to be in the public domain.

There are, of course, legal advantages to formally registering a work with the Copyright Office (with a $20 fee), and registration is important in the event that you want to recover economic damages from copyright infringement.

A copyright lasts until 50 years after the work's creator dies. This means that you could post the entire set of Shakespeare's plays on a Web page (as has been done) and not have to worry about copyright infringement.

At one time, a creator could never regain a copyright once a work was in the public domain. With the ratification of the North American Free Trade Agreement and the Uraguay Round Agreements Act (P.L. 103-465), however, some exceptions to this provision were built in to the copyright law.

It makes sense to use a copyright symbol on works you want protected, although in theory, this is not really necessary. This is done by putting on the work a © (insert year of copyright) by (insert name of creator). If you want the added protection of registration, you should apply to the Copyright Office.

You can be charged with infringement whether you use a work for commercial or non-commercial purposes, although the type of use could affect the damages that could be recovered from you by the creator of the work.

In most cases, quotes or excerpts must be attributed to the creator, and must be such that the commercial value of the work is not harmed.

Public Domain

This term refers to works that are not protected by copyright. It includes works created before copyright protection existed, works created by government employees in the scope of their employment, works once protected by a copyright that has since expired, simple facts and figures, and works the creator permits to be in the public domain.

For the most part, creators of works desire to have their works seen by as many people as possible. If you want to put something on your Web site that is the work of another person, it makes sense to simply ask for permission, and get it in writing. If the creator is not willing to grant this permission for free, the offer of a few dollars may make the difference. If it is an article written by a professional writer who makes a living from, in part, electronic distribution of his or her work, expect to pay a fee.

When in doubt, ask. Copyright infringement law is changing; what once was restricted to the civil damages arena is slowly evolving to the criminal arena, and some violations are likely to be felonies by the time you read this. Even if you win a case, the risk is time, legal resources, and a lot of sleepless nights.

Trademarks

Trademarks and service marks provide legal protection to words and symbols that identify a product or service in a way that is intended to distinguish it from the goods and services of others. Federal law provides for registration of trademarks used in commerce. Trademarks are acquired as a result of the first use of a valid mark in commerce. No registration is required, although registration assists those who claim an infringement. Those who register their trademarks are entitled to use a symbol ® after the mark. Registration applications are not routinely accepted by the Patent and Trademark Office. Examining attorneys consider whether the word or phrase is already in common use and therefore ineligible, or if the mark is confusingly similar to another already registered.

The full details can be obtained over the Internet from the Web site of the U.S. Department of Commerce's Patent and Trademark Office *(http://www.uspto.gov)*.

For additional information, see see *http://www.eff.org/pub/Intellectual_property/*

Personal Issues

Security

As a social worker, you probably work with confidential client files and information, so the security and privacy of the computer files you generate and send over the Internet is especially important.

Software such as PGP Mail encrypts messages, so that the only person who can see the message is the intended user. Encryption scrambles the message when it is sent, and the recipient deciphers it. The message looks like gobbledygook to any third party without the "key" to open it.

In Chapter 15, we will discuss in more detail the issues you should think about and precautions you should take to ensure privacy and confidentiality in electronic communications.

Virus transmission

A computer virus is an unwelcome and uninvited program that is designed to execute a frivolous or, in some cases, destructive action on your computer. In the worst case, viruses can cause your system to crash and all of your data to be lost.

They may come in the form of worms (programs that replicate themselves and devour your system's memory resources) or Trojan horses (programs that appear on the surface to be benign or useful, but are destructive in some way to your system).

You cannot get a computer virus by opening an e-mail message, because everything is in ASCII format (a format that uses only numbers and letters and is not conducive to making the commands that constitute viruses) rather than binary files. One way viruses can be transmitted in e-mail is through attached binary files (files that contain symbols and other instructions to your computer). But millions of binary files travel through the Internet every day. Just as it is good advice never to put a disk into your computer from a source you do not trust, you should never download a file or open a file attached to your e-mail from a source you do not trust. The major online services routinely check their shareware/freeware libraries for viruses, although this is certainly not a fail-safe system, because it is run by humans.

Even if you have a virus checker, new viruses are created all of the time. Vendors of anti-virus software typically update their products several times each year to respond to new strains. Most virus checkers will check to see if there is a virus already on your system, and have a terminate-and-stay-resident (TSR) component that stands as a sentinel on your system whenever it is turned on, alerting you when a new virus is introduced into your system.

It is important that you routinely and frequently employ the use of a virus checker, particularly if you are a frequent Internet user. It is also wise to back up important data frequently, so you can recover it, if necessary. It's good advice to have a general idea of how much empty disk space you have on your hard drive. And if you notice that your hard drive is inexplicably filling up despite the fact that you are not knowingly adding files, it's time to get some professional help.

We are not alarmists with respect to viruses. We know people who are so terrified of picking up a virus that they refuse to even go online. That is their choice, but they are missing out as a result of a myth that viruses are a significant worry. Our view is that picking up a virus is just one of many things that can go wrong as a result of using a computer. There are millions of long-time computer users who have never picked up a virus. In contrast, there are few who haven't had the pleasure of having a floppy or hard disk fail and losing hours of work, having software they depended upon get corrupted, or having their Internet Service Provider go down for a few days.

There are many false alarms about viruses circulating on the Internet. You can access a file on the Internet that uncovers false reports about viruses at this URL: *http://www.kumite.com/myths/*

Pathological Internet Use

Some mental health researchers have studied pathological use of the Internet, or "Internet addiction." They say this pathology can result in decreased productivity in the workplace and missed workdays. Social workers may recognize the warning signs in themselves, as well as in their clients.

Dr. Kimberly Young, a psychologist at the University of Pittsburgh at Bradford, has been a leading researcher on this topic. In August 1997, she presented ground-breaking research to the American Psychological Association. Dr. Young developed an 8-question screening instrument to assess Internet addiction, as follows (reproduced with permission from "Internet Addiction: Symptoms, Evaluation, and Treatment," by Kimberly S. Young, posted at *http://netaddiction.com/articles/symptoms.html*):

1. Do you feel preoccupied with the Internet (think about previous on-line activity or anticipate next on-line session)?
2. Do you feel the need to use the Internet with increasing amounts of time in order to achieve satisfaction?
3. Have you repeatedly made unsuccessful efforts to control, cut back, or stop Internet use?
4. Do you feel restless, moody, depressed, or irritable when attempting to cut down or stop Internet use?
5. Do you stay on-line longer than originally intended?
6. Have you jeopardized or risked the loss of significant relationship, job, educational or career opportunity because of the Internet?
7. Have you lied to family members, therapist, or others to conceal the extent of involvement with the Internet?
8. Do you use the Internet as a way of escaping from problems or of relieving a dysphoric mood (e.g. feelings of helplessness, guilt, anxiety, depression)?

According to Dr. Young, a person is considered "addicted" if he or she answers "yes" to five or more of these questions and when the behavior cannot be better explained by a manic episode.

There is some controversy among mental health professionals surrounding the diagnosis of a person as "addicted" to the Internet. One argument against the addiction model is that the Internet is not a substance that is ingested—however, many other non-substance related behaviors have also been defined as addicting (such as gambling or exercise). Another difficulty in diagnosing extensive use of the Internet as addictive is that the Internet does offer positive benefits. Even if a person meets 5 of the 8 criteria above, an argument can be made that it is necessary to use the Internet for school or work, for example. A skilled clinician will need to probe further to determine if such an argument is "legitimate" or if the client is exhibiting "denial" of his or her addiction. Another question mental health professionals might ask is whether overuse of the Internet is indeed a sign of Internet addiction, or whether it is an indication that the user is suffering from another mental health disorder, such as obsessive compulsive disorder or depression.

For a more complete discussion of Internet addiction, see Dr. Young's article, "Internet Addiction: Symptoms, Evaluation, and Treatment," posted at http://netaddiction.com/articles/symptoms.html, and published in the book *Innovations in Clinical Practice: A Source Book, Vol. 17.* Dr. Young has also written a book on the topic, *Caught in the Net.*

Among the sites that have information about Internet addiction are:

Center for On-Line Addiction: http://netaddiction.com (Dr. Young's site)
Internet Addiction Information: http://www.seanet.com/~gtate/addict.htm
CyberWidows: http://web20.mindlink.net/htc/4_1.html

When working with clients who use the Internet extensively, social workers may need to ask themselves and their clients: Does the client's use of the Internet represent healthy information-seeking and relationship-building, or does it represent signs of something less healthy? The resources listed above provide useful information that can help social work professionals develop their skills and competence in assessing and providing services to clients who need help with this new and developing mental health concern.

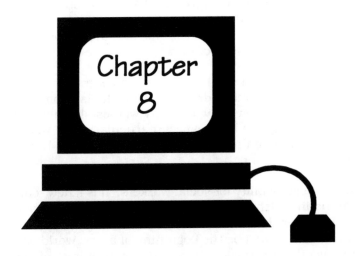

Chapter 8

That's It?

by Robert Tell

"That's it?" is the typical response when I show someone the World Wide Web for the first time. They have come to catch a glimpse of the Information Superhighway, that rumored, incredible convergence of information, technology, and art that is the beginning of a new world order, but instead they find themselves looking at a picture of a student's dog in Ohio. Just as typical is open-mouthed awe with seeing a Web site (particularly one that is designed attractively) for the first time, using a "graphical user interface" (GUI) browser like Netscape, compared to a text-based browser. And where else might you expect to find the entire text of a U.S. Supreme Court opinion that was handed down yesterday? Certainly not in your morning paper.

The Web can be a phantasmagoria of sight and sounds (can smell be technologically possible?) or can be rather anticlimactic. When you heard about the Web for the first time, it may have sounded like the ultimate reference tool where you could look up any fact and get all the latest news, and, in many cases, it's true—you can. At least if you know where to look.

The Web is completely disorganized. Eventually, you will find the information that you want, but before you do, you will have to read boring and tedious descriptions of people you don't really care about. Of course, that's after waiting a couple of minutes for a very large picture to download. The problem with the Web is that anyone can create a page that's accessible to millions, creating an instant platform to inflict his or her particular and sometimes twisted view of reality on the rest of us.

Cyberspace is a mirror of the society that developed and uses it. It has crime and virtue, deception and genuineness, love and hate, passion and indifference, heroism and cowardice. And it is a rare day that I spend a few hours surfing the Internet that I don't find at least one posting that puts a smile on my face.

This is the Web's problem, but it is also its strength. Whatever your passion or cause, you can create a page that is accessible to an incredible number of people. The Web is the Digital Age's printing press, and just as Thomas Paine provoked the colonies with *Common Sense,* an individual can provoke "the Web" with his or her own digital manifesto. Rumors (such as the many about viruses, true and imagined) and conspiracy theories (for example, what caused the crash of TWA Flight 800) flourish on the Web. And jokes that took months to saturate through the fabric of society after a first airing on Letterman now take days.

Some large corporations and agencies have put together really impressive Web sites, but there are sites equally as impressive that have been created by individuals or small groups. This raises one word of caution about the legitimacy of the information you read on the Web and the importance of knowing your source and its reputation for dependability and accuracy.

As you wander the Web, it is not always apparent whether a particular page has been put together by a large organization or an individual. In fact, the Web is really driven by individuals. Companies are scrambling to set up Web pages, while individuals all over the world have well-established pages that incorporate all of the latest features and technology. In this respect, particularly, the Web has the potential to be a great equalizer. For the first time, an individual can present his or her own views on an equal footing with large organizations.

The Web is therefore both an opportunity and a responsibility for social workers. It is a new tool for advocating and educating. It's also a new arena in which many voices are still being left unheard. Social workers can utilize the Web not only to better their work, but also to speak for those who don't—yet—have access to the Web. The Internet may well be the beginning of a new world order, and social workers who, perhaps more than any other professionals, are on the front lines of meeting human service needs, must make sure that it becomes even more inclusive.

So, the next time you set out to wander the Web and you start to think to yourself, "That's it?" say instead, "That's it!"

PART II:

SPECIFIC SOCIAL WORK USES OF THE INTERNET

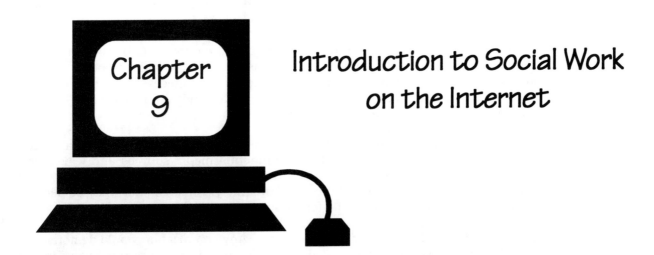

Chapter 9

Introduction to Social Work on the Internet

Just look at any recent social work conference brochure or social work journal, and you will see how the Internet is being injected into the profession. At the 1997 national conference of the National Association of Social Workers (NASW), for example, there were 35 technology-related workshops—the most workshops in any one category other than clinical practice. Among them:

> *Chat Room Psychotherapy: Considerations for Ethical Practice*
> *Wiring Social Work Education: Prospects and Pitfalls*
> *MOOing on the Internet*
> *Virtual Community for Learning and Activism*
> *Integrating the Internet into Child Protective Practice*
> *Using the Internet as a Resource in the Management of Chronic Medical Problems*
> *Web-Based Technology in the Implementation of Career Services for Social Work Students*
> *California: 10,000 Child Welfare Workers Go Online*

This list gives you some idea of the many ways the Internet is already being used by social workers. Similarly, standing-room-only workshops have been presented at the Association of Baccalaureate Social Work Program Directors (BPD) annual conferences, as well as at the Annual Program Meetings of the Council on Social Work Education (CSWE) for the last several years.

On September 7-8, 1997, a conference was held on *Information Technologies for Social Work Education: Using to Teach—Teaching to Use*, sponsored by the College of Social Work, University of South Carolina. Beyond the chance to teach each other what they have learned so far in using the Internet and other forms of communication and information technology, this conference served as a way for professionals and educators in the field to come together and think about what the profession is doing.

The Internet raises an interesting dilemma for the field of social work—for any field actually. The dilemma can be summed up in this way: how do we all coordinate the content we build online efficiently and cohesively?

To elaborate on this, we can look at the Internet from two perspectives: that of the content provider and that of the recipient of information.

As a content provider (an organization or even an individual), I may decide to build into my, or my organization's, Web site what I think will be a useful resource for all or some subset of the social work profession or the people it serves. This resource might be in the form of a useful listing of online content or connections to people or places—a links page as it may be called. Or it could be a specific form of content or a new tool.

Why am I doing this? My goal is probably in part altruistic and in part a way to take my personal or my organization's mission online and establish its role and relevance in this medium.

But before I commit to doing this, I would surely want to search the Internet to discover if anyone has already committed time and energy to the task I envision. If I do find my idea has been developed by someone else, then I may decide to abandon the idea as unnecessary. Unfortunately, this is rarely done. Instead, most organizations simply go ahead and build their sites—in part because there is no place to turn for coordinated action.

Let's give some concrete examples. Numerous organizations' and individuals' sites contain such information as lists of events, job openings, tools for contacting media sources and legislators, current news in the field, and so on. Almost every organization builds a links page, offering it to the professional world as a possible starting point for online content. Each such effort may be personalized and unique in its way, but the overlap of effort is substantial.

As a profession, this would seem to be a poor way to operate. Any organization would demonstrate a great failure of leadership were it to allow its individual staff and teams to continuously re-invent the wheel and compete with one another haphazardly.

Now from the perspective of the particular audiences, we can also see how this dilemma manifests. The key question becomes: where do I go to find what I am seeking when there are multitudinous options? Which is the best? It is an unnecessary burden on Internet users to force them to review the quality of each alternative resource they find.

Perhaps there is an answer.

Several of the participants at the conference held a special meeting to discuss these issues. They envisioned the profession uniting its disparate efforts into some cohesive structure. What this will look like is yet to be determined. The group decided to form a mailing list to continue the discussion. To date, this has grown and continues as a way to collaborate among organizations on the future of the Internet in the field of social work. This mailing list is called "Social Work Education on the Web" <SOCIALWEB@social.syr.edu> and welcomes any new participants to join the discussion.

While it is too early to tell what the result of this will be, the possibilities are exciting for the field.

This is just one example of the many ongoing projects and developments for social workers on the Internet. The remaining sections of this book are devoted to discussing "social work-specific" uses of the Internet. We will look not only at resources labeled "social work," but also at other resources that could benefit social workers and their clients. For example, we will look at family/parenting sites, children/educational sites, and various political, social, fund-raising, and other resources of interest and applicability.

In addition, we will discuss sites and other resources that are helpful more to your clients than to you—sites for example, that help people participate in the political process in their communities, states, or nations, or sites that can be used by adults and children to learn important life skills.

In approaching this wide variety of uses of the Internet, we are aware that it would be impossible to cover every site, every resource, or even every category of use. While we strive to be as comprehensive as possible, the most important objective is to give you a clear and thorough sense of the uses you can make of the Internet. More than anything, your imagination will ultimately be your richest resource. As you explore these sections, try to anticipate the kinds of sites that would be valuable to you if they existed. Chances are they do. And if they don't, then you might be the first person to discover and implement a great new idea.

Another helpful thing to keep in mind as you read on is whether the particular application of the Internet being discussed relates to things you already do (which are especially important as potential time savers or cost savers), or whether they represent exciting new ideas (which are to be approached with caution, assuming your schedule is already busy).   If the Internet can save you time and improve your primary and essential work activities, then it should be quickly embraced and utilized. If, on the other hand, it represents a way to do more and different kinds of things, then it should be recognized that while these new things may be efficient, you will have to prioritize your ability to commit to online activity.

In many cases, the things you can do online that are new will have a secondary nature and will not be directly related to your primary responsibilities. This is not to say that these uses are unimportant. To the contrary, you will likely find them enormously beneficial and satisfying. In essence, the Internet can expand your capacity as a social worker, with a minimal additional time and money commitment.

Thus, for example, you can expand the reading sources you use for professional growth and news without incurring the expenses and time associated with subscribing to every journal, newsletter, and newspaper. Similarly, you can expand your communication network using e-mail. Professional development activity you might have done without in the past becomes possible online without burdening either your budget or schedule. Discussing issues with professionals around the country and introducing your clients to online resources that can help in your work with them and for them are some other ways to increase the reach and breadth of your activities.

Besides giving examples of resources and ways social workers are using the Internet in their work, we will also discuss social work ethics as they apply to your use of the Internet in your practice. And we'll give tips on using the Internet for specific non-direct service functions, such as fund-raising and advocacy.

So, as you look at the following sections, consider not only whether there are Internet resources that can affect the core work you do, but also investigate its uses for activities you have pushed aside in your efforts to shape the scope of your daily responsibility. This will open the widest possible application of the Internet to the work you do and will enable you to make the priority judgments necessary to integrate the Internet into your social work practice.

Chapter 10

Professional Development and Connecting to an Internet Social Work Community

I would like to network with colleagues in my field of expertise. Where can I go to do this on the Internet?

I would like to learn about an area of practice or hone my skills and understanding of a specific topic. Can I do this on the Internet?

I would like to learn about opportunities for professional development or conferences online. Where can I research such information?

How can I share my professional experiences and increase knowledge about particular treatment models, interventions, strategies, or programs that work?

You can do all of the above activities on the Internet, if you just know where to look or how to search. In this chapter, we will look specifically at four ways to enhance your professional development online. They are:

- Online conferences and continuing education
- Online Communities and Professional Organizations
- Networking—Mailing lists, newsgroups, and online chat
- Online journals

Online Conferences and Continuing Education

We all know the value of attending a conference, symposium, or workshop. Besides learning new skills and information, conferences offer the opportunity to network informally with colleagues and take a break from the everyday routine of the office. And increasingly, they provide continuing education credits that are required for state licensure renewal for social workers.

We may experience a certain amount of tension when we see a brochure for a great conference we want to attend. The costs seem to get higher every year while the budget is tighter. We wonder how the agency will survive if we are gone for a few days, and how hard it will be to catch up when we return. We may rationalize, "What do I really need professional development for anyway? Work is going fine now. Do I really need this? Will I really learn anything new?"

Much of the concern about taking time out from our busy schedules (and money from our skimpy budgets) to attend costly conferences is legitimate. Sending one person in your office to a conference can cost as much as a computer that will allow Internet access for the entire staff.

Can you more efficiently network and develop professionally using the Internet instead of traveling to conferences? To preview, our answer is both "yes" and "no." Yes, much of the value you get from going to conferences can be supplemented with online networking and professional development. But no, there are many aspects of getting away from the workplace, taking time to meet people face-to-face, and hearing experts speak in a "live" situation, that the Internet cannot replace.

Online Continuing Education

A development we are beginning to see and will likely see more of in the future is the emergence of online "courses." An online course can allow people to access expertise without having to travel to attend programs and can use any of the tools we've already seen, including mailing lists and Web sites. Chat rooms can be utilized for shorter-term classes. Classes can be scheduled during specific time periods, or they can be permanently available as self-taught presentations of material with access to the author possible as necessary.

One example of the distance learning projects we found is the CyberTowers Distance Learning Center *(http://cybertowers.com/ct/dlc)*, which offers online courses such as "Sex Online: An Addiction?" CyberTowers courses are composed of modules that are read online and discussed by students in a chat room at a specified time. Each course has its own message board for interaction among students and instructors.

Behavior Online provides ongoing discussions on a variety of specialized professional topics, including shame and affect theory, classical Adlerian psychotherapy, cognitive therapy, EMDR, Ericksonian therapy, and others. These specialized message boards are frequented by the leading experts in these areas. For example, on the discussion board on the shame and affect theory of Donald Nathanson, one can interact with Nathanson himself. There are also clinical case conferences and private meeting rooms on this site.

Another form of continuing education for social workers is supervision. Joan Steinbock, LCSW, offers a weekly online peer supervision group through her Web site's chat room. (See her site at *http://www.designsrus.com.)*

Finding these opportunities can be difficult. We have not found a site that comprehensively indexes and announces online courses. Participation in the forums, mailing lists, and professional online communities relevant to you is the most likely way to find out about them.

The Internet is also a natural way to advertise traditional professional development opportunities. Universities, agencies, associations, and other training institutions will likely use their Web sites to provide a calendar of such opportunities. Also, resources like Mental Health Net's Calendar *(http://www.cmhc.com/calendar/)* and PsychScapes *(http://www.mental-health.com/)* list such programs.

Online Professional Communities and Professional Organizations

In most cases, a professional organization exists to serve the interests of its members and the interests of the subject area around which it is based. The organization brings people together around a particular topic or profession, and they can get to know one another and be mobilized, if necessary. Professional organizations typically provide members with educational opportunities, knowledge and resources, and networking possibilities.

Along these same lines, a "community" Web site serves some of the same purposes. It provides a "place" for people who share a common professional focus to meet, exchange ideas, obtain helpful resources, and mobilize regarding policies that affect them.

Joining an Online Community

Perhaps the first thing you will want to do in order to begin using the Internet as a networking tool is to look for an appropriate "online community." By online community, we refer to any Internet resource that is directed to a particular group and includes some of the following characteristics:

1. *Comprehensive*: An online community site based on a particular topic area usually aims to provide a one-stop place for accessing information about the relevant subject area. An online community for mental health professionals, for example, will probably link to many other useful sites giving information, resources, and tools that are helpful to people in this area of practice. In short, it seeks to provide the best gateway to the Internet for mental health professionals and hopes to serve as the best starting point for accessing information online for this field.

2. *Interactive*: Such a site will also likely be interactive, not just providing information, but seeking feedback and participation of some kind. In some cases, this might take the form of membership, so users feel that they are part of the online project. In other cases, it might mean the ability to chat or write comments that are posted online for others to read, or "vote" in an online poll.

3. *Networking*: Many of these sites also seek to serve as the connecting point for professionals in the area or field that the site is about. One way this might be done is to list individuals' names and e-mail contacts at the site.

4. *Timely*: Online communities typically attempt to maintain regular and timely information. They hope, for example, that you will visit with frequency to keep abreast of what is happening in the field as a whole. While many sites provide timely news relating to the work of the particular sponsoring organization, a professional community site would tend to provide a broader scope of current news.

Thus, a typical professional community site is one that is often larger than most other sites, provides connections to a broad array of information relating to its topic, organizes itself as conveniently as possible so that it can serve as a launching point for the rest of the Internet, and involves people outside of the organization in its project. It tends to be multi-functional, bringing a package of information and resources together on a particular topic, and is often membership-based.

A highly effective, but simple form of professional community is the e-mail mailing list or Usenet group. Here, professionals congregate and communicate about a specific field or topic. These provide—in essence—an ongoing conference or symposium that is, in theory, never ending. Treat these as you would a real-life conference. If you walk into a discussion in progress at a conference, you might listen in and get a sense of what everyone is talking about before jumping in with your own contributions. So, too, should you take the time to listen (or "lurk") and explore online discussions and communities before leaping in and commenting.

One example of an online community is HandsNet (see next page). Others are the Social Work Cafe (*http://www.geocities.com/Heartland/4862/*) and Mental Health Net (*http://www.cmhc.com/mhn.htm*). There are many other online communities, some of which are described in the reviews section of this book.

Professional Organizations

Besides professional communities that exist only online, traditional professional organizations like the National Association of Social Workers (NASW) and the Clinical Social Work Federation (CSWF) also have a presence on the Internet. By visiting their Web sites, you can quickly and conveniently find out what they have to offer, if you are not already a member. If you do already belong, your

Up Close: HandsNet
http://www.handsnet.org/

To give you an idea of what we mean by an online professional community, let's take a look at HandsNet. HandsNet is an organization whose sole purpose is to provide a national online human services community. While most Web sites in this field are sponsored by organizations that exist independently of the Internet and have other goals and activities associated with their missions, HandsNet is unique in having been formed and dedicated completely to the communication and connectivity of organizations online.

Thus, HandsNet is an online service (a separate special online network) that is similar in theory to services like America Online. Unlike America Online, however, HandsNet serves the human services field exclusively, rather than the general public. HandsNet is now completely accessible via the Internet. While it is an independent network, all of its content can be accessed through any Internet browser.

Handsnet is a membership organization that operates on both grants (it is a non-profit organization) and annual membership fees.

HandsNet is an important online community that everyone in the human services should know about. Within HandsNet are numerous sub-groupings of people organized around a variety of topics (substance abuse, housing, homelessness, AIDS/HIV, legal services, and others) or around a variety of populations served (children, youth, families, elderly). While members have access to any of these groupings' information, the typical member will likely focus primarily on the area closest to what he or she does.

Participating members in HandsNet are encouraged not only to obtain current and archived information, but also to input information in the form of articles, stories, experiences, calendar events, job announcements, data, evaluations, and any other news of interest to other members.

Some information is made available for non-members, including some current news articles, and some of its forums are made public. Freely available forums include Action Alerts *(http://www.igc.apc.org:80/handsnet/hn.action.alerts/)*, where members provide critical and timely news; the Weekly Digest *(http://www.igc.apc.org:80/handsnet2/hn.weekly.digest/index.html)*, in which HandsNet summarizes some of the important daily postings; and Welfare Reform Watch *(http://www.igc.apc.org:80/handsnet2/welfare.reform/index.html)*, which includes current information and resources for people involved in this area. Also included is the Members Exchange *(http://www.handsnet.org/handsnet/hn.community/mex/index.html)*, where community members can request and share information with one another.

HandsNet is highly interactive. Members, in addition to posting their own documents to be added to the wealth of archived and current information, can also communicate with one another. Every HandsNet member gains a special e-mail address, which can be used for simple internal communications or for communication across the Internet. Each member is added to a published directory and can use HandsNet as a forum for collaborative projects.

HandsNet's strength is in the combination of its narrow focus and its broad structure. What makes HandsNet unique is that it both narrows your topic area, allowing you to get specific targeted information and to network with people who are closest to you in the work they do, while at the same time, its overarching organization allows for the cross-fertilization of ideas and organizing the whole of human services. For this reason alone, if you are so inclined, HandsNet is a recommended service.

At the same time, HandsNet has a distinct public policy cast and may not include nearly as much in the category of direct practice. HandsNet, therefore, overlaps broadly with social work, but is not all-inclusive of the areas considered in the domain of social work. If you practice as a clinical social worker, while you should be aware of this service, it might not be as relevant to you and you may find little information that applies to you directly. In addition, HandsNet membership has been geared in the past primarily to organizational members, not to individuals.

But it is increasingly becoming a good service for individual members, as well, with membership rates and services that can be most valuable to sole practitioners. In addition, if HandsNet is short on clinical social work material now, the participation of more members interested in this area will naturally lead to more content and perhaps the opening of an appropriate forum for clinical social work. These factors might encourage you to join and build upon HandsNet's successes.

HandsNet provides weekly communications to its active members. One, the *Weekly Digest*, summarizes new information that has been posted over the week. The other, the *Members Exchange*, summarizes requests members have made to one another in the open forum area. Thus, even if you do not set aside the time to review HandsNet, you will have a way to keep abreast of a great deal happening in the field across the country.

For anyone who needs to disseminate information to others, HandsNet can be an outstanding resource. There are currently thousands of participating members. For these members, HandsNet serves to foster collaboration and partnerships. It enables agencies separated by geography to work almost seamlessly together, sharing databases of information and resources with one another. The potential of this resource is most dramatic. One might think of HandsNet as working to bring the entire field of human services together into a single mega-organization of collaborators and information sharers. Its current state makes it a valuable resource and tool, and as it grows, it becomes increasingly valuable to its members.

Handsnet home page. Courtesy HandsNet. Reprinted with permission.

organization's Web site is another benefit of that membership. In fact, some association Web sites have "Members Only" sections that offer some special information or services that only paid members can access. For members and nonmembers alike, the sites are excellent sources of information on such topics as social work licensing, ethics, up-to-date news of professional importance, upcoming conferences, available publications, and so forth. They may include online chat rooms or provide information on subscribing to an organizational e-mail list.

Some social work associations that are online are:

Association for the Advancement of Social Work with Groups (AASWG)—*http://dominic.barry.edu/~kelly/aaswg/aaswg.html*
Association of Baccalaureate Social Work Program Directors (BPD)—*http://www.rit.edu/~694www/bpd.htm*
Association of Oncology Social Work (AOSW)—*http://www.biostat.wisc.edu/aosw/aoswhello.html*
Clinical Social Work Federation (CSWF)—*http://www.cswf.org*
Council on Social Work Education (CSWE)—*http://www.cswe.org*
National Association of Social Workers (NASW)—*http://www.socialworkers.org*
School Social Work Association of America (SSWAA)—*http://members.aol.com/SSWAAWeb/SSWAA1.htm*
Society for Social Work Leadership in Health Care—*http://www.sswahc.org/*

Networking

One value of attending a conference or joining a professional organization or community is the ability to network with others in your area of practice. People in the same field of interest, separated by geography, can gather to talk and exchange ideas with one another. These connections can give you, or your staff or colleagues, valuable contacts and resources for the future. The kind of expertise available at a conference or through professional organization contacts may not exist locally.

On the Internet, these kinds of connections can be achieved through participation in mailing lists, Usenet groups, and (increasingly) real-time chats.

Mailing Lists

In some ways, mailing lists are a much more modest enterprise than an online community Web site for networking in the profession. They are, for example, much simpler, allowing you to send a message that is "mirrored" to all others who subscribe to the same list and in turn receive new messages and responses from others.

Almost everyone who has become truly active online subscribes to at least one mailing list, if not four or five. For those ambitious enough, a list can be created by most online service providers, so if there is not one on the topic you want to discuss with other professionals, you might consider starting one.

Mailing lists are intrusive—that is, subscribing to one will mean that you will receive, via e-mail, all of the messages that any other subscriber sends to the group, whether they are of interest to you or not. The intrusiveness, however, is also its strength. Since the messages come to you automatically once you subscribe, you do not need to change your daily routine or remember to take the time to participate. It is, therefore, easy to integrate your mailing list participation into your regular schedule.

You will most likely want to find a list on a topic that is as close as possible to your interests *and* not too heavily trafficked. The number of messages a day varies from list to list. The SOCWORK list, for

Up Close: E-Mail Mailing Lists of Interest to Social Workers

To subscribe to most mailing lists, send an e-mail message to the *administrative address*. In the body of the message type: SUBSCRIBE NAMEOFLIST

If you are subscribing to a LISTSERV list, type: SUBSCRIBE NAMEOFLIST YOURFIRSTNAME YOURLASTNAME

Once you have subscribed, you can send a message to everyone subscribed to the list by sending it to the *list address*.

Here are a few social work lists to get you started.

AASWG (Discussion of groupwork issues)
Administrative address:
listproc@martin.barry.edu
List address:
groupwork-aaswg@martin.barry.edu

BPD (Association of Baccalaureate Social Work Program Directors)
Administrative address:
listserv@listserver.isc.rit.edu
List address: bpd@listserver.isc.rit.edu

BSW Student Discussion List
Administrative address:
listserv@listserver.isc.rit.edu
List address:
bswstudent@listserver.isc.rit.edu

CSOCWORK (Canadian Social Work Discussion List)
Administrative address:
listserv@pdomain.uwindsor.ca
List address:
csocwork@pdomain.uwindsor.ca

CUSSNET (Computer Use in Social Services)
Administrative address:
listserv@listserv.uta.edu
List address: cussnet@listserv.uta.edu

FEMSW-L (Feminist Social Work)
Administrative address:
listproc@moose.uvm.edu
List address: femsw-l@list.uvm.edu

INTSOCWORK (International Social Work)
Administrative address: listserv@nisw.org.uk
List address: intsocwork@nisw.org.uk

SCIOFSLW (The Philosophy and the Science of Social Work)
Administrative address:
listproc@lists.vcu.edu
List address: sciofslw@venus.vcu.edu

SOCTECH (Technology and Social Work Discussion)
Administrative address:
listserv@uafsysb.uark.edu
List address: soctech@uafsysb.uark.edu

SWEAIDS-NET (HIV-AIDS Social Work Education Canadian Network)
Administrative address:
listserv@morgan.usc.mun.ca
List address: sweaids-net@morgan.ucs.mun.ca

SOCWORK (General social work discussion list)
Administrative address:
majordomo@uwrf.edu
List address: socwork@uwrf.edu

SW-FIELDWORK (Discussion of fieldwork issues)
Administrative address: listserv@nmsu.edu
List address: sw-fieldwork@nmsu.edu

example, may generate 50 messages daily, whereas a more specialized list like SW-FIELDWORK may go several days or weeks without any activity. Some lists offer a digest version, which is useful if the number grows high. The digest version allows you to receive one message a day containing all the individual messages of the day. You can skim it at your leisure.

How will you know the rate of messages on a list? In most cases, you won't. It's a trial and error process. First, you subscribe to the list that seems interesting to you, and if you find that you receive ten messages in the first half-hour, you might want to immediately unsubscribe. Instructions for unsubscribing are usually sent to you just after you subscribe, so don't lose that message or you will have to ask the entire list what to do (and this is considered very poor Netiquette).

Mailing lists are accessible by everyone with Internet e-mail. Some, however, are exclusively designed to serve only invited participants. An organization, for example, might use its own mailing list for internal communication.

Since mailing lists are created by anyone with appropriate software, they may be difficult to find. They can typically be found at relevant community sites, or through various resource lists on the Web. Michael McMurray has developed one of the most comprehensive such lists, and it is available at *http://129.82.209.104/lists.htm*. SWAN also has such a list at *http://www.sc.edu/swan/listserv.html*.

For a large directory of mailing lists (as well as Usenet groups), see *Liszt (http://www.liszt.com/)*, a directory of over 71,000 lists on every topic, or *Tile.net (http://tile.net/listserv/)*, which is organized by subject, description, name, country, and sponsoring organization.

Newsgroups

Usenet provides an alternative to mailing lists that are too heavily trafficked. The major difference with a Usenet discussion group (also called a newsgroup) is that it is non-intrusive. When you have the time, you can go and see what discussions are taking place and can contribute or read as you wish, following a discussion, or catching it in the middle. You can skim messages, eliminating them if they are of no interest.

Usenet groups' availability varies according to your Internet access provider. Each provider subscribes to a variety of discussion groups, and only these can be accessed by its members. There are some Web sites that provide similarly designed bulletin boards, and anyone can access these. True Usenet groups, however, vary from local groups such as "alt.chicago," which would tend to be subscribed to by providers in and around Chicago, to those that are international or national in scope and are almost uniformly subscribed to by Internet providers everywhere. The creation of new Usenet groups is a rather involved process. Often, members of an existing group decide to split into two subtopic areas to maintain a workable size and focused discussion.

Some newsgroups that may be useful to social workers and their clients are alt.child.support, alt.support.cancer, alt.support.depression, alt.support.divorce, and alt.support.grief, for example.

Chat

Chat rooms can be useful networking tools, although being based on real-time or "live" discussion, the number of participants is usually limited.

Thomas Cleereman has set up a Web-based social work chat room, which is open at all times. To get to this chat room, go to *http://www.sparknet.net/~tjcleer/chat.htm*. There are specialized social work chat rooms, such as *The New Social Worker's* Social Work Careers Chat, which can be accessed through *http://www.socialworker.com*, and the Social Work Cafe Chat at *http://www.geocities.com/Heartland/4862/*. (See page 9 for more information on social work chat rooms.)

America Online has a very active Social Work Chat on Thursday nights from 9-10:30 Eastern time. Each chat is focused on a particular topic. (See pages 9 and 66 for more details about these chats.)

When you participate in a chat, you can "talk" to another person in "real time." You type something on your computer, and the other person sees what you typed almost immediately. He or she can then respond right away. It's as if you are having a live conversation, but using a keyboard instead of talking out loud.

One can even accomplish the dubious task of "being two places at one time" by presenting a workshop or being a "guest speaker" via chat. Two social work professors scheduled such a presentation. The conference where they were presenting was in Baltimore, but the presenters were in other cities. Of course, the topic of the workshop was live chat and its implications for social work! When scheduling a presentation or meeting by chat, however, you may run into technical problems. This particular presentation didn't work out, because the server was down. Linda Grobman, co-author of this book, had a similar experience when she couldn't get in to her own Web site's chat room during a scheduled chat on social work careers. She has since set up an alternate chat room just for such emergency situations.

Online Journals

Another way social workers develop professionally is by reading professional journals. Again, we all face a certain tension. We wish we could take the time to read and absorb every professional journal relating to our work, but time is a factor, as is the cost of subscriptions. We may not subscribe to all of those that are relevant for us (which would be costly) or we may only focus on those that are most specifically related to our practice area and interests (because this is the most efficient way to spend our time).

The availability of online journals and articles offers several potential advantages. First, you automatically have access to them through your computer (except, perhaps, those that charge subscription fees to read online). Even if a fee is charged to read online journals, it may be less than subscribing to the printed version.

Of course, there are other advantages to taking some of your professional reading online, such as the ability to search by words or phrases, save articles to your hard drive, the ability to cut and paste quotations into documents (within the legal limitations of copyright law) in which you use them, and the ability to correspond with the article's author.

Online Journals in Full Text

There are two types of journals online—those that are published only in electronic form, and those that are online versions of print publications. We have listed some of these in the Publications section of the reviews in the back of this book.

One example of the first type is *Perspectives (http://www.cmhc.com/perspectives/)*. This mental health magazine is published exclusively on the Web. No print or e-mail version of this electronic journal is currently available. Submissions are invited from professionals and others. Examples of recent articles are "The Role of Counseling in Illnesses" and "False Positive: What You Should Know Before and After the HIV Test."

An example of the second type, an online version of a print publication, is *The Advocate's Forum (http://www.chas.uchicago.edu/ssa/advocates_forum.html)*. This is a student-run, mostly student-written, journal published by social work students of the University of Chicago School of Social Administration. The online version includes the full text of all articles published in current or past issues of the print journal.

Right now, the amount of online publishing probably serves a relatively small online readership. Simply put, many people have not adapted to the differences between online and print publications. While your newspaper, magazines, and other journals probably come to your mailbox, regularly updated Internet journals must be visited by their readers. This means that to get the full value of them, a part of your week or month must be spent remembering about the journal and checking in to read the latest volume. While some online journals allow people to register and receive e-mail alerts when new issues are available, even this takes the proactive step of visiting the site when you have the time.

For many, the actual reading of articles on the computer is another difference that is hard to get used to. Magazines are things we fold up and take with us on the bus. We highlight in them with yellow markers, and cut out articles of interest. Our computers have been used for over a decade for entering information, and not so much for retrieving it, especially in the form of passively reading. Doing so now, feels strange—even unproductive. But it is a great opportunity for learning.

On some level, most online authors probably realize they are writing for a small handful of people, if any. One justification is the theory that readership will grow as the Internet grows. Another theory is that only by publishing worthy content will readers be attracted to the Internet. A third possibility is that while online regular readers may not be there, posting articles online will contribute to the available research information that can be found and called upon when needed (e.g., through the use of search engines).

Without commenting on the accuracy of these assessments, we can say that there is a great deal of good content free for the reading. While it is incumbent on the reader to know the source as part of evaluating its value, the underutilization of the Internet for reading is something people should probably try to overcome. Articles can be read on the bus, because they can be printed. They can be stored for future reference on your hard drive, or you can bookmark them. They can be shared with others by simply sharing the URL address. Unlike magazine articles, the Internet sometimes gives readers the chance to write to the authors, helping to use the Internet for a broader exchange of ideas. Interactivity is one of the major advantages of online journal articles. Another is the inclusion in these articles of hypertext links to other pertinent material online.

The only change people need to make is to build into their schedules the time for reading identified sources and to develop the inclination for this form of professional development. Consider some of the online journal sites (defined as any site that publishes articles on a regular basis) in the Review section of this book. Are there any you would want to return to in the future?

How to Find Online Articles

One resource for finding articles is the *Electric Library* (http://www.elibrary.com/). This fee-based resource allows you to search an extensive database of over 1,000 journals for articles on particular subjects. Articles are available in full text. The *Electric Library* brings thousands of offline journals to your fingertips, archived and searchable. Perhaps more than any other single spot on the Internet, this one will make you feel as if you have tapped into a library.

NewsPage (http://www.newspage.com/) is free for a basic membership, but charges a fee for premium and advanced memberships. The service provides you with a personalized Web site, organizing and prioritizing topics of interest to you, from health care to business to general interest topics. Once created, the personalized site becomes a source for clippings from various periodicals with access to the full text of articles.

MY Yahoo! (http://my.yahoo.com/) is a free service that allows you to create a personalized news source for online articles.

You may be able to use your home or office computer to remotely search card catalogs and data-bases at a public or university library. Some databases will require you to use a password. If you are a student or faculty member at a university or college, contact your school's computing center to find out how to get a password. If you have graduated, check with your school to find out if alumni are allowed access to the library's electronic resources.

Writing for Online Journals

Internet journals also provide new avenues for social workers who want to write for publication. For example, the journal *Perspectives (http://www.cmhc.com/perspectives/)* is a peer-reviewed, multidisciplinary, APA-style journal that is published only on the World Wide Web, not in print. The submission guidelines for this journal reflect some of the special issues in writing for an online audience. "There is no definitive length on articles; authors, however, are reminded that they are writing for a Web-oriented audience. That means smaller is likely better, but if you have to make it long, so be it. Maximum article length is 2,000 words (15,000 characters or bytes). Ideal article length is 1,600 words or less (10,000 character bytes)," the guidelines suggest. And, of course, manuscripts are accepted via e-mail.

Citing Online Journal Articles

The availability of journal articles and other resources online is a great convenience for researchers. It also presents the question of how to cite such sources in academic writing.

The 4th Edition of the *Publication Manual of the American Psychological Association,* published in 1995, began to address the issue of how to cite electronic media. However, the standards are expected to change with frequent changes in technology. There are several Web sites that provide updated information on citation of electronic sources. On the APA's own site, you can find a page on "How to Cite Information from the Internet and the World Wide Web" *(http://www.apa.org/journals/webref.html).* At another site, you will find "Web Extension to American Psychological Association Style (WEAPAS): Proposed Standard for Referencing Online Documents in Scientific Publications" *(http://www.beadsland.com/weapas/).*

Here is an example of how a reference to an article on *THE NEW SOCIAL WORKER's* Web site might look:

Grobman, L. (1996). Is There a PhD in Your Future? *The New Social Worker, Vol. 2, No. 2, pp. 30-31.* Retrieved March 15, 1998 from the World Wide Web: *http://www.socialworker.com/phd.htm*

In this particular case, the document is available both electronically and in print. The citation tells the reader where the article can be found in both versions. It says that *as of March 15, 1998,* this resource was available at this URL. However, if the article is removed from the Web site or moved to a different URL, the reader will still be able to find it in print.

If you are citing an e-mail communication in your writing, this is treated as a personal communication. In APA style, personal communications are not listed in the Reference section. They are cited in the text only. For example, if you are referring to an e-mail message sent to you by Gary Grant on March 1, 1998, this is how the citation will look:

G. Grant (personal communication, March 1, 1998)

Chapter 11

Networking and Finding Resources Through Online Services

The major online services, such as America Online, Prodigy, and Compuserve, all offer services and information that are not available on the wider Internet, while at the same time offering Internet access to their members. We decided to take a look at these services and find out what they have to offer social workers and their clients. We found that they vary greatly in quantity and quality of social work-related content.

America Online

The largest of the three major online services we will discuss, America Online (AOL) has over 10 million subscribers and is organized around "keywords." Once a member signs on, he or she can type in a keyword and immediately go to that area of AOL. One of the keywords on AOL is "ssSocial Work." If you log onto AOL and type "ssSocial Work" in the keyword window, you will be taken to a screen that lists services for the Social Work Forum. This forum is sponsored by Allyn and Bacon, a publisher that provides the College Online area on AOL.

Susan Mankita, LCSW, a hospital social work director in Miami, Florida, hosts the Social Work Forum, which includes a message board, a weekly social work chat, links to social work related Web sites, information about social work Internet mailing lists, and information about Allyn and Bacon's publications.

One chat, for example, focused on the topic of what to do when people with clinical needs find social workers online and try to get them to "do therapy." What are the social worker's responsibilities and liabilities? Each weekly chat is focused on a specific professional topic.

The AOL Social Work Forum also provides message boards where social workers and students can ask questions, share experiences, and network. Message board topics include Introduce Yourself, Job Bank, Retirement, Licensure Issues, MSW Programs, and others.

There are other places on AOL where social workers gather. On a message board called "Health Professionals Exchange," there is a folder for social workers. Also, under "Professions," social workers can be found. Until recently, there was a Child Abuse Forum moderated by social workers.

Another feature of AOL is that each member has the option of posting a "Member Profile." In this profile, the member can list his or her name, city and state, occupation, hobbies, and other information. The profiles can be searched by any of these categories. So, if you want to find AOL

Up Close: An Interview with Susan Mankita, AOL Social Work Forum Host

Susan Mankita, director of social work at a hospital in Coral Gables, Florida, has developed a national online constituency as moderator of America Online's Social Work Forum, a part of College Online sponsored by book publishers Allyn and Bacon. She has been running the weekly chat for social workers and social work "wannabees" since the Spring of 1995.

Mankita's responsibilities are three-fold: First, she maintains the site, keeping the bulletin boards free from spam (unwanted commercial or other inappropriate messages), as well as developing topics for and facilitating weekly chats. She secures content and Web links to keep the site up to date and informative, and she uses her social work training to encourage newcomers to the site to connect with others who share their interests.

Second, Mankita maintains a 500-subscriber mailing list of forum members who wish to be notified of weekly chat topics and other information. "People are constantly sending e-mail messages that they want to be added to, or removed from, the list," she says. "Often these requests include questions about social work. I feel it's important to answer them. Although my affiliation with the Social Work Forum leads some to consider me an expert in all social work matters, my real expertise is the ability to connect these social workers to relevant material, colleagues with similar interests, and informed experts."

Third, Mankita leads the chats. "This is by far the most interesting aspect of my responsibilities for the Social Work Forum," she admits. "Being a chat host is something of an art form. In addition to focusing a room 'full' of participants on a particular topic, I have to greet newcomers and clue them in. If someone enters the room by mistake, I have to steer him or her in the right direction. Often we get students looking for homework help, and they can really disrupt the flow of conversation. I try to answer their questions through internal messaging, but that can take my attention from the room, where it's most needed."

Leading a chat means balancing structure with flexibility. "If you envision the chat room as something of a town square, or local pub, a place where community develops, it's easier to understand the role of the host," explains Mankita. "It's his or her job to make the members feel they're part of something comfortable and welcoming. Without the smiles, hugs, and handshakes offered in real time, the host has to convey warmth creatively through the text."

Why is that so important? "The Internet is a huge, scary place," suggests Mankita. "There are many social workers who use the Social Work Forum as a vehicle to safely explore the larger, less-friendly online world. If they feel secure, as if they're among friends, they'll take more risks in their exploration."

What is a typical chat session like? Susan's chat group meets every Thursday from 9-10:30 p.m., EST. Participants are about equally divided between social workers and social work students, and represent all age groups from high school through retirement. They are disproportionately from the East Coast because of the time schedule. Men and women participate in equal numbers—a change from about a year ago, when the chats were comprised primarily of women.

An average chat draws 15 participants, with as few as 10 and as many as 30. Mankita chooses topics from current events—such as welfare reform, health care, and managed care—and from chatter requests. Some chat sessions are devoted entirely to case presentations.

How is chatting like, and unlike, other communication? According to Mankita, chatting has several features unique to synchronous communications, such as telephone or speaking face-to-face. "There are few widely shared norms," she says. "The Internet community actively makes these up, and they show up on the net as 'Netiquette.' One advantage of chatting is that people may feel freer to share intimate details that would be difficult to say face-to-face. But there are also negative outcomes, such as 'flaming.' That occurs when all social norms are flung aside and one communicator assaults another." And, Mankita warns, "people can be lulled into believing that communicating online, and talking about action, is the same as actual action. It is not."

Text-based communications such as chatting may be preferable for some individuals, but not others. "They're marvelous for those folks who enjoy talking through their fingertips, or feel they can be clearer by writing," Mankita explains. "On the other hand, they pose difficulties for people who aren't crackerjack typists, or who are more comfortable verbally."

For herself personally, the absence of "physical distractions" in chatting is appealing. "It enables you to consider ideas, devoid of environmental or personal features," she says. "But again, the absence of social cues can be problematic at times. In ordinary conversation, we can usually tell if others want to continue—they look at us with interested expressions, and their mouths might drop open a bit when you share something a bit shocking. We oftentimes hear small gasps and other auditory cues. With chatting, we don't know who's waiting in the background to make a point, or who is being sarcastic. Some people find this freeing. I find myself doing everything I can to add cues as to my mood, such as using emoticons." She reports that she also types "uhm," "er" and "hmmm" a lot, because it adds a human rhythm to her online communication.

Chatting has at least one unequivocal advantage: it's accessible to people who otherwise might be isolated by geography or illness. Several social workers who participate in the forum are unable to work because of chronic illness, but they can participate fully online. Internet communication also offers equality, at least for the computer-literate. "It doesn't matter if you're a student or a professor in the Social Work Forum," explains Mankita. "Everyone gets equal time, and all opinions are considered important."

"The Internet has a lot to offer, but there is also reason for caution," Mankita suggests. "Using the Internet—especially if you start signing up for things, developing a Web page, or making your presence known—is creating a permanent body of data that can be used, copied, or misused. In particular, all agencies should ensure that client information not be included in an accessible way, or confidentiality would be at risk."

Mankita recommends that agencies that consider use of the Internet do everything possible to connect clients as well. "Social service agencies tend to have clients who are disadvantaged, and these are the people who will really be left behind, as more and more people access the Internet," she emphasizes.

The AOL Social Work Forum can be accessed by AOL subscribers at keyword **ssSocial Work**.

subscribers who are social workers in Seattle, you can search for "social worker Seattle" and get a list of people that match your criteria. As an example, we did a search for "social worker criminal justice" and got back 5 names. "Social worker mental health" yielded 101 AOL members, and "social work Atlanta" gave us 49 Georgia social workers.

Prodigy

Prodigy was one of the first of the major online services to give its members Internet access, in the early 1990s. Many flocked to the service for the inexpensive Internet access, although somewhat limited at that time. Now, a few years later, Prodigy offers more Internet services, but a search of this service yielded very little in the way of a social work community.

Prodigy has "jump" words, similar to AOL's keywords. In Prodigy, members access the "Go to" menu, then click on "jump" and type in the word they're looking for. When we typed in "social work," we were taken to the Adoption Bulletin Board, but in looking through that board, we found little evidence of social workers there. In fact, there seemed to be little professional input in general on this or other client-issues-related boards, such as divorce and family matters.

Some of Prodigy's bulletin boards and Interest Groups may be of interest and use to social workers' clients. The Interest Groups include adoption, child abuse, autism, divorce, self-help, family matters, health and fitness, and others. We found an "Ask the Therapist" bulletin board under "Health—Emotional Issues." There was no indication of the credentials of the "therapist." This consisted of a public bulletin board where a writer wrote a question, such as, "My daughter is driving me crazy staying out til all hours of the night. What can I do?" and the therapist wrote back publicly with an answer, sometimes asking more questions of the original writer. Occasionally, the "therapist" suggested that the writer seek "in person" therapy.

Prodigy has a "member list" that can be searched only by name or location, so there does not seem to be a way to search for categories of members, such as social workers, on this service.

There is a Prodigy Web site *(http://www.prodigy.com)*, where you can find information on the services offered, as well as download the Prodigy service software.

CompuServe

CompuServe is known for its strengths in the areas of business and research. When we signed on to CompuServe, we liked the graphical interface. It was pleasant to view and easy to understand and navigate.

The "Professional" icon looked like one that might lead to social workers. However, it took us only to a screen of business-related information.

Next, we tried the "Education" icon. It took us to a section called "Reference and Education," then to "Business and Career," where we found such resources as the E-Span Job Search, and Business and PR Newswires.

We tried the "find" icon and searched for "social work." Three items were listed—AARP, Authors Forum, and Retirement Living Forum.

One of the service's major strengths is its "Forums." These are special interest group areas that consist of message boards, article libraries, chats, and other services. These seem similar to the Social Work Forum on AOL, but there is not one specifically for social work on CompuServe. Presumably, there is the potential to start one, if someone has the interest and takes the initiative, and if there is enough interest among CompuServe subscribers.

Some Compuserve forums that might be of use to social workers and their clients include the AARP forum, African American Resources forum, ADD forum, Missing Children forum, Survivors' forum, Public Health forum, and others.

For more information on forums available on CompuServe, see the Web site at *http:// directory.compuserve.com/forums/forumsindex.asp.*

Making a Decision

These services provide easy and fairly inexpensive avenues for connecting to the online world and, potentially, a professional community. If you are not familiar with the Internet, it may be a good idea to get connected through one of these services first, before trying a local Internet Service Provider, which may be less expensive, but also less user-friendly.

All of these services have price plans that are similar—around $9.95 for the first five hours per month, and $2.95 for each hour thereafter. In late 1996, AOL began to offer its $19.95 per month unlimited usage plan, which initially led to access problems and busy signals, resulting from the response to this new plan. The price for this plan increased to $21.95 a month in April 1998.

These services have extensive networks of local access numbers, making it possible for most customers to access them by dialing (through the use of a modem) a local telephone number. For those in rural areas, however, the closest access number may be a long distance one, therefore adding the cost of long distance fees to the cost of the service itself. If you live in a rural area and cannot get local access to one of these services, you may find it less expensive to use a local ISP instead.

All three services offer free trial memberships, so you can try out each one and decide for yourself which one, if any, fits your needs. They all provide Internet access, and they offer members their own space to publish Web pages. They each provide additional content, besides Internet services.

If you are looking for a social work community on one of these services, we would recommend AOL, where it is easy to find not only individual social workers, but also an organized group of colleagues.

Chapter 12

Staying Linked, Online

by David Grotke, CSW
(aintdave@aol.com)

I retired recently after more than 30 years as a social worker, six years of that in child protective services, and the rest as a psychiatric social worker in a community mental health center. I enjoyed the work and intellectual stimulation.

About a year before I retired, I purchased a nice little Mac LC and signed on to America Online (AOL), learning how to use the machine and navigate in cyberspace. I didn't want to be left behind on the new information superhighway. It was easier than I thought. I've upgraded machines twice and now use a fast new PowerMac and a speedy modem.

I've found that this is now my main connection to the profession. Over the past few years, I've subscribed to several mailing lists, including the Forensic Psych list *(forensic-psych@sjuvm.stjohns.edu)* and the Child Maltreatment list *(child-maltreatment-research-l@cornell.edu)*. I've "lurked" (read, not contributed) and contributed to lists, having fun and keeping up on current issues, adding my two cents and experience when something strikes me. I interact with other social workers, psychologists, psychiatrists, lawyers, GALs (Guardians Ad Litum), consumers of mental health services, and the general public with questions about social work and mental health issues—very synergistic and multidisciplinary.

I particularly enjoy responding to e-mail requests by students for information about careers in social work, psychology, forensic work, and child protective services. I tell them my experiences and offer encouragement, tips on alternatives, types of work and agencies, pros and cons of the profession, and readings they can explore. They really appreciate the help and often say this information is otherwise hard to find.

Some of my friends in the child abuse and neglect field have regular chats on AOL, and I often join them. I've hosted a few chats myself, including one on child abuse and the media, and another on child abuse and criminal justice reforms. I was "nominated" to be one of four hosts on AOL's Child Abuse Forum (which has since been discontinued), a message board devoted solely to that subject. My "job" is to peruse the lists each week and do my best to answer inquiries and provide useful information to AOL members. In return, I discovered they give me credits for online hours! Nice. AOL has many resources for children and families looking for support or mental health information.

I browse lists and sites on AOL and the World Wide Web (WWW) for other psychological and behavioral information and discussion. I've discovered new readings and resources. It's like having the stacks of a huge library right on my desk. It's the first place to go for information on anything. I learn what's going on in other countries, other states. I see a lot of feedback and frustration from "consumers." I have found odd places and perspectives, like the support group for self-mutilators I stumbled into one day—teenagers, discussing their cutting practices and feelings. Never got that in school. It's a well of human thought, behavior, and emotion to explore.

In 1996, I decided to build a Web site. Initially it was just an exercise to see if I could do it. It was a little work, but again easier than I'd thought. Nothing complicated, just a site I could manage as a sort of hobby. In the spirit of the free and open nature of the Internet, I decided to call it "Dave Grotke's Free Advice!" I found information on how to set up the site, use an HTML (Hypertext Markup Language) program, make a few graphics, and upload the files to AOL, which acts as the "server."

I provide a variety of mental health and social work links to other good sites, basic information, a disclaimer, a personal résumé, and an e-mail service to answer questions submitted by Web surfers. It's user-friendly and reflects my personality. I tested it out with friends, then "advertised" it by submitting my URL (Uniform Resource Locator) to major search engines, such as Yahoo!, Excite, Webcrawler, and AltaVista. You can check out "Dave Grotke's Free Advice!" at *http://members.aol.com/ aintdave/*.

I had over 400 site hits (visitors) in the first three months. About 35 of those were actual requests for help, none of them phony, with some repeaters. Suicide, loss of control, sexual problems, child abuse, parent-child issues, relationships, work problems, just like at work. Teenagers and adults. The difference is the near anonymity, and several people have said that they could *not* have presented these problems face-to-face with anyone. It's not therapy, and I tell people that. Several have referred friends. It's also free, and they have mentioned that. I find that I'm providing a useful service that appears to meet people's needs. I can continue doing some of the work I enjoy, at a pace I can handle, without an insurance company or HMO second-guessing me. I run it as ethically as I believe I can (that's another issue), and I feel freer to say what I think than I did as an employee of a public agency. I speak as an individual now.

Another thing about the process is that it requires you to write everything. There are a few video links, but they're not used by most people yet. All your input must be typed. You are forced to write, and to put into words things that you ordinarily might not write about. When I worked in an agency, most of the writing was notes, memos, letters, filling in forms—all functional stuff. Occasionally, I would have to write a piece that required serious thought and cogent argument, but not usually. In order to respond to online inquiries or discussions, you must write, and you want it to be sensible, understandable, and represent what you really think. You respond as an individual, not as a representative of an agency.

Using the computer like this will force you to practice writing on a daily basis. It will make you write more, make you examine your own views more carefully, and expose you to a wide range of ideas to play with and respond to. You'll get feedback and criticism, too. When you're finished, if you remember to "save," you'll begin to accumulate a collection of your thoughts and ideas, perhaps useful to you or others in the future.

So my Mac, AOL, and the Internet have kept my "processors" running for the last few years. The desktop box has been my main connection to social work since I quit working. Because of it, I am still working, doing what I enjoy, in a new environment, learning new things. If I ever decide to do real work again, I'll be ready.

Using the Internet With and On Behalf of Clients

Chapter 13

There are many places on the Internet that speak directly to people's emotional and social needs. There are resources for mental health, child abuse, chronic illnesses, hospitals, forensics, community organizing, substance abuse, homelessness—you name it, and there's bound to be a Web site, chat room, mailing list, or newsgroup about it. There is no limit to the potential here, and your imagination will be more important than ever in using these resources.

Imagine, for example, that hospitals offered Internet access for patients. People confined to hospital beds often feel isolated. The future may see the Internet available from every hospital bed, allowing patients to engage in conversations (at any time of day or night in either real-time or posted discussion boards), to explore reading material, and much more. On one occasion, Gary Grant played chess through e-mail with a man from Norway who was in the hospital with Parkinson's Disease. In this example, the hospital allowed the patient to use its Internet e-mail address for the game. He could send Gary one move a day and, at the same time, share his experiences. It was very rewarding for Gary as his chess opponent expressed how important it was to him to have this activity to look forward to each day. The breadth of activity online offers a multitude of possible ways to deal with isolation, whether it is due to a short- or long-term hospital stay, disability, or other circumstances.

Other examples already emerging as primary Internet uses include helping children identify and keep up with pen pals from other countries or finding sites for helping students do their homework, sites for helping people obtain tax forms and other basic life resources, and helping clients with disabilities network with others who share the same condition.

Internet sites for your clients may not be listed in one place or under a list of "social work" resources. It will be up to you to think about the needs of your client and whether there may be an Internet solution for that need. It will then be up to you to help locate a solution on the Internet. Often, the sites that will be relevant will have been created by non-social workers, or perhaps by others who are in similar circumstances to those of your client.

You may also need to think about access to the Internet for your client or client population. Can your agency provide clients with access? Increasingly, community-based agencies are developing on-site computer labs for those they serve. Funders are often willing to support such projects. Companies might donate computers they are replacing. Some computers that a company might consider out-of-date are still sufficient for basic Internet access, especially e-mail. Alternatively, can you find other places—libraries, nursing homes, or other community organizations—that can help provide computers for your client? You may even consider advocating for publicly accessible Internet-ready computers at appropriate locations in your community.

Finally, you may need to be able to demonstrate the Internet and to guide clients in how to use it for the purposes you think would be valuable to them. Using the Internet does not require an extraordinary amount of knowledge. The Internet has grown increasingly user-friendly, and most can understand how to navigate it without a great deal of expertise.

In addition to being able to locate sites that are helpful for clients, a social worker might want to be able to point some of these out to others working with the clients, such as teachers, parents, or home health nurses.

Let's now begin to explore in more depth some of the possible uses of the Internet for your clients.

Learning About One's Condition or Needs

Well-prepared agencies will have available for clients various forms of printed material to help them understand a condition that they or a family member may have or to detail how to address particular circumstances in their lives. Consider the Internet an excellent resource for finding more. Social workers can obtain educational information and print it out for their clients, or they can direct clients to sites that will help them understand a particular problem and demonstrate how others deal with it in their lives.

Below are a few examples of sites containing information that might be helpful for clients to use.

School Psychology Resources Online: (http://www.bcpl.net/~sandyste/school_psych.html)
Online resources for the school psychology community. Counselors, educators, parents, psychologists, students, researchers are welcome. The site contains a directory to numerous articles and information about such issues as Anxiety Disorders, Behavior/Conduct Disorders, Eating Disorders, Mental Retardation, Suicide, Attention Deficit Disorders, Deaf/Hard of Hearing, Learning Disabilities, Mood Disorders, Tourette Disorder, Autism, Dissociative Disorders, and Substance Abuse.

Habit Smart: (http://www.cts.com/~habtsmrt/)
This site was created and is maintained by Robert Westermeyer, Ph.D., who says: "This Web site has been constructed to provide an abundance of information about addictive behavior: theories of habit endurance and habit change as well as tips for effectively managing problematic habitual behavior." For clients, this site contains an online self-scoring form for determining if one is addicted to alcohol. Articles are often directed to clients, offering such advice as ways to get back on track, tips for moderation, and ways to help parents cope with children with addictions. There is also a great deal here for professionals.

Yahoo! Health Related Resources: (http://www.yahoo.com/Health/)
Yahoo's list is enormous, enabling you to find information on just about any health-related issue. Here, one can find resources on death and dying, disabilities, procedures and therapies, and reproductive and women's health.

Yahoo! Family Resources: (http://www.yahoo.com/Society_and_Culture/Families/)
This section of Yahoo's directory leads to content for parents on all aspects of parenting, to adoption-related information, and to a variety of sites for children on such topics as domestic violence. One good example is *Dianna's Domestic Violence Page (http://www.geocities.com/Wellesley/1488/index.html)*. Here one can find a variety of information, such as discussions directed to teens on date rape and teen abuse.

These are only a few examples of the many, many sites where individuals can find out about problems they face. Many others are described in the *Reviews* section of this book. The Internet offers the ability to research a problem in privacy, with simplicity and ease. It also helps people to get a

When the Professional is the Client

For social workers who themselves have a physical disability or mental health diagnosis, are recovering from addiction or abuse, or otherwise need support for themselves, the Internet has some interesting possibilities.

First, the same sites that are available to any client of social workers are also available to social workers as clients themselves. One social worker who is diagnosed with bipolar disorder, for example, told us that she participates regularly in an Internet mailing list for people with this diagnosis. Participating in an online support group can help social workers avoid the stigma they might face (or fear they would face) if their colleagues found out about their impairments. It can help them preserve a level of confidentiality for themselves that might not be possible if they attended a local support group in the same community where they practice.

Some sites have been developed specifically for social workers and other professionals with issues of their own to resolve. *The Wounded Healer Journal*, an online publication started by social worker Linda Chapman, offers "points of departure for psychotherapists and others on the healing journey." This site has a searchable database of professionals for networking and referral purposes.

The *Professionals with Disabilities* page, also by a social worker, provides some useful statistics and links to other resources that have been designed with this group in mind.

One such site, *The Independence Bank (http://www.ind-bank.org/)* is a résumé bank for individuals with disabilities. When we searched it, we found 3 social workers.

wide range of perspectives, both from professionals and from others like themselves. They can find a wealth of information and see vividly that they are not alone.

Using the Internet can be empowering for clients, allowing them to help themselves in researching and networking. Information and discussions are available and possible at any time of day or night. It offers more privacy, allowing clients to read material online without having to carry around printed material, fearing the stigma they might face if someone found these materials.

The Internet also gives the social worker a rich source of supporting material. By showing what others have discussed on the Internet, the social worker may be able to more thoroughly demonstrate that he or she understands the problem than would otherwise be possible. Exploring a client's problem using the Internet can be a way to enhance his or her trust and confidence. It brings before them a more global and representative sample of other people sharing their opinions and facts.

On the other hand, social workers should be aware that it is likely there will be differences of opinions presented online. While this may require the social worker to explain such differences, the Internet is still a good starting point for engaging the client in discussion about issues. Social workers should be prepared to explain why someone at a Web site makes a claim contrary to what they have presented to the client. It is especially helpful if the social worker can identify those sites that are sufficiently concise and well-organized and contain information that is accurate and can be trusted.

Life Skill Resources Online

Social workers must often be Jacks-and-Jills-of-all-trades. Clients may need information on basic resources for daily life. Using the Internet, you can find tax forms for a client, help give directions to an interview, find the bus schedule, find job opportunities in their area, learn about day care resources close to where the client lives, and so on.

While many of the sites referenced in this book will lead to general life resources, the Yahoo! directory is a good starting point for more of these, especially in urban areas where Yahoo! has specialized regional directories. Federal, state, and municipal government sites, as well as sites of individual local resources, can also help. Your proficiency in searching for and locating resources will be the best tool for finding these when needed. Once found, it might be a good idea to begin collecting them for future use. You can begin recording useful Web site addresses, newsgroups, and mailing lists. You can even develop your own Web site, providing links to sites you find valuable to clients in your area.

Thinking of the Internet's value in daily life requires a mindset change and especially important is anticipating when it may *not* be helpful. One useful tip may be to turn to the Internet when there is no other tool handy. If a client needs a writing workshop, do you know of one? If not, then you might explore whether there is an Internet site that provides this function and is of sufficient quality for the client's needs.

As this discussion suggests, one important way to use the Internet is to start by thinking, "Hmm, wouldn't it be great if there were a Web site offering some recipes and advice on low-cholestorol cooking for this person?" Chances are that such a site exists, or if it does not, then at least a reference to a book can be found (and typically accompanied by an order form) online. What other solutions might exist? Is there a newsgroup for those who cook where a particular question can be asked?

It will generally be more effective to think of the need first and then determine if a useful Web site exists to address this need. The opposite approach, researching Web sites and then applying them to your clients' needs, will likely enmesh you in a very time-consuming process that is less likely to result in finding the right sites.

Let's try a few more examples to see how this might work.

Catherine is a Senior Adult Coordinator at a community center in Atlanta. The members' program committee has asked her to find a speaker for a prospective lecture on art and culture. Turning to the Internet, she could use "Art and Culture and Atlanta" as a search term. Doing so, she would quickly find a wide range of sites referencing museums, university departments, cultural organizations, and individuals with interests in this area. Contacting any of these by phone or e-mail should lead to someone willing to visit and present to the group.

Jennifer is a social worker who works for a home health agency. On her first visit with an elderly woman, she discovers that the client is not eating a healthy diet. She has difficulty getting around, and hasn't always been able to find a ride to the grocery store. Jennifer remembers reading a magazine article about *NetGrocer (http://www.netgrocer.com)*, a nationwide online grocery store that delivers groceries to the customer's house. Although her client doesn't have a computer, Jennifer makes arrangements for a volunteer to take the client's order each the week and place the order for her via computer.

Tom is advising a client who is preparing for a job interview. The client needs to know what to say and ask in the interview, how to write a good résumé and cover letter, and even how to dress appropriately. Turning to the Internet, he finds many sources for advice and tips on all these areas, as well as examples. He finds that the company has a Web site, so Tom helps his client research the company and prepare specific questions and comments for the interview.

Think of other examples from your own experiences in which you might use the Internet to access everyday information useful to your clients' needs. Clients can be linked to places where they can learn parenting and infant care, access professionals in other fields, get health, safety, and nutritional resources and advice, and much more. As a social worker, being the gateway to these resources can enhance your ability to serve clients effectively and address their needs.

Client Networking

The Internet can be a tool for client-to-client interactions, allowing people to network and meet others who share some of the same problems, issues, or conditions they face. Clients can network with others through newsgroups, mailing lists, or Web site communities. The social worker's role is to connect them to existing resources, or to start new ones. Connecting with others in these ways can give clients the opportunity to "practice" interaction skills, for example, or to communicate with others in similar situations in order to gain or give information or emotional support.

Social workers who work with groups or particular populations may appreciate the Internet as a tool for helping people connect to others in their specific group. There are sites for broad categories of people (women, African Americans, Hispanics, elderly, and people with disabilities). There are sites for somewhat more narrowly defined groups (children who suffer from cancer, interracial families, women with eating disorders) or combinations of the above (minority women in business). There are even sites for extremely specifically defined groups (Bostonians who are tall).

One of the particularly exciting things about the Internet is its ability to help people form communities by interests rather than by geographical location. An online community shares many of the same attributes as an "offline" one. There are people who feel a sense of being joined together. Each member has an opportunity to voice comments, concerns, and questions. Typically, the members even share some level of authority in what happens in their community. Even if one person "owns" the site, the ability to create competing communities focusing on the same topic encourages democratic participation at some level.

For those who enjoy involvement in any online community, the people they meet there may become a sort of extended family of resources and supports they can draw something from. Those they know geographically close to them may still be their primary network, but the online community extends more widely.

So, what actually goes on in a Web site community? Collections of online and offline resources may be detailed, often with commentary from those who have used them. Online discussions are frequent, either live or in a format similar to newsgroups. Often, participants will be listed by name or alias and describe themselves, also offering communication with one another. Sometimes the community will act as a whole in advocating change. In short, it does much the same as any organization might do—just doing it mostly online. In fact, it is often hard to tell the difference between an offline organization that has developed a Web site component and a group that has formed entirely online.

Social workers should be especially interested in this kind of online activity. Perhaps you work frequently with or advocate on behalf of a particular group. The convenience of online sites might allow you to monitor some of the discussion that takes place at a relevant site to keep abreast of the major issues. Similarly, you can use such sites to research and ask questions relevant to working with a client who has issues you are not so familiar with. Naturally, if you know of a great site that might be relevant to some clients, there might be occasions to connect them to it for helpful interactions and information.

A Hypothetical Internet Session for a Children's Social Worker

by Linda May Grobman

I had never even heard of the Internet when I worked at a children's hospital in the mid-1980s. But if I had, and if the Internet had been widely accessible then, how could I have used it to enhance my practice? In what ways could I have used it to gain more information on conditions that my patients had? Could I have found other professionals with similar experiences with clients? Would there have been resources that my clients could access directly that would provide them with information and support for their situations?

I decided to take a ride on the information superhighway and find some stopping-off points for a children's social worker.

First, let's say that I'm a social worker in the oncology unit of a children's hospital. Since I am the only oncology social worker in the hospital, it is sometimes difficult for me to get constructive feedback on my work with the patients and their families. I have a good network of oncology social workers in my city, but I'd really like to expand that network of people I can call upon to "bounce ideas" off, and I'd like to find more resources to use with my patients and their families.

I decide to use the Alta Vista search engine, and I do a search for "oncology social work." One interesting resource I find is a Web page for Talking Lady Press *(http://www.canadamalls.com/talkinglady/)*. This company publishes books for children, including one written by a social worker, called *Having a Brain Tumor.* I can even order it online, although the form on the Web page is not secure, and the publisher suggests printing it out and mailing it in.

I also find a Web page for the Association of Oncology Social Workers *(http://www.biostat.wisc.edu/aosw/aoswhello.html)*. Although I could find information about this organization by other methods, it's nice to be able to access the Web page to get updated information.

Next, I do a search for "pediatric cancer." This leads me to a site called POWR—"Pediatric Oncology Web Resources" *(http://www.hmc.psu.edu/depts/pedsonco/index.html)*. This site was developed at Pennsylvania State University Children's Hospital and includes links to patient and professional resources.

I also find a great site called "The Never-Ending Squirrel Tale" *(http://www.squirreltales.com)*, developed by a mother of a childhood leukemia patient. This is a site for parents of children with cancer, and includes this mother's own story of her daughter's diagnosis, treatment, and coping; an online newsletter; a questionnaire; a Frequently Asked Questions (FAQ) page; and a page of links to other resources. Because this mother is also a professional copywriter and graphic designer, the page has nice graphics and is well designed. I think to myself that this would be a great resource for parents of children in the hospital, and I think of the following idea.

The idea is to set up a computer at a central area in the hospital. This computer could be in a waiting room, in a children's activity room, or even in the social work department itself. Parents and patients would have Internet access through this computer, and at the computer would be a list of Internet resources that the hospital's social workers have put together. As parents and children find new resources, they could also add them to the list. This idea could work in other hospitals besides children's hospitals, and could be used in other types of agencies or settings, too, but I think it would work especially well in the hospital setting. Parents could benefit from accessing pages like "Inkan's Preemie Home" *(http://hem.passagen.se/inkan/index.htm)*, a personal Web page of a premature infant and part of the Preemie Ring, a collection of non-commercial premature infant Web sites. To get a list of all the sites in this Web ring (99 altogether as of March 1998), go to *http://www.webring.org/cgi-bin/webring?ring=preemie&list.*

I move on to look for resources for my colleague who works with adolescents and children in the hospital's outpatient mental health center. She recently began working with a couple of new clients—one a young child recently diagnosed with ADHD, and the other an adolescent who needs residential treatment. She asked me to look up some resources on my computer, since she doesn't have one, but these clients do. She has found that kids are often more computer savvy than the therapists or the kids' parents. They may use the information they find online more readily than they will listen to the adults who are trying to help them live their lives more effectively.

In my search, I find a NAMI Helpline Fact Sheet on ADHD *(http://www.nami.org/helpline/ adhd.htm)*. This might make a good handout for parents, or they can read it online. I print out a copy and make note of the URL.

Next, I search for "residential treatment." I find online brochures for several treatment programs. One, Brandon Residential Treatment Center in Natick, MA *(http://205.161.11.2/brtc/ home.html)* has a fairly extensive, graphically sophisticated site, including information about its program, as well as links to special education-related sites. The site even has an online referral form, which makes me wonder about confidentiality issues. Is it a good idea for a social worker to send a client's name and other identifying information to another agency in this manner? My colleague and I discuss this at length, and decide it would be best to use the site as a sort of online brochure, but to follow up looking at the site in the more traditional ways—by calling the agency and getting more information before making a referral.

Menninger Residential Treatment Program *(http://www.menninger.edu/tmc_prof_chdsrv_restrt.html)* has a link to e-mail the admission office, but not an online referral form. Island View Residential Treatment Center for Adolescents *(http://www.qcontinuum.com/~ivrtc/index.html)* has a site similar to Menninger's, in that it provides information about the program and contact information for making the traditional type of contact (by telephone or mail).

When I narrow my search to "residential treatment Pennsylvania," to try to find something closer to home, all I get is a listing of residential real estate sites! Oh, well! The Internet doesn't always know what we are searching for, I guess.

Through this search, I realize there is much on the Web that can help me, the children I work with, and their families. I decide to, at a minimum, develop a list of these sites for social workers in the hospital, and another one for patients and their families. Setting up an Internet station in the hospital is something to work toward, but may take a little more time. Perhaps I should go on the SOCWORK list and ask if anyone else has been successful in doing this....

Examples

To give you an idea of the types of communities we're talking about, we'll look at a few now.

PlanetOUT (http://www.planetout.com) is a relatively recent attempt to create "the" online resource for the gay and lesbian community. The site attempts to provide something for everyone: news updates and archives; community discussion areas that allow participants to pose and respond to questions, entertainment information, and Internet links.

Chicano Latino Net (CLNET) *(http://latino.sscnet.ucla.edu/)* is a general Latino-focused Internet site serving all segments of the community, and a gateway to Chicano/Latino research efforts being carried out at the University of California. The site has a lot of good information and links that help it encompass many aspects of the Latino community, including: sections for job postings and employment seekers; a virtual museum on Latino art, music, dance, theater and film; online exhibition of the life of a famous Latino educator; calendar of events; links to Latino student organizations nationwide; and more. A really nice feature is a page where Latino faculty, staff, students and professionals can fill out a form asking a series of questions, and have CLNET create a Web page for them that will be added to a long list of Latino personal pages the site stores—thereby giving visitors a true sense of interaction with the site, and literally letting them become part of a virtual Latino community.

ElderWeb (http://www.elderweb.org/) is an online community of older adult computer users. Most areas are restricted to registered members only. Activities include the Elder Village Cafe, a place to link up for discussions about general issues, and sharing memories. Similarly, *Seniornet (http://www.seniornet.com/)* offers online discussions for older adults, as well as computer learning centers in various communities, where senior citizens can meet and take computer classes.

Pen Pals

For children, one way to "network" has always been through correspondence with pen pals. There are sites now that link children to one another for sharing discussion through e-mail or by writing. The advantage of e-mail is that it is so much quicker and less expensive than "snail" mail. There are places for finding pen pals, such as *Cool Kids and Teens E-mail Club (http://www.geocities.com/Heartland/Hills/3415/)* created by a 12-year-old who instructs children on using Penpal Soup, a service that matches children to pen pals and provides a unique e-mail address for the purpose, or KeyPals Club International *(http://www.worldkids.net/clubs/kci/)*, started by an 11-year-old. KeyPals Club is for 8- to 16-year-olds and includes opportunities to have pen pals from other cultures, chat, develop home pages, get homework help, and join mailing lists. It is part of World Kids Network *(http://wkn.org/)*, which is "dedicated to the advancement of children's education worldwide" and strives to "inspire them to thoroughly explore the possibilities of their world in the creative atmosphere of the Internet, to become computer literate, and to achieve their full potential in this dynamic new field."

There are also sites where children can find pen pals who have a common medical or social situation. One example is *Winners on Wheels (WOW)* at *http://www.wowusa.com/*. This non-profit organization for children in wheelchairs exists offline as well as on the Web. Kids who are WOW members can get a password to enter the WOW Kids Connection online to find a directory of WOW kids' e-mail addresses. The site also has a gallery of WOW kids' artwork, poems, and stories, and offers guidelines for submitting these materials.

Finding Referral Resources

Another way social workers might use the Internet is to find places to refer clients when other referral options don't pan out. Most social workers have at their fingertips (and at the tips of their tongues) the more common places to which they refer clients, but what about those times when you have a client who needs something out of the ordinary?

Some communities have community service directories posted on the Web. For example, the Columbia County Human Services Coalition in Bloomsburg, PA, makes its Human Services Directory available in this way. It can be found at *http://www.bafn.org/human-services/alpa-dir.html,* as a part of the Bloomsburg Area Free-Net. This listing is similar to those you can get in print from most local and regional United Ways, but it is online.

The New York City Public Advocate's office has a "cyber-hall"—"a customer-friendly tour guide to NYC government." Among other things, this site includes a People's Green Book listing contacts for services related to children, health, emergencies, courts, food and shelter, disabled people, seniors, discrimination, and others. The site is at *http://www.pubadvocate.nyc.gov/~advocate/greenbook/greenbook.html.* Such online directories could come in handy when looking for resources in another city, or when looking for very specialized resources that may not be readily identifiable in other ways.

In the next chapter, a social worker in private practice, Sheila Peck, tells how she has used the Internet with clients.

Up Close: Hyde Park/Kenwood Community Conference
http://www.hydepark.org/

One effective example of building support for a non-profit community group through the Internet is reflected in the fledgling efforts of The Hyde Park/Kenwood Community Conference. At present, the conference—maintained by a community organization—doesn't seek contributions online. As a local group, it has a narrow reach, and people in the community wouldn't have a reason to visit the site unless they were already involved in the organization.

Hyde Park/Kenwood obtained free server space donated by a company, Ganymede, Inc., which is recognized at the Web site.

With this server space, the organization offers to establish a "beginning" Web site for any non-profit or business member as a part of membership. Small-budget non-profits can have a Web site built by the organization's volunteer designers at no cost; all others pay a small fee. Businesses and organizations with existing Web sites can join as "link" members, supporting the organization and in return being linked to its directory.

Free consultation is provided to members seeking to develop more elaborate Web sites. Through these services, and by organizing a community directory, HPKCC helps organize a Web site where community members and potential visitors can access existing online information and resources in a single place.

In addition, over time, the Hyde Park/Kenwood Community Conference is using the Web site to enhance its own mission—improving the quality of life in the community and increasing participation by all community members in the decisions, policies, and issues that affect them.

This is just one example of how the Web can be used to organize and empower a community.

Hyde Park/Kenwood Community Conference home page. Reprinted with permission.

Chapter 14

Clinical Social Work, Computers, & Cyberspace

by Sheila Peck, LCSW

Keeping in Touch

Martina (all client names have been changed), my client, was going to Moscow for the summer. We had known about the trip for months—in fact, the trip was a direct outgrowth of therapy. Her family lived in Moscow, and she had not seen them for years. Now she needed to. It was time to resolve certain issues, particularly with her elderly grandmother, who was not physically able to visit the States. We had been targeting this visit for months—and now it was time for Martina to go. She was frightened, nervous, extremely cautious about speaking to these people who were used to acting out their feelings in dramatic, stereotypically Russian ways, but who never actually *talked* about them. The matriarchal grandmother was the most formidable of all. Therapy had centered around her and now it was time to work some of it out.

But Martina felt alone and unready. There was NO ONE in Moscow, no friend, no relative, to whom she could turn for support in this troubling task. And in Moscow, therapy isn't what it is here in the U.S. For years, psychiatry meant social control. People were supposed to conform, not feel. If you went to a therapist, you were not conforming. You could get into political trouble. And even if that's changed, Martina didn't really know any such professional there who she could trust.

I knew Martina had a laptop computer, and she knew that I, too, was online—we used the computer for scheduling or changing appointments, on occasion. She asked if she could write to me via e-mail when she did her therapeutic work in Moscow. Of course, I said, "Yes." But should this really have been, "Of course"? Would we be doing therapy? Support work? Online chats? Neither of us was sure. But we were both comforted by the fact that she would not have to be entirely alone in this process. Nor should she be. But without the computer, she would have been.

Making Difficult Communication Less Painful

"Margaret," a client, was an abused and battered child. She has never been able to confront her father in person because he is too intimidating. Recently, after much therapeutic work in which it was difficult even for her to fantasize what she might say to him in person, she decided to try it via e-mail (they live in widely disparate parts of the country). First, she informed him she had much to say to him and she preferred to do it via the Internet— would he hang in with her? Intrigued—and both of them are computer buffs—he agreed. Through e-mail, Margaret poured out all that she had been holding within for so many years. Her father became defensive, overwhelmed, and eventually denied most of the history she was relating to him. Nevertheless, the process was therapeutically helpful for this client in three basic ways. She was able—finally—to ventilate; because she had his replies in writing, she could e-mail them to me and I could validate, where appropriate, her perceptions; and finally, she could at last understand that he would not change and that if she wanted to continue a relationship with him (which she did) it would have to be on a superficial level. This latter was an important realization for Margaret, because she was finally able to let go of her intense need to please him and her subconscious belief that all of what had happened might have been her fault.

A New Medium

The use of the computer in clinical work is still being defined. With each new situation, each new bit of client work utilizing the computer, we clinicians need to make new rules for ourselves. There are issues of boundaries, confidentiality, malpractice, liability and anything else that relates to the practice of psychotherapy and clinical social work.

John Augsburger, LCSW, is past-president of the Virginia chapter of the Clinical Social Work Federation (CSWF) and the first Webmaster of the CSWF Web pages *(http://www.cswf.org)*. In a description of a workshop that he, two colleagues, and I presented for the CSWF's conference in February 1997, John wrote, "The growth of the Internet and the advent of the World Wide Web present unique opportunities for the profession of social work. Contrary to the fears of some that developing technologies would lead to further isolation in our society, the advent of Internet technology offers a greater possibility of connection and relatedness to us and to our clients. The Web has the potential to impact all spheres of practice: direct patient contact, the education of social workers, the 'business' of social work and the political realities of the profession."

As I prepare to submit this chapter (via e-mail, of course), I've been talking about it with many of my colleagues. And I hear more and more of a diversity of reactions—some of it about matters I have not previously considered. And, of course, this is as it should be. The idea of using the Internet in clinical practice—of even having the possibility arise as it did with Martina—is so relatively new that we must all define and redefine it.

So, I will include some questions, some caveats, and some case examples in which I've utilized this new technology. It will be highly incomplete as to any final interpretation. I hope that each reader will decide for her or himself what is personally acceptable to use in clinical work. Perhaps, however, some of my ideas and my questions may help other clinicians to define their own rules.

The computer, although I've been using it in a number of ways for more than ten years, is still as much a source of excitement and "magic" for me as it was in the beginning. Actually, even more, since I now have a much clearer sense of what I'm doing compared to the fumbles and bumbles that marked my computer attempts in the beginning. Now, instead of sitting over a word processor in a stuffy office, I can take my laptop outside in my green and leafy July garden, plop a glass of iced tea down right next to my lawn chair, and with my portable phone by my side, create a delightful outdoor office bower. This is not technology, this is being alive in a beautiful place.

One of the more obvious uses of the computer in clinical work is to make or re-arrange appointments. In these busy days when people seem to play "telephone tag" with answering machines, it's helpful to have a way to connect with each other, in writing, in order to schedule sessions. One of my clients has a highly variable work schedule, so we cannot have a standing appointment. Every week, she e-mails to me her arrangements for the upcoming seven days, and I send her back a choice of two appointments. Then she picks one and e-mails me back. All of this happens within a few hours.

In discussing the writing of this chapter with various colleagues, most of them envisioned exchanging e-mails or engaging online "chats" as if in a written therapy session. For me, however, the clinical use of the computer is something quite different. My decision has been to use cyberspace as an adjunct to therapy or in a way that may creatively enhance the regular therapy.

In thinking over whether to do "sessions" online, I decided that this wasn't comfortable for me, in the same way that telephone sessions are unsatisfactory. Thus, I do not charge clients fees for any computer work that may take place. Charging a fee makes it therapy. I prefer to see it as therapeutic, but *not* therapy. This does not imply, of course, that if you don't charge a fee, it's *not* therapy. It's merely that if there is a charge, the client will probably regard it in that light and have the mindset that we are "doing" therapy. I want to avoid this assumption. In addition, I am careful to prevent the level of communication, fee or no fee, from rising to what might be considered therapy. This is, however, a decision that each clinician will decide on a personal level.

Referrals

Recently Clara, a new client who was about to move to a country in Europe for a year, scheduled an initial session. She knew of no English-speaking therapists there but wanted to be able to engage in therapy (we can leave it to her future clinician to examine why she waited until she was on the brink of leaving). She asked if we could do sessions online while she was out of the country. Perhaps if she had been in treatment for a while, I might have said yes, at least to supportive therapy. In this case, having little background knowledge of this client, I thought it inappropriate.

Instead, with Clara's permission, I contacted the mailing list of the Clinical Social Work Federation (CSWF) and asked if anyone knew of a therapist in the city where Clara would be. I got back three responses, all of which I forwarded to her. She is currently in treatment in Europe. Although it would have been possible to unearth an appropriate therapist without being online, use of the Internet made everything so much quicker and easier, And it is indeed the instant availability of resources that is one of the immediate advantages for clinicians of entering cyberspace.

In connection with referrals, some may question whether a social worker can be sure of finding a competent therapist in this manner. In the example given above (of contacting the Clinical Social Work Federation), I specifically asked my colleagues for referrals whose work they knew, so this is no more or less reliable than any other word-of-mouth referral would be, except that I knew the credentials of the therapist would be real and I trusted my colleagues' opinions. There is no specific referral list on the CSWF Web site. In another instance, looking for a therapist in a different part of Long Island, but still relatively local, I (with the transferring client's permission) telephoned the potential new therapist and had a long talk before referring the client. I believe that searching for a therapist within professional mailing lists is as reliable as looking in a professional directory.

Support Groups

Support groups are another important way the Internet gets used, and there are new ones all the time. In addition to the obvious possibilities, such as Twelve-Step programs, there are a few that may not have occurred to you. For example, many of the families of the Flight 800 tragedy of July 1996 belong to an online support group. This is also true for Oklahoma City bombing victims and survivors. One of my clients participates in a group for cross-dressers. Another belongs to an adult ADD discussion group. There are bulletin boards, news groups, chat rooms, mailing lists, and a host of resources available for almost any issue one could name.

Online Promotion

Some clinicians have seized the existence of the Internet to create a new therapeutic niche for themselves. In a recent practice management newsletter, one clinician was quoted as saying he charges for Internet psychotherapy for clients with whom he has had no personal contact. He believes that professionals wishing to work in this fashion should be prepared to work really hard and to begin the initial e-mail contacts or chats without charging a fee. Some clinicians have done therapy in this way, enhanced by the use of a tiny, two-way camera and Internet phone software, which can be attached to both computers. This seems more like tele-therapy. Another clinician who specializes in supervision for newer clinicians is researching ways of doing this (for a fee) on the Internet.

There are a number of ways to advertise one's practice on the 'Net. Some mental-health oriented Web sites provide a forum for practitioners to list their services, free of charge. In addition, the Social Work Forum on America Online (keyword "ssSocial Work") is a place where clinicians can informally interact with colleagues. If you point your browser toward the pages of the Clinical Social Work Federation *(http://www.cswf.org)*, you'll discover CSWF's mailing list for professionals, which you can join free of charge. Frequently, clinicians on this list ask for referrals in various geographical areas, although as previously stated, there is no specific referral list.

Finding Information

One resource I have found useful on the 'Net is the ability to research various medications, both for my own information and to be able to inform clients when I think they may require such treatment. You can enter the name of the medication into any search engine and come up with numerous references. Further, I find it helpful to research any physical problems from which my patients may suffer. If I educate myself about these conditions, I can probably do better therapy with the client. Only recently, I saw a woman whose daughter had leukemia and was about to undergo a bone marrow transplant. Because the Internet makes so much of the world's knowledge available almost instantly, I was able to find out more about this difficult process and to understand the demands that would be made on my client and the impact of the process on the entire family.

Convenience

Cyberspace in clinical practice offers much convenience, both in rapidity of research and resources and in staying in touch with clients. It allows connection without intrusion. You can receive or reply to e-mail at any hour of the day or night. Several clients have told me that e-mail feels far more comfortable to them than a phone call, so those who might hesitate to call in a sticky situation are at ease sending e-mail. According to one client, "I didn't want to call because I thought I might disturb you, so I sent an e-mail instead." I check mine every two hours, either manually or by setting up the software to do it automatically.

Not only that, when I go on vacation I can "stay in touch," if necessary, via my laptop, with those clients who use e-mail. The client need not know where I am in order to be able to reach me. No matter where I am geographically, I'm there. This helps preserve the therapeutic boundary, since knowing my e-mail address, unlike the area code of a telephone number I might give out, will not identify my location. I don't experience this as an interruption, since I choose the time, usually early in the morning, to read my e-mail. Actually, most clients are comforted by my giving them my e-mail address and don't bother to use it. Some clinicians I know use a specific e-mail address just for communication with clients. Most ISPs (Internet Service Providers) allow subscribers to use several different such addresses for the price of one account.

Novelty

Some clients (and some clinicians), are so intrigued by e-mail and the Internet that staying in touch in this way can truly help move the therapy forward. The novelty of the process helps the principals commit to continuing it.

Josephus was once well-known as a television set-designer. Then he became disabled and was no longer able to pursue his career. Sinking deeper and deeper into depression, he eventually required hospitalization and medication after a serious suicide attempt. Traditional therapy maintained him, but the depression remained. Because of his physical limitations, he was nearly a shut-in. Arriving for a session, Josephus noticed the empty carton of my laptop computer placed on the curb for a trash pickup. Remarking on this when he limped into the office, he asked if I thought a computer would be beneficial to him, although he wasn't sure what he would do with one if he got one.

When asked if he wanted to experience what it was like to use a computer, his face came alive with a surge of interest I had never seen him display. Bringing the laptop into the office, we spent the rest of the session surfing the 'Net and "playing." We even found some information about a support group relating to his particular disability. When Josephus left the session, even his cane moved almost jauntily. It was as if he had found a new "pet." He ordered his own computer that week and became quite active all over the 'Net, joining the support group and making a number of "e-friends." Interestingly, he has never sent me an e-mail, although he has my address.

Caveats

There are, of course, many caveats to consider. The most obvious concern is that of confidentiality. When clinicians think about this issue, they usually are concerned about the possibility that someone might intercept e-mail not intended for them, by design, much as a phone tap might work. However, it is unlikely that a random e-mail will be seen by unintended eyes outside the household of a recipient.

However, what clinicians *must* remember is that other members of the household might, if they know the correct password, have access to a client's e-mail. Therefore, always check this out with your client and be careful about what you say. Unless you know for sure that the e-mail address is secure, remember that someone else might have access to it. Take the same care you would take when leaving a voice message on your client's answering machine.

Mark, a clinical social worker from Michigan who often uses the Internet, warns that, "It is open knowledge that e-mail is not a protected or confidential medium (unless you incorporate an encryption scheme). Without some sort of protective mechanism, you can't even [be confident] that the correspondence hasn't been intercepted — or whether or not it's been truly delivered. In addition, some programs [tell Net users] when a selected user is online anywhere in the world. Thus, a client would know when you were online."

Mark also points out that a client who becomes frustrated with a therapist might choose to "spam" the therapist's e-mail address. "Spam" is computer-speak for flooding a particular address with hundreds of messages.

It's also important to remember that whatever you send via e-mail is recorded for all time. Phone calls and sessions are usually not taped or recorded, but e-mail is eminently reproducible. So be careful what you say. You don't know who your client might let read your note. The possibility of its being used in a potential malpractice suit later on should always be considered. And you should always keep a copy of *any* correspondence, electronic or otherwise, that takes place between you and a client, even if it's as simple as setting up an appointment. Your computer records may be excellent for reproducing session notes, but once you've sent an e-mail message, you are no longer in control of what happens to it. A wise but down-to-earth supervisor told me, a long time ago (before e-mail), to be careful about what I wrote down for my clients, and to ask myself the scary (but important) question, "Would I want this letter to be found on the body of a client who committed suicide?"

One of the authors of this book noticed my statement that I hope that each individual clinician will make a personal decision regarding the degree of therapy done via e-mail and whether to charge. In contrast, the author hopes "it will be an ethical issue that the profession wrestles with as a whole and sets guidelines for everyone to follow. If it is not, then the profession would move with the money—so that those willing to do it regardless of the ethical considerations that could limit its use would profit." I believe it will be a long wrestling match and we'll need to deal with this well before such guidelines are established. Right now, each clinician is making his or her own decisions. Many of us don't even have access to the Internet. Inasmuch as it's all changing so quickly, we are not yet at the stage of setting the rules, other than those Codes of Ethics that already apply. Social workers who are willing to be unethical in this arena are probably going to be professionally unethical elsewhere, as well.

I suspect, too, that managed care companies will latch on to the idea of e-mail therapy (as they have on tele-medicine) and might well start to structure this area so they can profit, too.

Even with all these considerations—and more arise every day as clinicians use their computers to transform therapy into an even richer and more varied experience—clinical social workers, computers, and cyberspace form a partnership that will continue to grow. Four years ago, before I became Internet-active, I would not have conceived of writing a chapter such as this. It didn't occur to me that I would use my computer in my practice in any way other than administrative. Then I went online and discovered a creative and challenging world that is changing its shape and possibilities daily. Martina, my Muscovite client, will attest to this. I wonder what I'll be able to write on the same topic after four more years have gone by.

Chapter 15

Ethics and Other Problems of Social Work Online

By Linda Grobman and David Grotke

Ken was ecstatic when the Internet became accessible to the general public. He could now offer a support group to clients scattered across his large city who could never come together in a face-to-face group because of time conflicts and other constraints. All he had to do was make sure his clients were connected to the Internet, and they could participate in this new service. It would be the first support group of its kind in the city—a great marketing tool for the agency. But Ken had never led an online support group, and he didn't know anyone else who had, either. Ken's supervisor wondered if this was a responsible way to practice social work, and if she could competently supervise him in this new endeavor.

Cathy, a social worker new to the Internet, discovered the SOCWORK mailing list and joined right away. Being excited about this new resource for professional networking and consultation, she posted a message asking for assistance with finding resources for a client. To explain the situation, Cathy gave a brief case history, similar to the following: "I have a 29-year-old white male client in a rural area of Kentucky who is...." She went on to give specific information about the client before explaining the nature of the request. This set off a flood of responses not answering the request itself, but questioning the ethics of posting the amount of information about the client that Cathy had posted.

Jan ran into a different kind of online ethical dilemma. She was a regular participant in a social work bulletin board on a popular online service. Suddenly, one day, she found in her e-mailbox a desperate plea for help from someone she had never met—Susie, a suicidal teenager. While Susie had a therapist in her hometown, she felt more comfortable expressing her feelings "anonymously" to someone online— someone with the credentials to help her. Jan wondered: Should I try to respond to her online as I would to someone who walked into my office? Should I encourage her to tell her therapist the things she is telling me? What is my responsibility? What is my liability?

Do Social Work and the Internet Mix?

The above examples are hypothetical, but they illustrate some of the very real issues facing social workers using the Internet. Social workers face some special online ethical dilemmas, whether they are using the Internet for professional networking, for client contact, or for recreational purposes. The NASW Code of Ethics provides guidelines with respect to the social worker's responsibility to clients, colleagues, in practice settings, as professionals, to the profession, and to the broader society. In using the Internet, social workers need to look at this code in new ways and be aware of ways that it applies to this new form of communication.

Among the basic ethical concerns we will take a look at are competence, confidentiality, informed consent, and questions about appropriate uses of the Internet for social workers.

Competence

Let's go back to the example of Ken at the beginning of this chapter. Ken wants to start an online support group, but his supervisor questions his ability to lead such a group and her own competence in supervising him in this new endeavor.

The NASW Code of Ethics tells us that "Social workers should provide services in substantive areas or use intervention techniques or approaches that are new to them only after engaging in appropriate study, training, consultation, and supervision from people who are competent in those interventions or techniques" (NASW Code of Ethics, Section 1.04 (b), 1996, p. 8). The Code further states that "social workers should exercise careful judgment and take responsible steps...to ensure the competence of their work and to protect clients from harm" (Section 1.04 (c), p. 9) when engaging in new areas of practice.

Since providing an online support group is a new technique for Ken, according to this section of the NASW Code of Ethics, he should get some training, consultation, and supervision in its use. This could be difficult, since he doesn't know of anyone else who has done it. However, because the Internet makes it easy to communicate with others who are using the Internet, he may be able to locate someone in another part of the country or the world who has had some experience in this new realm. And as the Internet develops, continuing education courses are being developed on its use in social work, professional conferences are including increasing numbers of workshops on Internet use, and social workers are writing and publishing accounts of their experiences in this area. So, it is becoming easier for social workers to get the information and training they need to become competent in this new territory.

If Ken subscribes to SOCWORK or another social work-related mailing list, he can post a message saying, "I am planning to start an online support group. If there is anyone out there who has done this kind of thing, please e-mail me. I'd like to discuss how you did it, what worked, what didn't, and any suggestions you may have. I appreciate any responses." Once he has heard from someone (or several people) by e-mail, he can follow up with phone calls for further consultation. He may then be on his way to competently and responsibly leading such a group.

Confidentiality

Confidentiality issues come into play when using e-mail with clients, colleagues, and other agencies. In the case of Cathy on page 89, was this an example of an overzealous social worker giving out too much information to people she didn't know, or was it an overreaction on the part of the list members who flamed her for presenting case material on the Internet?

Public Communications

The NASW Code of Ethics addresses the issue of confidentiality of information transmitted through computers, e-mail, fax machines, and other technology, saying that "social workers should take precautions to ensure and maintain the confidentiality" of this information (Section 1.07 (m), p. 12) and that "social workers may disclose confidential information when appropriate with valid consent" (Section 1.07 (b), p. 10).

The question is: Did Cathy post so much information that someone reading her post would be able to identify the client? And if so, did she have the client's permission to do so? Was Cathy, herself, identifiable to the online group, or did she remain anonymous by not posting her full name or where she worked? Depending on the type of information or assistance Cathy was requesting, it might have been necessary for her to give some background information in order to put the request into the right perspective. But if she needed to give enough information that the client could possibly be identified, she would need to get the client's consent first. If the client perceived the request as a useful one, he or she might be quite willing to give this authorization.

The Code of Ethics also says that "social workers should not discuss confidential information in any setting unless privacy can be ensured. Social workers should not discuss confidential information in public or semipublic areas such as hallways, waiting rooms, elevators, and restaurants" (Section 1.07 (i), p. 11).

This wasn't written about online communication, but if taken literally, it would preclude discussion of clients on a public electronic forum or providing any personal online services, because they are not secure, and are public or semi-public areas. It is possible for dishonest people to intercept e-mail or eavesdrop in chat rooms. You can be traced and found. There's no way to know how many people avoid online services for this reason, but many people alone at their computers don't think of this as a significant threat.

Private Communications

"Whatever you write can be passed on any place without your knowledge," warns Sheila Peck, a social worker in private practice on Long Island, NY, and author of Chapter 14 of this book. She suggests that, unless the social worker knows that a client is the only one with access to his or her e-mail account, the social worker should only use e-mail to send very general messages, such as, "Call me." "Sometimes e-mail doesn't go through," she adds. "If you don't get a response, follow up. Keep e-mail and back it up, to protect yourself in case of a lawsuit. It is inherent on the social worker to educate him or herself about what can happen [with e-mail]." And keep in mind the risk that one e-mail communication might be used as evidence in a lawsuit, out of context from other related messages or communications. Be careful with regard to each communication independently of any other. Not only can it be passed along, but it can be altered.

When providers of online advice, counseling, or other services reply to an inquiry that they receive online, it's important to get the e-mail address correct. One man wrote to Dave Grotke from one address and requested the answer be sent to a different address. Each time Dave replied he had to double check, not just hit the "reply" button. It's important to read e-mail carefully for specific requests people make to ensure confidentiality and to make themselves comfortable with the transaction.

Some consumers of online advice and information may feel more secure and anonymous using e-mail and chatting than walking into a professional office. No one can see or hear them seeking help. They feel in control at the computer. They can sign off or pull the plug. They can disguise their identities. They may think it unlikely that someone would take the trouble to intercept a particular piece of e-mail out of the millions of messages on the 'Net. People run a quick risk-benefit analysis and bet they won't have their privacy violated. As encryption technology improves and proliferates, so messages are scrambled while in transit, confidentiality may become less of an issue.

Online providers should remind seekers of information, though, that replies they receive may not be secure in transmission, and that e-mail stored on their or the provider's computer may be subject to access by others. If either the seekers or the providers are on a network, in an office, or a home where people can access their e-mail, messages can be intercepted deliberately or accidentally.

Sheila Peck brings up another problem that can occur in e-mail correspondence with clients. "There are considerations of 'Are you a good typist?' If you aren't a good typist, it could have a negative effect. If someone else types for you, there's the issue of confidentiality."

But some social workers, like Dale Fitch, LCSW, associate director of the Child Protection Program at University Hospitals and Clinics in Columbia, MO, are not as concerned about confidentiality. He thinks it's an overstated issue. "[My] peers seem to get hung up on confidentiality; then they'll put 'confidential' paperwork in the mail basket for who knows who to come by and pick it up hoping it gets to the intended party. Or they'll use the phone or fax saying it's more confidential than e-mail! Finally, we seem to overlook the fact that our clients can now participate with us equally in this flow of information. They may be more inclined to want their 'participating' agencies to use this technology than we think they are." Of course, the argument could be made that Fitch's colleagues should be more careful with their paper files!

Confidentiality of Electronic Records

If you're storing confidential information on your computer, you need to take precautions, just as you would when storing confidential paper files. If you keep client records (the paper kind) in a locked file cabinet, it makes sense to keep similar electronic files in a password-protected directory, on a floppy disk in a locked cabinet, or in files encrypted with software such as Pretty Good Privacy's Viacrypt or PGPMail. Not every social worker has the technical knowledge (or wants it) to encrypt files, but if you have sensitive or confidential information on computer disks, it provides an added safeguard.

This relates to Section 1.07 (l) of the Code of Ethics, which implores social workers to "protect the confidentiality of clients' written and electronic records and other sensitive information" and to "take reasonable steps to ensure that clients' records are stored in a secure location and that clients' records are not available to others who are not authorized to have access" (p. 11-12).

Rita Vandivort, Senior Staff Associate for Mental Health and Addictions at the national office of the National Association of Social Workers (NASW), heard about a different perspective on confidentiality of electronic communications when she attended a conference on managed health care. "The issues that many therapists are upset about—giving confidential information to managed care companies—will be exacerbated, because they'll be asked to chart right there [on the Internet) to the managed care company. I'm not saying that's all bad. You can see that the client went to the emergency room last Saturday [from the Internet files]. You can see their last blood level from Lithium, or you can access the latest literature on the list of systems. That would be a benefit," she says. But, she adds, "Some of the confidentiality issues are going to become front and center. I don't think social workers see it coming."

Informed Consent

Jan, in our third example on page 89, was faced with the issue of fully informing the client. But first, she had to determine: what exactly was her role with Susie, or with others like her who might seek Jan out online? *Was* Susie her client? Was she providing services to Susie?

According to the NASW Code of Ethics, Section 1.03 (a), "Social workers should provide services to clients only in the context of a professional relationship based, when appropriate, on valid informed consent. Social workers should use clear and understandable language to inform clients of the purpose of the services, risks related to the services..." (p. 7-8).

The Code specifically states that social workers providing services through electronic media "should inform recipients of the limitations and risks associated with such services" (NASW Code of Ethics, Section 1.03 (e), p. 8).

In addition to the competence concerns discussed previously, Jan should consider the risks and limitations in this situation. If she decides to engage in an online relationship with Susie, she will need to explain to Susie that the help she can provide by e-mail is limited and does not take the place of her therapist's services. She should explain that she is not Susie's therapist (unless, indeed, she decides to take on that role and provide some form of online or in-person therapy to Susie) and that, while she can offer emotional support to Susie, it is risky for Susie to get dependent on her rather than letting her therapist help her work out her problems. Jan does not know who Susie really is, or where she lives, so she can't intervene in the same ways Susie's therapist can in a time of acute crisis. In fact, Jan may decide not to get involved in this situation at all, but instead to refer Susie back to her own therapist.

The Disclaimer

Dave Grotke calls his site *Dave Grotke's Free Advice!* (See Chapter 12.) He wants his personality and style to come through, and he wants to make people feel comfortable. He's not in it for the money. He also wants to be serious and ethical, so he identifies himself as a social worker, but he doesn't want to pretend that he's doing psychotherapy online. He doesn't want that kind of responsibility, and he tells people so in the following disclaimer:

> *Free Advice is like any advice. You take it at your own risk.... You are responsible for your own words and actions and their consequences.... Free Advice is not therapy. It's no substitute for a real face-to-face meeting with a professional counselor.... Free Advice is mainly educational and informative.... Free Advice is no substitute for seeing a doctor or psychiatrist.... Always follow the advice of your physician or therapist about any treatment or medication you receive.*

He includes a link to his résumé and another page about confidentiality and its limits, particularly with respect to electronic transmissions, child abuse, and harm to self and others. Anyone who reads it can see what he or she is getting into if they e-mail him. If they want to, they can check Dave's credentials and track him down.

Many professionally-run sites that offer some type of mental health service include a disclaimer warning people in one way or another of the risks involved, limits of what is offered on the site, and pointing visitors to "real" help offline. Disclaimers are a part of doing business on the Internet, and they provide one way for social workers with such Web sites to cover themselves in terms of ethics and legal liability.

At "The Counseling Room" *[http://www.kobe-net.or.jp/counseling/index-e.html]*, for example, we find a simple professional disclaimer:

> *The purpose of this site is to help people who are worried about their mental health. If you think you have serious mental problems, please consult with a mental health professional as soon as possible.*

Here's a short one from the State University of New York at Buffalo's self-help site *(http://ub-counseling.buffalo.edu)*:

> *Welcome to the Counseling Center Self-Help Home Page, at the State University of New York at Buffalo. We have collected here a wide selection of documents, Internet resources, referrals, and reading lists, all to help you with day-to-day stresses and difficult periods in your life.*
>
> *Please note, this service is NOT meant to replace a face-to-face consultation with a trained counselor, nor does this service provide "on-line" counseling (see the entry under Services for referral suggestions).*

If you plan to offer advice or other social work services online, we advise that you consult a lawyer regarding development of an appropriate disclaimer for your site.

Online Therapy?

"Advisement or counseling—yes. Therapy—no," says Sheila Peck of providing online clinical services. Many social workers tend to echo this sentiment.

"I have a great deal of concern about online therapy from a couple of perspectives," Rita Vandivort-Warren of NASW says. "You never really know who you're talking to on the other end. I also have concerns about...nonverbal communication that's very important in therapy that you don't get in a text-based environment. I think the text-based environment is fragile. I don't know if it's a lack of the person being in the room, social control loss, but I think it's easy to misunderstand people. That's why people use emoticons [such as smiley faces]. It's okay if you're planning a meeting—I think it's far more serious if you're talking about the vulnerable issues that come up in mental health and addictions."

Nathaniel Prentice, a social work doctoral candidate at the University of Pennsylvania, agrees. "Psychoeducation and info/referral? Sure. Counseling? Never. I would hate to have an actively suicidal client in Saskatchewan, and not in my office [in Philadelphia]," he explains.

"Information and referral is okay. It's easy to locate a self-help group for nearly every problem by searching the Internet. Self-help or hot-line services where trained listeners offer encouragement and support seem okay. Similar services are already available on the telephone, radio, and TV," says Sheila Peck. "Online psychotherapy is much more problematic. It would be difficult to provide accurate assessment, and the Internet provides opportunities for people to disguise themselves. The credentials of the therapists would be difficult to verify."

But not all social workers think online therapy is a bad idea, and there are certainly social workers and other professionals providing these services. Gary Stofle presented a workshop at the 1997 NASW national conference on chat room therapy. In regard to questions of the therapist's competence in providing online psychotherapy, Stofle wrote in a paper posted on his Web site and handed out at his workshop, "Being a competent therapist by itself is not enough to make one a competent online therapist. We need to take into account and adjust for the differences that exist in the provision of text-based psychotherapy, as opposed to face-to-face psychotherapy. Even the most noted therapist could not conduct online therapy sessions without skills in typing, spelling, grammar, and navigating online." He pointed out that "the therapist needs to focus intently on the session, while the potential for distraction is quite great."

Stofle outlined other ethical and practical considerations in his paper, which is posted at his Web site at *http://members.aol.com/stofle/index.htm.* And he warns, "If we proceed too cautiously in this journey because of the ethical issues, or decide not to provide online therapy services because of the unknown, who will be available to treat the clients who won't, for whatever reasons, seek face-to-face therapy?"

Dale Fitch agrees. "As long as that [online clinical services] is what the client wants and they are fully informed of all the possible ramifications [then it's ethical]," he says. "In my opinion, preventing the use of online clinical services for a homebound quadriplegic should be considered unethical."

Dick Shoech, professor of social work at the University of Texas at Arlington, contends that the question is not really whether online therapy is ethical or not. "Yes, if provided in an ethical manner [it is ethical]," he says. "The tools you use to practice are not the source of unethical practice." Instead, he says the concerns lie in the applicability of social work ethics and standards to Internet therapy and in getting liability insurance to cover Internet therapy.

In any event, the number of social workers providing therapy or counseling services online is growing. We found them at several Web sites, including:

CounseLine—*http://www.counseline.com/*
Poppins Valley Therapy—*http://home1.gte.net/poppins/index.htm*
Wired Senses Online Counseling—*http://www.revisions.com/wiredsenses.html*

For more information about online therapy and links to sites that provide it, see the *Metanoia Guide to Internet Mental Health Services (http://www.metanoia.org/imhs/intro.htm)*. This site provides information about how online therapy works, ratings of and links to psychotherapy sites, and a "Credentials Check" service.

Other Online Treatment Issues

What happens when the online social worker isn't online? Section 1.15 of the Code of Ethics calls on social workers to "make reasonable efforts to ensure continuity of services in the event that services are interrupted by factors such as unavailability, relocation, illness, disability, or death."

Dave Grotke posts a notice on his Web site when he won't be available and recommends other sites, emergency services, and seeing a local therapist if the person needs help. Providers who work in groups cover each other, and the Web sites run by organizations usually have Webmasters who watch the traffic and keep the site functioning. Responsible sites recommend local services for urgent situations.

And what about termination of services? Section 1.16 states: "(a) Social workers should terminate services to clients and professional relationships with them when such services and relationships are no longer required or no longer serve the clients' needs or interests, and (b) Social workers should take reasonable steps to avoid abandoning clients who are still in need of services...."

Most sites are for short-term advice and information. Most online hosts suggest or refer to local therapists and services. If a provider clearly states the limits of the service, and watches for very needy or troubled people, the recommendation for private therapy and termination of online service should be acceptable. Requests for direct intervention in a situation can lead to role-confusion and trouble, unless a provider is in proximity to the consumer and has face-to-face resources available.

Online Group Concerns

Barbara Nielsen, a social worker in Canada, ran into some different ethical dilemmas in the course of running an online support group for parents of children with bladder extrophy, a rare condition in which a child is born with his or her bladder on the outside of the body.

First, as a social worker interested in conducting research on this rare condition, she saw "a wonderful opportunity for a qualitative research project." All the interactions of the group—essentially an Internet mailing list—are archived, so the technical ability to analyze these interactions is there. But there is the issue of informed consent for research subjects. (Section 5.02 of the Code of Ethics addresses this issue.) "The potential is there for me to say, 'Forget about getting consent for research,' but I won't do that.... People starting out on the Internet certainly aren't aware that people can do what they want with their words." Nielsen may at some point do this type of qualitative research with another Internet support group, but she would do it only with the consent of the group's members.

Another ethical concern for Nielsen relates to whether to use the Internet as a marketing tool for her employer in the course of running the online group. "Someone from Spain had a young baby, and he was thinking he needed a second opinion. Various members of the group said, 'Come and see Dr. So-and-So.' I felt Sick Kids [her employer] had a good reputation, but this is not an advertising ploy for Sick Kids." She felt it was inappropriate to "put in a plug" for her own hospital, although she would respond to questions about its services. The doctors told her to tell the patient to come to the hospital. She said no. "One side says no. The management says yes, we could make money." (See Sections 1.06(b), 3.09(d), and 4.07(a) of the Code for related concerns.)

Confidentiality is an issue in the group, as well, when Nielsen knows some members of the group from working with them in person, while she does not know others other than through the online group. "I know the people in the group who I've had contact with. Do you take information you know about the person from another context? I wouldn't disclose the information, but I might phrase things differently to elicit a response from them. That might be a dilemma." This is an issue in face-to-face groups, as well, not uniquely an Internet issue. Some group workers advocate that therapists not have individual contact with people they see in a group. However, the reality, as Nielsen points out, is that this is not always possible. She won't deny services to someone because there is not a separate individual and group therapist available.

Plagiarism and Copyright Violation

"It's very easy to violate copyright laws by downloading others' material," says Diane Falk, NASW-NJ president and assistant professor of social work at Richard Stockton College of New Jersey. "There are sites where students can download term papers, then print them out and present them as their own work. Although getting others to write term papers for them has always been possible, it has never been so easy. Such dishonesty is very difficult to prevent or detect." The NASW Code of Ethics, Section 4.08 (a) states: "Social workers should take responsibility and credit, including authorship credit, only for work they have actually performed and to which they have contributed."

There are legal questions, too, when it comes to passing along any material that is not the individual social worker's creation. Any material that is copyrighted is clearly not to be distributed without permission. If you wish to reproduce another person's work, electronically or in print—whether it's an e-mail message, a Web page, an online article, or anything else—the best course of action is to ask permission. The exception is if there is a clear statement indicating that your intended use is allowed without permission.

Codes of Ethics Online

For social workers who want more information about professional ethics, whether those applying to online or offline behavior, there are several Codes of Ethics available online. The National Association of Social Workers Code can be found at NASW's Web site at *http://www.socialworkers.org/code.htm*. The full text can be downloaded as a Microsoft® Word document.

Similarly, other social work organizations have made their ethical codes available online. Here are a few:

American Board of Examiners in Clinical Social Work (ABECSW)—*http://www.abecsw.org/ethic.html*

British Association of Social Workers (BASW)—*http://www.basw.demon.co.uk/pages/info/ethics.htm*

Clinical Social Work Federation (CSWF)—*http://www.cswf.org/clinical/coepre.html*

International Federation of Social Workers (IFSW)—*http://www.ifsw.org/4.4.pub.html*
This file includes the *International Declaration of Ethical Principles of Social Work* and the *International Ethical Standards for Social Workers*

Irish Association of Social Workers (IASW)—*http://homepages.iol.ie/~iasw/Code_of_Ethics.html*

Ethics Under Construction

Is there is a particular way a professional "should" present herself or himself online, or is there a place for disclaimer-defined services, different styles, marketing ploys, and hype? Is it possible to do therapy on the Internet? Practitioners already charging money for such contacts seem to say yes, with qualifications. Consumers eagerly accept what they're getting. Where does a profession draw the line in a sea of information, advice, and entertainment?

How can you evaluate someone you can't see or hear? How can you diagnose a person or situation by reading a few paragraphs? Maybe we'll need to learn more about statement analysis techniques. Someone will want to research the effectiveness of online practice versus traditional therapy to sort out the risks and benefits of different delivery systems.

NASW and other professional groups will have to revisit these issues and revise their codes to reflect current practice and consumer input. One approach might be to develop realistic and ethical disclaimer statements for online professional services. Another might be to insist on more effective technology to ensure confidentiality. Time will have to be spent online looking at the variety of help-givers and how they already operate. There's not just one way to do it; many strategies succeed in meeting different needs.

Those working out the ethics and standards now are the people online, doing the work, exploring the technology. They're joined by consumers who are present and active, more so than in office-based practice. This makes the process dynamic and challenging, improves the variety and availability of ser-

Welcome to Dave Grotke's Free Advice!

Get Free Advice from an experienced therapist on any personal problem! Dave has counseled thousands of adults, young adults, adolescents, and children. Now he's here, with a personal response to your questions. This is not a scam or commercial enterprise. It's real. He likes doing it.

Notice:

Free Advice! will be ON VACATION 2/9 - 3/1/98.

If you're willing to wait for an answer, go ahead and write for some Free Advice. Dave will answer when he gets back. If you can't wait, try some of Dave's Links for Free Advice. There's a lot of good stuff there. If you're cracking up or want to end it all, better call 911 or a local crisis center pronto! Otherwise hang in there and we'll see you next month.

Free Advice is one year old!
Read our 1997 Report

"Stickman" wants YOUR Free Advice!

Are you, or somebody you know, confused, worried, depressed, angry, in conflict, or miserable about something? Think you're going nuts or losing it? Can't afford a shrink? Wondering about something? Something weird? Tossing and turning? Need help with a serious problem? Or a little problem. Get a checkup here. Dave's heard it before, won't think you're strange for asking, and almost always has good ideas for you based on years of clinical experience. **Free!**

For **Important Stuff** about this site please see More About Free Advice, Confidentiality, the Disclaimer, and the less important Dave Grotke Retirement Fund.

See what Satisfied Customers have to say about Dave Grotke's Free Advice! Then ask away!

If you want even more Free Advice, check out:

Dave Grotke's Free Advice home page. Reprinted with permission.

vices, and seems a healthy development. With a lot of misguided information out there as well, it makes sense to have a serious and ethical presence on the Internet. If we do, we minimize the chance that people will be harmed or misled, and increase the likelihood that good information gets to people who need it.

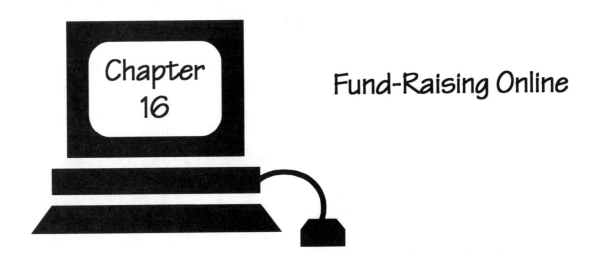

Chapter 16

Fund-Raising Online

by Gary Grant and Steve Roller

Social workers in administration, program planning, on boards of directors, or in a wide variety of other roles may find themselves involved in fund-raising. While no one would recommend that you base your fund-raising strategy solely on the Internet, it can help in a number of ways, both directly for raising funds, and indirectly saving you time and money.

A good way to begin thinking about the Internet's uses for fund-raising is to consider which individuals or organizations are most likely to use the Internet for reaching you, or hope you will reach them. If you use a Web site for fund-raising, what audience do you expect to reach?

For example, one might expect, and would in fact find, that foundations are among those leading the way in using the Internet. At least one-third of the top foundations have Web sites, and others are moving quickly to put proposal information and other content onto Web sites. But foundations are unique in this regard. Few individual donors would feel as interested in making it broadly known that they want to contribute to a particular cause.

Overall, it is probably safe to say that there are more people online seeking donations than there are offering funding. Even in the category of fund-raising educational material, there are more Web sites describing books for sale than there are free online books or articles on the subject. Simply put, there are few who have an incentive to give you information about how to raise funds. On the other hand, people are usually collegial by nature, and are often more than happy to share their experiences and expertise to at least some extent.

For more information about how to use the Internet in fund-raising (and why), see the online article *Fundraising and the Internet: Another Arrow in the Quiver (http://www.fund-raising.com/ intfundart.html)* According to this article, a 1995 survey found that the average household income of a "wired" family was $66,700, compared to $42,400 for non-wired families. It also found that Internet users were younger, more highly educated, and were using the Internet more for handling financial matters and making purchases. It reasons that charitable organizations should consider this group an important one to reach out to now and in the long-run.

Educating Yourself About Fund-Raising

If you want to learn about fund-raising and want to use the Internet as a starting point, perhaps the best way is to use it to access other professional fund-raisers who may be willing to share and discuss issues pertaining to the field and to answer questions for newcomers. You may find colleagues on some Usenet newsgroups, such as soc.org.nonprofits. Also, there are some mailing lists you can join, including the following:

CFRNET, a list for people involved in Corporate and Foundation Relations. (To subscribe, send e-mail to: *cfrnet-request@medicine.wustl.edu* and type message: subscribe cfrnet <your real name>)

FUNDLIST, a general mailing list for fund-raising professionals. (To subscribe, send e-mail to: *listproc@listproc.hcf.jhu.edu* and type message: SUB FUNDLIST <your real name>)

GIFT-PL, a list on planned giving (To subscribe, send e-mail to: *listserve@vm1.spcs.umn.edu* and type message: subscribe GIFT-PL <your real name>)

Fundraising Online, E-mail to *majordomo@igc.org* with the message: info fundraising online—which should give you basic information about this list.

More fund-raising mailing lists can be found at:
E-mail Discussion Forums—*http://weber.u.washington.edu/~dlamb/apra/lists.htm*

Creative Fund-Raising Ideas

Depending on the kind of fund-raising you do for your organization, you might be interested in exploring creative fund-raising ideas: fun things to do, items to sell as a fund-raiser, and the like. Besides getting ideas from others sharing their success stories, you might also search for companies that offer products for sale by charities. An example of one we found was: *Music Brokers for Charities (http://www.quiknet.com/dimple/used2.html)*. Your organization can collect used CDs and videos, and Music Brokers will purchase them from you.

Of course, you should be wary of anything you find on the Internet, especially when it involves any financial transactions.

Prospect Research

Prospect research can take many different forms. Are you looking for information about an individual someone recommended to you as a possible supporter? Are you seeking to broaden your appeal to new individuals and corporations who have not yet been involved in your organization?

Below are some examples of the sites used by prospect researchers.

Internet Prospector
http://w3.uwyo.edu/~prospect/

David Lamb's Prospect Research Page
http://weber.u.washington.edu/~dlamb/research.html

Hoover's Online
http://hoovweb.hoovers.com/

CASE List of Prospect Research Sites
http://192.203.212.6/256/frprspct.htm

The Association of Professional Researchers for Advancement
http://weber.u.washington.edu/~dlamb/apra/APRA.html

Finding Funding Sources

For finding individual supporters, prospect research provides a tool to identify prospects and to collect relevant public information helpful to the fund-raiser. Many other funding organizations, however, use the Internet to make information available to those who may want to apply. Finding these sites is a matter of meeting the funder half-way. The approaches you can use for finding funding sources online can range from "hunting" to "gathering."

"Hunting" for funding sources involves embarking on a search through the Internet for support from any variety of sources at a single time when funding for a particular purpose is needed. A "gathering" approach involves identifying particular funding sources and visiting them on a periodic basis or otherwise collecting their information as it is updated, so that you can be first in line to learn of the availability of support. There is no necessarily preferred method of finding funding but, in general, if you can identify the sources that might regularly be appropriate for you, it is probably best to take a "gathering" approach and to accumulate references to sites of value to you.

Many federal agencies have their own Web sites and use them to post the availability of funding opportunities and detailed information on grant programs. A good place to visit is the Library of Congress's Internet Resource Page for official Federal government Web sites *(http://lcweb.loc.gov/ global/executive/fed.html)*. This page covers virtually the entire executive branch of the federal government, with links to the other branches.

Good places to start when looking for funding sources are:

The Foundation Center—*http://fdncenter.org/*
The Internet Nonprofit Center—*http://www.nonprofits.org*
Putnam Barber's Information for Nonprofits—*http://www.eskimo.com/~pbarber/index.html*
Goodwill Industries of America—*http://www.goodwill.org/*

News, Articles, and Publications On Fund-Raising and Philanthropy

Using the Internet can be helpful for accessing information from sources that are either available only online or which are secondary in importance to you. Even if you don't read your online sources for news regularly, it may be helpful on those occasions when you want to look through a variety of perspectives on a hot topic.

The following sites are among the online publications relating specifically to fund-raising:

Philanthropy News Digest—*http://fdncenter.org/phil/philmain.html*
Philanthropy Journal Online—*http://www.philanthropy-journal.org/*
Chronicle of Philanthropy—*http://www.philanthropy.com*
NonProfit Times Online—*http://www.nptimes.com/*

Using E-mail to Attract and Solicit Support

One question that is often discussed is whether e-mail can be used for direct solicitations. The newsletter *Successful Direct Mail & Telephone Fundraising* cites a recent study that projects that 130 million people will be using e-mail by 1998. More than twice as many people use e-mail than are using the World Wide Web. If all of our supporters *and* prospective donors used e-mail and if it were acceptable to solicit them in this way, then non-profits could in theory eliminate their direct mail costs. Of course, there are design limitations when soliciting by e-mail.)

Up Close: Trolling the Internet for Grants

Steve Roller works for the Chicago Housing Authority and is particularly interested in grant programs through the U.S. Department of Housing and Urban Development. Each month, Steve visits the HUD Web site *(http://www.hud.gov/)* and finds his way to the funding opportunities page *(http://www.hud.gov/fundopp.html)*. Here, he reviews the current HUD Tentative NOFA (Notice of Funding Availability) Schedule *(http://www.hud.gov/nofas.html)* where he gets the earliest possible news of soon-to-be-announced programs. For example, seeing that the HUD Office of Community Planning and Development has already made available information on the Continuum of Care Homeless Assistance program, he downloads the complete document to his computer and prints it out the day it is released.

Other funding information on the HUD site includes details of programs by categories, including help for the homeless, youth programs, drug prevention programs, counseling services, research support, and more.

Similar information is available at sites for the U.S. Department of Education *(http://www.ed.gov)* through its Money Matters page *(http://www.ed.gov/money.html)*, the U.S. Department of Health and Human Services *(http://www.os.dhhs.gov/)* through both its Funding page *(http://www.odphp.osophs.dhhs.gov/nonprofit/funding.htm)* and its Partnership page *(http://www.hhs.gov/partner/)*, and other social service-related federal departments and agencies.

There are comparable resources available at the state level. For example, at the State of Illinois Web site *(http://www.state.il.us)*, you can click on "state agencies" to find a long list of links to various state departments, agencies, and offices. You may need to navigate around these sites a bit to determine if they have information posted on grants they award. If you don't see a heading for grants, or Requests for Proposals (RFPs), then look for such headings as "Programs," "Services," "Resources," or "About the Agency."

For a list of the Internet World Wide Web home page addresses for the 50 states and the District of Columbia, see Appendix A.

Up Close: Development At a School of Social Work

Gary Grant is a development officer at a school of social work. His interest in funding opportunities covers the gamut of topic areas, providing that the funding applies to research in areas of social work. Reviewing all the applicable agency sites online each month is impractical for him; however, several key agencies and organizations provide automated searches or reports as funding announcements are made. Gary receives the weekly National Institutes of Health (NIH) guide via e-mail, as well as several other alerts. Skimming these for the ones applicable to social work research, he forwards them by e-mail to the faculty and doctoral students at his school. Most of what he receives could be obtained in printed form, but by using e-mail, he gets it into the hands of those who need it almost immediately, for less cost, and with less time spent in the effort than ever before.

Information like that provided at agency sites makes possible a level of searching and information-gathering never before possible. But to be realistic, only if you have a narrowly tailored interest area can you spend the time necessary to search each one. You may want to find sites that either do the gathering for you and provide a comprehensive listing of opportunities, or enlist the assistance of a service that searches for you while you are offline. Once you identify a possible funding opportunity online, the site describing the opportunity is likely to contain more helpful information necessary to you as you work through the application process.

But these "ifs" are very big. The Internet is too new to be sure one way or another, but so far, it appears that the culture of the Internet frowns on soliciting people online. In general, there is a degree of fear among many e-mail users that they will soon be inundated with e-mail. Already, the presence of e-mail advertisements or "junk e-mail" (also referred to pejoratively as "spam") is raising fears and sending some back to their more traditional ways of communicating. Many just delete e-mail advertisements without giving them much thought. In addition, e-mail is an informal method of communicating, and solicitations should probably still be made in a more formal manner, such as a letter on your agency letterhead with an original authorized signature.

This could change. When the telephone first became popular in the general population, it was quite unclear what etiquette it would demand. In fact, the earliest practice was to send a letter to the person you wanted to call, announcing that you planned to call at a particular date and time, rather than surprising him or her with an unexpected call. It was not until much later, well into the 1970s, that phone solicitations began to be well accepted—at least those from institutions with which people were already involved, if not "cold calls" from organizations seeking new supporters. Even now, it is common to precede phone solicitations with a letter informing your prospect base that you will be phoning to request their support. And many people are still annoyed by these calls.

E-mail solicitation is tempting on one level. It offers an opportunity to solicit gifts from the largest possible audience in a way that is less expensive and less time-consuming than either direct mail appeals or phone solicitations. As such, it may one day help to minimize the dollars spent raising funds, but some of the same factors that make this a tempting opportunity also make it a danger-ous risk. Step without caution on the wrong toes, and your organization could be the talk of the Internet in all the wrong ways. Angry words about your organization's overzealousness could spread quite quickly and create problems far exceeding the advantages of the dollars you might raise.

One place to be especially cautious is on mailing lists and newsgroups. In both cases, participants defend the topical turf of their particular group with ardor. Even the most well-meaning appeals for action or support of ideological values not inherent in the subject that brings the group together may be attacked. The reason for this is that most of these groups suffer from (or at least fear) being overwhelmed with irrelevant dialogue. To prevent this, they stamp out such tangential discussions immediately.

So, unless you are participating in a group you know welcomes solicitations, you should refrain from this. As with any group, you should always read the discussions first, until you get a feel for what is proper and not proper in the group.

But what about your existing constituency? Would they be put off by an e-mail solicitation? Even here, it's hard to tell for sure, but right now it is probably not advisable, except perhaps in the most special and extraordinary cases. A routine of doing this could lead people to request that they be taken off your list.

Perhaps a better use of e-mail is to simply interact with your constituency and to provide them with information and services that make them feel closer to your organization. E-mail can be a most convenient means for increasing the direct communication between you and your organization's actual and potential supporters. Sharing timely and informative news about what you are doing can keep you on donors' minds and make sure your work has visibility.

One way to do this is to organize a regular e-mail newsletter. Providing a consistent and dependable flow of information can allay fears of being overwhelmed by e-mail. As use of the Internet and e-mail grows, this can help ensure that your e-mail lists grow, bringing a larger portion of your audience closer to your organization. A large multi-faceted organization may want to have several alternative topic newsletters, allowing its constituency to choose from among them. For example, there might be an advocacy/action newsletter, a volunteer newsletter, and a program announce-ment newsletter.

Another way is to develop a mailing list that you use to encourage dialogue among your organization's constituency. Some organizations, such as the Children's Defense Fund, provide an advocacy alert by e-mail and encourage their members to share information with others. This gives CDF the ability to almost instantly get word out to untold numbers of people, and in turn may bring many of these people closer to the organization.

Finally, e-mail is used frequently to inform people of updates to a Web site. This can help to bring people back when, although they find your site useful, they do not remember to return on a regular basis or know when to do so. A good way to increase your organization's constituency is by including a "guestbook" at your site. Visitors "sign in," perhaps sharing what attracted them to your site. Those so inclined to sign an online guestbook are probably more likely than the average person to be involved over time. Web site administrators of organizations can collect a list of guestbook signees and add them to the list of those who are kept up-to-date by e-mail.

Using a Web Site to Attract and Solicit Support

Increasingly, social service agencies with Web sites are including information or even special areas of their sites dedicated specifically to soliciting visitors for gifts. These range from noting the mailing address for donations to providing secure online forms for making credit card contributions.

Sites asking for donations may:

> (1) Detail how funds are used by the organization,
> (2) Elaborate on the need for or impact of support,
> (3) Detail giving vehicles such as charitable gift annuities,
> (4) Recognize current supporters or sponsors, and
> (5) Allow for inquiries about giving.

How effective these sites are is still to be determined. Some organizations, particularly larger ones, have reported substantial success in raising funds through their Web sites. In general, many today are hesitant to give online—either because of the lack of security of the Internet, or because of uncertainty about whether the organization is legitimate. The larger agencies overcome the latter fears and may even offer secure pages for sharing credit card information.

In general, good common sense and an understanding of cyberculture should be applied to any organization intending to build a fund-raising site.

As with e-mail, one of the best fund-raising uses for a Web site is simply to begin attracting prospective donors. Cultivation, online and through traditional means, can then be used to involve people in your organization and to develop their interests in the long-term.

For more thoughts on using the Internet in fund-raising, see *http://www.fundraisingonline.com/*.

Chapter 17

Social Policy and Advocacy Online

by Gary Grant and John Aravosis

Can I participate in existing advocacy efforts online? How can I build an online constituency for advocacy purposes? What are some of the ways to carry out advocacy efforts online? Does online advocacy really work? What advocacy resources exist?

The Internet is a natural resource and tool for advocacy on any number of issues. It is a resource for obtaining information necessary in the quickest possible way, and it is a tool for networking and making information available to others. The sites included in this book are considered advocacy sites if they do one or more of the following: (1) make advocacy-related information, alerts, press releases, and reports available in a timely manner; (2) organize people or generate action; (3) collect or report opinion data on current issues; (4) describe advocacy efforts and events on or offline; (5) urge specific political responses on particular issues; or (6) present political positions on a topic along with arguments in favor of one side in the debates.

There are many advocacy organizations that have established a Web presence describing the kind of work they do. Our exploration of advocacy Web sites, however, will focus primarily on those that use the Internet for actual advocacy efforts. These may include, for example, sites that organize online events, network people and agencies, or provide direct online responses for people who want to do something about an issue. These online advocacy activities and online supports for advocacy efforts are where the Internet really begins to realize its largest potential.

In 1995, for example, Antonia Stolper and Bob Fertik, the publishers of *Political Woman Newsletter*, brought their in-depth coverage of women's issues online as *Political Woman Hotline*. They invited their print subscribers to subscribe by e-mail, and offered it free to the Internet community as a benefit of joining *Women Leaders Online*. They announced WLO on the Internet in March 1995, and had 1,000 subscribers within a month. They then held a press conference with U.S. Representative Nita Lowey, Frances Fox Piven, and other feminist leaders to announce it to the world at large. Since then, they've built their list to over 5,000 subscribers. While the e-mail list initially started as a comprehensive compilation of short interesting news stories and advocacy tips (sometimes as many as 50 per e-mail), the newsletter has since evolved into a more standard issues update/action alert.

Political Woman Newsletter is not just a good example of using an online effort in conjunction with other more standard approaches—the newsletter itself was unique (at that time) in its ability to solicit a large number of quality submissions from its growing list, and then redistribute those that were relevant to the list at large.

HandsNet and Policy.Com—A Comparison

Two important online sources for social policy research, reports, and other documents are *HandsNet (see pages 56-57 for a full description)* and *Policy.com.*

HandsNet *(http://www.handsnet.org)* is a major online service relevant for those involved in the social services. It is a membership-based site and members (usually agencies and organizations) contribute all of the content. HandsNet facilitates the organizational structure, which assists at all levels—searching for archived information in the form of stored documents, summarizing current documents weekly and e-mailing this summary to all users, and organizing content into relevant folders according to their topic areas such as children, youth and family, welfare reform, substance abuse, health, or housing.

Policy.com *(http://www.policy.com/)* is a similar site in that it aims to be a "comprehensive public policy information service and Internet/online community." Policy.com targets both a professional audience and the larger general public, whereas HandsNet focuses primarily on professionals. Information is provided by the site owners as well as by participants—both agencies and individuals, usually linked directly to any provider's Web site. The site includes a news ticker for those who have Java-enabled browsers.

Policy.com features the following:

News and Events: provides headline style news of the day. Features include a calendar of weekly events, and a "Virtual Congress" where participants can learn about, discuss, and vote on current bills in Congress.

Issues of the Week: provides analysis, facts and figures, and interactive discussion on significant issues and the legislation relevant to these issues. Content from previous weeks is archived and searchable.

Issues Directory: is an area of particular note for researchers and students. Here, one can follow links to any of the following topics: Affirmative Action, Agriculture, Budget & Tax Reform, Campaign Finance Reform, Civil Justice, Civil Rights, Constitutional Issues, Crime, Defense & Foreign Affairs, Economics, Education, Energy, Environment, Government, Health Care, Immigration, Information Technology, Labor, Media, Political Process, Social Security, Society and Values, Telecommunications, Trade, Transportation, Urban Renewal, Welfare, and Women's Issues.

Within these issue areas, one will find reports and studies from a variety of institutions. For example, within "Education," there are the following documents: a policy analysis on school vouchers by the Cato Institute, a study on the effects of violence in schools published by the American Civil Liberties Union, a speech by Commissioner Susan Ness on connecting libraries and schools to the Internet, and a speech by the President on the same topic.

Feature Event: Those with Real Audio capability can hear actual current and relevant policy speeches.

Other Features

Policy.com's *Newsstand* links to articles of interest on national policies. There is also a *Student Union* area where high school or college students can enter areas according to their political interests. Discussions and debates take place in this area and links are provided to the Web sites of student groups based on political topics or partisan agendas. A *Job Bank* is also available here.

Finally, Policy.com links to Think Tanks, University Centers, Advocacy Organizations, Associations, Businesses, U.S. and Other Government sites, and Media resources of interest.

Summary: HandsNet vs. Policy.com

Users of either HandsNet or Policy.com need not struggle over which one to use—they can simply use both, and they may find other similar sites, as well. Information contributors can submit to both and be sure of the widest possible reach. But it may be helpful to be aware of the differences. Below are some points of variance we found:

(1) HandsNet tends to be a cooperative, collaborative site in which members not only share information but work together and collaborate. There seems to be a certain ideological unity among HandsNet members, although they often do disagree on points. Policy.com participants, however, seem to be more aggressively critical of one another. The ideological gulf between participants seems much wider.

(2) HandsNet, being the older and more established site, and being particularly driven to collecting data and documents from organizations, seems to provide more information in a tighter format than does Policy.com. Policy.com, perhaps through its discussion and chat areas, is lively and current and may provide a better "pulse" on how the general public perceives today's important issues. Policy.com also provides a centralized resource for accessing information already on the Internet in a way that HandsNet does not seek to do.

(3) Content on the two sites overlaps significantly, but not entirely. For example, HandsNet has a great deal of content from the legal services community, while Policy.com does not. Policy.com includes such topics as defense and foreign affairs, which HandsNet does not.

(4) HandsNet is a not-for-profit organization, funded by grants and memberships, while Policy.com is a commercial endeavor.

Online advocacy holds many actual as well as potential benefits but, so far, it is unlikely to replace the offline work advocates have always pursued. So, it should usually be considered "something extra." You will probably not be able to use the Internet to recruit hordes of demonstrators for your rally, for example. But with the simple and cost-effective ability to spread the word about such events, you may boost the numbers and serve to spread the word, while at the same time building for a future involving ever-growing use of this kind of technology. Simply put, the advocacy you do online is both advocacy for your particular cause and advocacy for the increasing use of the Internet for achieving such goals.

Perhaps the most exciting facet of online advocacy is that it is so much more convenient than traditional methods of civic participation. Anyone who has ever felt guilty about remaining silent on important issues merely because they did not have the time to write and send letters, make phone calls, or attend relevant events and demonstrations may find a rewarding and time-saving solution in the Internet.

For example, e-mail makes it a simple matter to send an editorial letter to your newspaper. Oftentimes, the newspaper will publish the e-mail address of the person commenting, who may then receive comments from other readers (for good or bad!). If you don't want your e-mail address published along with your comments, make sure to specify this when you send your message. Similarly, views can be expressed to legislators by e-mail. Many local newspapers routinely publish the e-mail addresses of elected officials on their editorial pages.

An example of the changes such tools are bringing to our society was demonstrated in 1997, when Air Force pilot Kelly Flinn faced a court-martial and possible imprisonment on charges of adultery. Through the ability of people to respond electronically, the Air Force was flooded with e-mail from people across the nation, mostly sympathetic to Flinn and viewing her treatment as overly harsh. What would have likely been a relatively private matter suddenly became a public referendum.

Many believe that the future of the Internet will include formal voting through online means. Referenda and regular elections may one day be as easy as logging in to the appropriate Web site. While this is probably some time away, there are many who are using online voting to collect their own data, survey people, and circulate petitions.

Getting the Word Out About Your Advocacy Efforts

You're representing your professional association on a coalition to plan a rally at the state capitol opposing welfare cuts. What can you do to make your event known to those online who might be interested?

One answer to this kind of practical problem is to do some preliminary work long before the event is to take place. Begin compiling an audience with whom you interact electronically, using both e-mail and the Web.

You might first start to ask those in your organization's existing membership or on your mailing list for their e-mail addresses, so you can keep them posted on happenings with your organization. Use your Web site to attract more interested individuals and give them the chance to submit their e-mail addresses to join your mailing list. Develop a regular (but not too frequent) schedule of communication to this group, urging them to pass your communications on to those individuals or groups they represent or interact with.

Asking people to forward your messages to the groups they correspond with electronically can greatly enhance your reach. Most individuals online for any length of time will have some group of colleagues or friends with whom they are happy to share appropriate communications. People in organizations are often happy to share such relevant information with their entire staff through e-mail.

The Children's Defense Fund, for example, has done this with great success. CDF sends advocacy alerts and calls to action to a list of interested subscribers. Since these messages contain a good deal of information and are more than just pleas for involvement, they are particularly easy to share with others. While there is no way to tell for sure how many actually get the CDF alerts, the evidence suggests that they get to many more than receive them directly from the organization. As a result, the alerts can have a widespread anticipated benefit and lead to unexpected successes, as well. Gary Grant, with a few clicks of his mouse, shares the CDF announcements with the 300 students at his school of social work.

Complement your e-mail communications with news on your Web site. You can, for example, use your Web site as a place for supplemental information, briefing people by e-mail and offering more substantive and complete additional information on the Web site. This will keep people visiting from time to time, which is something they are less likely to do unless they know there is new information there since the last time they visited.

With these strategies, you can, over a short time, find that you are spreading your influence and network in ways and to a degree you would never have expected. The quantity of your communications can be increased, and the quality of your relationship with your constituency can be enhanced.

Ultimately, when the time for your rally comes around, you can provide an e-mail alert and post detailed information on your Web site, if appropriate. You might even get a better read on the event by encouraging responses from those planning to attend.

Whether you organize your online network well in advance or not, there are measures you can take to get the word out about your event to targeted individuals and groups online.

By investing a few hours of work researching the appropriate places online to send news of your event, an alert, or a call for action, you will have available a ready way to respond electronically now and in the future. Here are some steps you might take in initially compiling such a list.

Step 1: Collect the e-mail addresses of people in relevant organizations and groups online.

By using some basic search techniques, you can locate the Web sites of national and local groups whose work is related to your own. These sites typically include the e-mail contact address for the organization. Collecting them into your address book will give you a way to instantly spread your word to people who can then pass it on within their organizations and among their constituencies.

Think of these contacts as "gatekeepers" for the lists they are likely to have compiled for internal or external communication. Your contact with them can seek to enlist their aid in building a network, starting with the urgency of the current event you are working on.

Over time, such gatekeepers are probably a good group to cultivate a relationship with for mutual advantage. Information and resources can be shared over time, making possible connections and the avoidance of duplicative efforts that may have been the norm in the past.

Through your continued relationship with gatekeeper contacts, you can begin to get a solid feel for how far and wide your message is spreading. Find out what groups they represent and with whom they communicate electronically.

To find possible gatekeepers, search the Web for organizations that are online. Once you find relevant organizations, visit their sites and locate the contact people. Cut and paste their e-mail addresses into your e-mail address book. Begin a list of related organizations, so you can send a message simultaneously to all of them.

Next, you can look for Web sites dedicated to relevant topic areas, such as the professional communities discussed in Chapter 10. Chances are you will uncover some more people who have gathered a collection of helpful contacts and who can serve as another kind of gatekeeper. Add these individuals' e-mail addresses to your lists. Online journals related to your topic might include your alert in their publications on the Web or via e-mail.

HandsNet is one excellent example of an online community covering a variety of areas. If you are a member, there are forums in which your alert can be posted and shared weekly with all other members. Even if you are not a member, you might find a contact person at HandsNet willing to post your alert for you.

When you have finished spending some time gathering possible gatekeeper addresses, draft an e-mail message describing your event or effort and encouraging others to participate. At the top of your message, provide a statement introducing yourself and courteously asking that they assist you by forwarding your alert within their organization and among their constituency, colleagues, and friends as they see appropriate. Encourage them to let you know which groups they are contacting on your behalf. If possible, promise to do the same for them if they need such assistance in the future.

Try to make your message as personalized as you can within the context of a general mailing. Make it short enough that it is easy to understand what is being asked, but try also to make it informative enough that it is not just a plea for involvement. Make it as exciting as possible, and state how important participation is. You might want to modify your letter for the specific kinds of groups contacted. You should probably also suggest that people print it out and post it in their offices for those not using e-mail.

Step 2: Locate related newsgroups and bulletin boards.

A few minutes of work is sufficient to uncover at least a handful of newsgroups to which you can address messages. It is recommended that you spend a little bit of time getting to know the tenor and type of discussion that takes place, so your message is not inappropriate to the topic of the newsgroup.

Examples of newsgroups that are likely to be appropriate for posting information about a rally are regional groups (such as chi.general for general discussion relevant to Chicago or whatever city you are in), topical newsgroups (such as alt.planning.urban or alt.activism or misc.activism.progressive), or organizational newsgroups (such as soc.org.nonprofit).

In all cases, post your message as a courteous request and make the subject line as clear as possible, so those not interested can avoid it. Your posting to larger newsgroups may very possibly generate some negative responses. These may, to some extent, be legitimate if your read on the group was wrong. Even if it *was* appropriate, an individual participant may feel otherwise. No matter what, it is best to ignore these. No matter how correct the complaining party is, an apology to the group is usually seen as making matters worse, since the apology is itself another off-topic communication. In general, one isolated slip-up in Netiquette will be forgotten, but don't let it lead to a month of discussion and ranting.

A number of Web sites have their own bulletin boards. These create the same kind of threaded discussion as a newsgroup, but they take place directly at the Web site. If you find such bulletin boards related to your effort, treat them like newsgroups and post your message.

The National Committee for Educating Students to Influence State Policy and Legislation
http://www.statepolicy.org

This committee was formed in 1997 to "assist faculty and students in learning how to influence effectively the formation, implementation, and evaluation of state-level policy and legislation."

The site, which has a text-only version in addition to one with graphics, offers a wide range of state policy resources, linkages with state policy makers, updated news, student projects, faculty assignments, bibliographies, membership listings, and a calendar of events.

There are links to sites related to state government, federal government, welfare reform, and social work. A bibliography of related articles includes links to those that are available online.

A page called "Breaking News" links to current and recent policy-related articles, many on the topic of welfare reform.

An especially interesting section of the site lists sample student projects and faculty assignments related to social policy. This could serve as an excellent resource for students trying to come up with a project idea or professors putting together a new syllabus for a policy course.

The National Committee for Educating Students to Influence State Policy and Legislation home page. Reprinted with permission.

The national chairperson for the Committee is Dr. Robert L. Schneider, a social work professor at Virginia Commonwealth University.

Keep your eyes on this site as it develops.

Step 3: Use mailing lists to spread the word.

The mailing lists you join can become places to spread the word about actions in which you want to encourage others to participate. In some cases, you need not join the list to get your message mentioned.

Just make sure that you post only to appropriate mailing lists. It is not uncommon for advocacy efforts in mailing lists to spill over into other forums on unrelated topics. People often carry their interests in one area to another. A person who posts to a gardening list might decide to mention the rally you are planning. While you really cannot prevent this, you should not encourage it, since people tend to be very protective of their discussion forums and rail against even well-meaning discussion that distracts from the main topic.

Mailing lists relevant to social advocacy efforts are too numerous to name them all here. There were state social work mailing lists in 22 states at our last count, and many of these have a state or local legislative focus. You may be able to find these through your state NASW office, or through Liszt's directory (http://www.liszt.com), which contains information on more than 71,000 mailing lists and 18,000 newsgroups. There is also a list of these state mailing lists on the Association of Baccalaureate Social Work Program Directors (BPD) Web site at *http://www.rit.edu/~694www/bpd.htm.*

Conclusion

The Internet is an important tool for advocates and promises to be even more significant in the future. Perhaps the greatest challenge for advocates in any area is to get information to people in a way that is quick, cost-effective, and in a form capable of motivating them to action. The Internet meets this criteria and only requires more universal access and usage to ensure the greatest possible benefit for advocacy efforts.

The Internet gives advocates the freedom to present information to a large, geographically diverse group of people for a negligible cost. The new challenge will be to make people care. But for those who do care, action is now easier.

More than just being a tool, the Internet is itself a community. Opinions are made and shaped online. People are expressing their volunteerism through online activities. The Internet holds the key to a higher level of civic participation by the broadest number of people than could otherwise be possible. The future may see policymakers turning increasingly to the Internet as a more cost-effective and convenient way to gauge public opinion. This could make the Internet an especially important ground for advocates to stake out now.

With so much possible online, it is sometimes difficult to know where to start. Even if the financial commitment is negligible, the time commitment is considerable. Enter carefully, but experiment and feel your way. Find linkages with other organizations, and see how they are pursuing their online advocacy efforts. Be a participant in the efforts of others as an advocate. Finally, be creative. The culture of the Internet is still forming, and what you do online helps to shape it.

Chapter 18

Job Search on the Internet

by Jennifer Luna-Idunate and Robert Canon

A 1997 newspaper article reported that a school district near Pittsburgh, PA, requires all its job applicants to download its job application form from the Internet. This is the only way they can obtain the form, because—as the article explained—the district wants every employee in every school to be computer literate.

Not all employers have gone to this extreme, but certainly computer literacy is increasingly becoming an asset that employers seek in job candidates, and it is a skill that will serve job seekers well in looking for new avenues for finding job opportunities.

Careers expert Joyce Lain Kennedy and writer Thomas J. Morrow wrote one of the first books on using the new technology in the job search process—*Electronic Job Search Revolution*—in 1994. In that book, they describe such possibilities as résumé database services, in-house applicant tracking systems, "armchair" job hunting, electronic employer databases, and computerized job interviews.

Using the Internet for your job search will expand your career opportunities by allowing broad access to professional development services and employment listings at your convenience—24 hours a day. You can research potential employers, areas of practice, and many professional organizations without ever having to leave your own computer. If you are considering a long-distance job search, you will find help wanted advertisements, relocation and salary calculators, and many online services that will even allow you to post your résumé for free. An additional bonus: using the Internet as one of the tools in your search demonstrates an important transferable skill that will definitely increase your marketability in social work—your familiarity with the computer and the Internet.

But are social work employers really using these methods? Or is it just technical jobs that are advertised and found this way? How many social work jobs are listed on the World Wide Web (and other places online), and how many social workers are looking there for jobs?

Elena Felipe, MSW, a hospital social worker in Miami, FL, is one social worker who looked online, and found her job through a posting on the commercial service, America Online. "The great thing about the online discovery [of a job opening] was that I was able to act on it right away," said Felipe. "I found the ad on Labor Day weekend. I e-mailed Susan [Mankita] and she responded the next day, which was Sunday. She requested my résumé, and we set up an interview for Tuesday after Labor

Day. Had I found an ad in the paper, it might have taken several days or weeks before I received a response...who knows if the job would still have been available."

Mankita, who coordinates America Online's Social Work Forum, had posted the job opening in the Forum's "Job Bank" folder. She also advertised in the traditional ways—in the local newspaper and a professional organization newsletter. She had already narrowed her search to three candidates and was ready to make a hiring decision when Elena's résumé arrived in her e-mail box.

"The Internet, especially AOL, is one of the best ways I've ever encountered of forging relationships with colleagues," says Mankita. "I like people who explore frontiers. In some ways, mastering the Internet requires bravery and some pioneering spirit. Finding that [in a job candidate] is an extra bonus."

"I would certainly recommend an online job search," says Elena, who became a social worker after a successful career in radiology. "This job is the best thing that's happened to me in a while. Had I not had the opportunity to market myself the moment I saw the ad, I would have been too late."

Madeleine Dale agrees. Now director of career development at Columbia University's School of Social Work, Dale found her job online after searching various sites and search engines. See page 118 for more on Madeleine's job search.

Where to Start

So, where do you start to find a job online, like Elena and Madeleine did? You can look for jobs online whether your connection is through a university, a commercial service, or an Internet Service Provider. Several sites offer assistance in all aspects of career development, including career path exploration, résumé writing, and negotiating salary and benefits. A good way to begin is to check out a few of the more popular sites at one sitting, using sections that link to other sites. You can use one of these services as your jumping off point, but remember every site is linked to other sites, so you may quickly find yourself 10 or 15 links away from where you started.

One such site, called *Career Planning Process*, is available at *http://www.cba.bgsu.edu/class/ webclass/nagye/career/process.html*. This site presents a career planning model that encourages people to gather information about themselves and their options, allowing them to make informed decisions about their careers. It includes self assessment, academic/career options, relevant/practical experience, job search/graduate school preparation, and career change components.

The *Career Development Manual* from the University of Waterloo at *http://www.adm.uwaterloo.ca/ infocecs/CRC/manual-home.html* offers similar tools for self assessment, occupational research, decision-making, employment contacts, and career/life planning.

The *College Grad Job Hunter* site at *http://www.collegegrad.com/* provides lots of tips on the job search process. The complete book of the same name is online, covering such topics as deciding what you want to do, preparing for the job search, what to wear to the interview, negotiating job offers, and salaries. There is an "Ask the Expert" question and answer section where author Brian Kruger answers Web site visitors' questions. There are also Real Audio files that allow you to listen to presentations of various job search topics.

Making Contact

Another way to get job information is to contact a professional organization or other social service affiliation, and many of these have WWW sites available for general information, research, and

Up Close: Social Work and Social Services Jobs Online
http://gwbweb.wustl.edu/jobs/

Since June 1996, this site has provided a place for social workers to look for jobs and career information online. Sponsored by the George Warren Brown School of Social Work at Washington University (St. Louis, MO), the site was created by Carol Nesslein Doelling, director of career services at the school, and Violet E. Horvath. A homepage committee oversees the site.

"Our intended audiences are social workers and employers who hire them in a wide range of positions," says Doelling, who is charged with the site's ongoing maintenance. "Given our traffic and feedback forms, I think we are reaching those audiences."

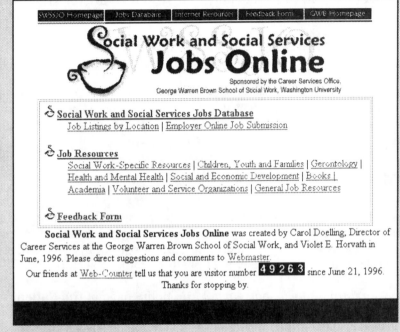

George Warren Brown School of Social Work's Social Work and Social Services Jobs Online home page. Reprinted with permission.

Visitors to the site will find extensive job listing and career resource links, in addition to an on-site listing of jobs throughout the United States and some international locations.

Employers can post job openings free for four weeks by completing an online form. Listings can be renewed at no charge by contacting the Web master.

networking. For example, licensure information and examination services nationwide, the Council on Social Work Education (CSWE), and the National Association of Social Workers (NASW) are all available for gathering information pertaining to professional development. There are also several state chapters of NASW online. Most of these sites have an e-mail address for requesting information, therefore eliminating long-distance telephone calls and possibly lengthy waits.

One helpful feature of the NASW Web site (http://www.socialworkers.org) is that it has a list of all the state chapters of the association. So, if you live in North Carolina but are planning to move to Utah, you can look on the NASW Web site and find out how to contact the chapter office in Salt Lake City by mail, telephone, fax, and e-mail.

Social Work Examination Services (http://www.tiac.net/users/swes/) is a company that offers licensing exam preparation courses and study materials. This Web site, besides telling about SWES's commercial products, has a listing of contacts for state licensing boards. The American Association of State Social Work Boards (AASSWB) site at http://www.aasswb.org has a similar listing.

Mailing lists can be useful in your job search. People often post informal job announcements on these lists. Also, as a new subscriber, you can post questions related to your job search.

When first joining a mailing list, think of it as a meeting and introduce yourself to the group, mentioning your job search goals. You may want to just read the list for a few weeks, to get a feel for the nature of each group before posting your questions/comments. Conduct yourself as you would in any other professional setting. Participating in an online mailing list of people all over the world may seem to give you anonymity at first, but you never know when the person you flamed on the SOCWORK list last week may be interviewing you for your dream job tomorrow!

The Association of Baccalaureate Social Work Program Directors (BPD) has posted a list of Internet Discussion Lists for Social Workers at the following site: *http://www.rit.edu/~694www/lists.htm*

To get started, you may want to join the Social Work Discussion Group, also known as SOCWORK, at majordomo@uwrf.edu. Write to this address with the command: SUBSCRIBE SOCWORK. Once you have subscribed, you can send messages to all members of the list at socwork@uwrf.edu. See page 24 for more information on SOCWORK.)

Employment Search Sites

Several employment search sites post nationwide job listings in almost every career field imaginable. At these sites, you can usually search by professional title such as "social worker" or "therapist" or by location. The key to searching these large databases is to use as many keywords as possible that relate to the type of position you are seeking.

JobWeb (http://www.jobweb.org), the home page of the National Association of Colleges and Employers, is one example of this type of site. It includes a variety of career-related services, which are updated and expanded regularly. You'll find an employer directory of career opportunities, a searchable database with job postings (including links to federal jobs), job search information and guidance, and links to other job-search resources.

A few employment search sites exist specifically for social work and related professions. One of the most comprehensive job search sites for social workers is George Warren Brown School of Social Work's *Social Work and Social Services Jobs On-line* at *http://www.gwbweb.wustl.edu/jobs/*.

This database allows you to search for national and international jobs by location in academia, administration, advocacy, case management, clinical social work, community development, direct practice, fund-raising, international social development, non-profit management, social policy, research, and other areas of interest to those in social work. The site also includes links to other job resources, career development resources, and an employer online job submission form for employers who want to post job openings.

The New Social Worker Online Career Center at *http://www.socialworker.com/career.htm* is published by White Hat Communications and was newly-designed in Summer 1997. It is part of *The New Social Worker's* Web site and includes job links for social workers, employment postings, and feature articles related to career development from *THE NEW SOCIAL WORKER* magazine. Interactive features added in 1997 include social work careers chats and a bulletin board for discussion of social work careers.

Several state Chapters of NASW have job listings at their sites, including California *(http://naswca.org/jobsindex.html)*, West Virginia *(http://members.aol.com/naswwv/naswwv.html)*, New Mexico *(http://www.naswnm.org)*, North Carolina *(http://members.aol.com/naswnc/jobs.htm)*, and Oregon *(http://home.earthlink.net/~nasw/jobs.htm)*.

Another place to look for job listings is on the sites of social service agencies themselves. Larger agencies, especially, may have their own Web sites, which may include job listings. Of course, while you're at the site, do some preliminary research on the agency, to give yourself an edge over the other candidates when you apply for the jobs listed.

Finding Internships

Many non-profit organizations have recently turned to the Internet to publicize and recruit interns for opportunities within their agencies. The National Assembly of National Voluntary Health and Social Welfare Organizations (the National Assembly) has an online database of over 2,000 paid and unpaid internships at youth development agencies such as Big Brothers/Big Sisters, Boy Scouts, Girl Scouts, YMCA, YWCA, and Volunteers of America. The database, located at *http://www.nassembly.org* (click on "Internships"), can be searched by state, city, and type of internship sought.

Those looking for social policy internships might want to check out the Student Union section of the Policy.com site *(http://www.policy.com)*. Internships with a variety of national policy-related organizations are listed, as are opportunities to be a "virtual intern" for Policy.com.

The Long Distance Approach

When conducting a "long distance" job search, the WWW can be your most useful resource. You can begin by using the national employment databases mentioned previously. Additionally, newspapers in some large cities publish classified ads in a searchable database. Once you have chosen to relocate, there are also sites available to help you calculate salaries and relocation costs. Many cities are online with information about real estate, local events, restaurants, and other businesses. These pages are often maintained by City Net or the local chamber of commerce.

CareerPath (http://www.careerpath.com) is a useful resource for long-distance job seekers, because it contains the Sunday classified want ads for 57 newspapers (as of March 1998), including the *Boston Globe, New York Times, Los Angeles Times, Chicago Tribune, Washington Post, Denver Post, Baltimore Sun*, and others.

City Net (http://www.citynet.com/) contains local information from over 30 cities around the nation. Information includes classified ads, entertainment, malls, phone book, news, and weather.

The Salary Calculator...Living, Real Estate (http://www.homefair.com/homefair/cmr/salcalc.html), *E-Span's Cost of Living (http://espan2.espan.com/career/p1/dir/relo/cost.htm)*, and *U.S. Cost of Living Comparisons from Datamasters (http://www.datamasters.com/cgi-bin/col.pl)* can help you decide if you are making a financially sound decision.

Publishing Résumés on the WWW

Most Internet access providers allow users to publish WWW documents, or home pages. These pages can be highly reflective of the developer's personality and serve as a showcase for technical talents, in addition to putting résumés where they can be accessed from anywhere in the world, 24 hours a day. Your personal WWW page can be used as an electronic portfolio of other achievements, including résumé/vitae, links to other WWW projects, links to pertinent organizations or affiliations, universities attended, presentations and workshops, papers published, and research projects. The basic HTML tags to create an attractive showcase for your accomplishments are easily learned and widely available on the WWW. Many universities provide information on WWW page development for beginners. The following sites will post your résumé for free.

CareerSite
http://www.careersite.com/index.shtml
You are required to sign up, but résumé posting is free.

Up Close: An Online Job Search

As Director of Career Development at Columbia University School of Social Work, it's Madeleine Dale's job to know how to conduct a job search and to teach those skills to students. But when it comes to Internet job search techniques, Dale isn't just a teacher—she's a role model.

Knowing that she wanted to move back to her native New York after living in Miami, FL, she set out on a long-distance search. After reading an article in a business publication that suggested using the Internet to find jobs, she began searching the CareerPath Web site *(http://www.careerpath.com)*. At that time (in 1995), the site listed ads from five city newspapers, including the *New York Times*. Now, it lists jobs from 57 newspapers.

"Careerpath.com was giving me a good number of ads to read, but I wasn't able to target my search for the right job for me, which I think is the best way to go about seeking a job," she says. "One Monday morning, I thought, 'This is it. You want New York. Go for it,' so, I booted up my computer and went to the Internet and typed in 'Jobs New York.' Scads of institutions popped up. I often joke I'd be at NYU if Columbia hadn't come sooner in the alphabet." She found the job announcements page off of Columbia's "beautiful homepage, passed on being a landscape gardener (although it had some appeal), saw the announcement for a Career Development Director at the School of Social Work, and said, 'That's it!'"

She wrote a well-crafted cover letter, stating at the very beginning that she had seen the listing online. "In that short article I had read in the business publication, it said something to the effect that if you indicate you found the job on the Internet, you would get ten extra IQ points from the employer," she explains.

The Dean who interviewed her said that since they were looking for a Career Development Director, they were paying special attention to how the candidates conducted their own job

E-Span
http://www.espan.com/
Allows you to put your résumé in front of thousands of hiring professionals.

Westech Virtual Job Fair
http://www.vjf.com/pub/Rsubmit.html
Will let you post your skills in two ways, one public and the other confidential.

E-mail Résumés

When conducting an online job search, you may be asked to submit your résumé and a cover letter via e-mail. Although you can use the same content for your online résumé as for a printed one, the format will probably need some changes. Since you will be sending your résumé electronically, it will have to be stored in plain text format with no bullets, boldface type, or underlining. In order to emphasize key points or section headers you may use asterisks or capital letters. After you have finished checking it for spelling and grammar errors, send it to yourself or a friend to see how it looks after it is e-mailed. When you're confident that it is picture perfect and ready to send off, don't forget to send both the résumé and the cover letter in the same file and use the advertised position title as your "subject" line in the e-mail message.

While using the Internet for your job search won't take the place of visiting your campus career office, face-to-face networking, scanning the local employment ads, and other traditional methods, it will certainly be to your advantage to use it as part of your overall job hunting strategy. Think of searches. "The implication was that I was computer literate! I think I got 100 extra IQ points!" Dale says. "After all, I got the job just as they were a day away from offering it to someone else. That line in my letter caught the employer's attention—he wanted to meet me when he read that word 'online.'"

Now, Dale is a strong advocate for other social workers' use of the Internet in their job searches. Her office at Columbia still keeps job postings in notebooks that students and alumni/ae can peruse. Until mid-1998, it still sent out a hard copy listing of opportunities for more advanced social workers, but a decision was made to discontinue that service. Says Dale, "That style of job searching cannot continue. It doesn't get the news of a job opening to candidates fast enough. If you don't look for openings on the Internet, then you are behind the times and behind...your competitors for jobs." She called her office's jobs bulletin "a dinosaur," saying by the time it got photocopied, collated, stapled, and mailed out, the listings were at least two weeks old. "Furthermore, it is unnecessary to do such a mailing, when everyone can get the information in a timely manner, since everyone has access to the Internet," she adds. "Everyone can go to the public library."

When Dale did her own job search, she didn't know where to find Web sites for employment, so she just went to a search engine and typed words that seemed to make sense to her, and that worked well. Now she knows of lots of resources, but she still uses the search engine method periodically for her students, updating a list of sites she has put together.

Besides that, she suggests that online job searchers "be creative and have fun." She also recommends that if you find a job on the Internet that interests you, you should respond right away and say you found the job online.

But what about those who aren't familiar with the Internet? Can they use it as a job search tool, too? Dale doesn't see it as a problem. "I tell people who 'resist' the Internet, 'If you can follow the directions on the back of a *Jell-O* box, you can use the Internet.'"

the Internet as a career development tool that can greatly broaden your professional network, enhance your computer skills, and expand your career options—all at the click of a mouse.

This Chapter is adapted from an article published in THE NEW SOCIAL WORKER, Spring 1997 issue (Volume 4, Number 2).

Up Close: The New Social Worker® Online
http://www.socialworker.com

The New Social Worker Online, like its print counterpart *The New Social Worker* magazine, is a resource devoted to social work students, new social workers, and their career development. It features, among other things, an Online Career Center. There are sample career development articles from the magazine, links to job search and career-related sites, and on-site job listings.

Developed in August 1995 and maintained by Linda Grobman, one of the co-authors of this book, the site was redesigned in the Summer of 1997.

With that redesign, the site became more interactive. In November 1997, the first "Social Work Careers Chat" was hosted on the site, featuring guest speaker Jennifer Luna-Idunate, co-author of Chapter 18 of this book. The plan is to hold similar chats on a regular basis, with other social work career development professionals "speaking" on topics of interest to job seekers.

A message board was also added to the site in November, with an emphasis on social work careers. Threads on the board include one on salaries and another on why people chose social work as a career.

The New Social Worker® Online home page. Copyright © 1998 White Hat Communications. Reprinted with permission.

Besides providing ways for social workers and students to network with each other and exchange ideas about job search and careers, *The New Social Worker*'s Online Career Center offers something more concrete and practical—classified ads for current job openings. "More and more social work employers are looking for places to advertise online. Many of them are coming to *The New Social Worker*, one of the few sites focusing specifically on social work careers," says Grobman.

Additionally, the Online Career Center features a list of over 50 links to general and social work career and job sites. For example, these include sites like CareerPath, which list jobs in all fields, and more specialized sites like the page that lists MSW jobs in the State of Louisiana merit system. Many state job sites are listed, as are NASW state chapter sites that include job listings.

To access the Online Career Center, go to: *http://www.socialworker.com/career.htm*

Chapter 19

Social Work Education and Research

I am an undergraduate student and I want to pursue graduate social work studies. Can the Internet help me find the right school? What should I look for at school Web sites?

As a social work student, I would like to enhance the resources available for my research and writing, but the Internet is so time-consuming to navigate. What sites can assist me without putting me behind schedule? Are there any helpful tips for making effective use of the Internet as an educational resource? How about connections to other social work students—are there any ways for the Internet to give me access to students at other schools?

I am a faculty member in a school of social work. It seems as if the Internet is changing our world. I just hope it's for the better. I would like to use part of the summer to review my course materials. Perhaps there are Internet resources I should include in my syllabi. I should at least know where to refer students who ask about research on the Internet. How should I start thinking about the Internet as a teaching resource? Should I develop Web pages for my classes and research projects? Should I make my writing available on the Web?

I am an administrator at a school of social work. Are there any Internet tools that might have an impact on my work? Should my department administer a home page?

I am a social work graduate. What should I expect from my school through the Internet? What resources might I find at my school's site or at other schools' sites?

Exploring Social Work Schools through the Internet

There is good news for students considering entering graduate and undergraduate degree programs in social work. Educational institutions have been among the leaders in making information available on the Internet. Virtually all universities and colleges now have Web sites. Almost all departments, graduate schools, and units have their own Web sites as well.

You can spend a single sitting at your computer touring schools across the U.S. and abroad. You can contact recruitment staff and request applications and brochures. You can read online versions of catalogues, read about courses, see pictures of faculty, and read about their accomplishments, interests, and writing. At many sites, you can get visual images of people and events, read faculty or student writings, or contact faculty, students, alumni, or staff with specific questions. You can explore the current research and learn about specialized training opportunities. You can see what field placement agencies the school offers. For example, before taking an actual trip to

Indianapolis, you can pay the University of Indiana social work program a "virtual visit" on its Web site *(http://www. uindy.edu/~socwork/program/vv.htm)*.

You can also expand your research and find out about the rest of the university campus and resources and the community.

Ultimately, a live visit is the best way to get a true sense of the school.   But the Internet offers students a wide array of information and opportunities that have never before been available or possible.

Online Directories of Social Work Programs

The first trick is to find the right list of social work schools to begin your research. There are several options. You can search for a desired school using a search engine, or find your way through directory topics such as "education" or "social work."   But unless you have a very short list of schools you are considering, you will almost certainly want to start from a site that lists schools of social work and social work degree programs.

The list you select should be the one that gets you to the information you need in the fastest way. The site descriptions below may help:

SWAN's List of Social Work Schools (http://www.sc.edu/swan/univ.html)
SWAN provides a simple and quick alphabetical list of social work programs. It is a comprehensive list of master's level programs updated with reasonable frequency. If you know exactly which schools you want to visit, SWAN will get you to them quickly. The drawback to using a list like this is that it provides no clues as to whether each school listed has a significant amount of information at its site or not. A school with a very detailed site is listed in exactly the same way as one with very little.

University of Chicago School of Social Service Administration's Guide to Graduate Schools of Social Work (http://www.chas.uchicago.edu/ssa/links/schools.html)
SSA's list of social work schools is another alternative and is run by Gary Grant, co-author of this book. This site is also a comprehensive, alphabetical, and regularly updated list of master's programs, but it includes a grid that lays out the various sections of each school's site and allows you to go straight into each area immediately. SSA's list provides much more information about each school up front, so it is helpful and can save a great deal of time primarily when you want to explore schools rather than visit a particular one.

Since this site allows you to bypass each school's "front door" page, it is helpful to anyone wanting specific information on each school. For example, suppose you want to scan through the student Web pages at several social work schools, or skim the publications of each school. These activities will be faster using the SSA list. The information you can access directly from SSA's pages include: the schools' addresses and phone numbers, contact people and deans, faculty directories, student and alumni Web pages, research and publications, event calendars, and other special resources each school makes available at its site.

Association of Baccalaureate Social Work Program Directors (http://www.rit.edu/~694www/bpd.htm)
BPD boasts the most up-to-date listing, with links, of accredited and "in candidacy" social work programs. The site provides a listing in alphabetical order by state, from which you can link to each school that has a Web site. BSW, MSW, and doctoral programs are listed.

Peterson's Education Center (http://www.petersons.com/)
Another option for researching schools of social work is to use the Peterson's online guide. Peterson's is also an extremely useful tool, although it may or may not lead you to the home page of the school. In some cases, it will lead you to the university's home page rather than the school of social work,

or it may not have a link at all. However, information exists for all or nearly all schools, even those with no Web site. In addition, Peterson's offers information that the Web site might not include, especially hard data. Furthermore, it is presented by an objective third party, rather than from the school's staff, who are naturally interested in promoting their schools and attracting applicants.

Some Words of Caution

How much does the quality of the school's Web site have to say about the quality of the school itself? Should you judge schools in part based on the amount of information made available on the Internet or the presentation? Or is this judging the book by its cover?

The Internet is a new medium, and schools are using it at different rates. A high quality program may not yet have a well developed Web site. An average program could have a highly skilled and creative Web master who makes an impressive and innovative site. So there is some need for caution. As you explore the Internet for information about schools, try not to evaluate them solely on their Web sites. On the other hand, it is appropriate to consider the quality of the Web site as one factor.

What can I expect to find at the average (or excellent) Web site of a school of social work?

If the school you are exploring has done all it can, you should be able to come away with most or all of the following:

1) Knowledge of the school's mission.
2) Understanding of its strengths, the areas of expertise of its faculty, and specialized programs offered.
3) Awareness of the degree requirements and curriculum.
4) Access to information about financial aid.
5) Exposure to faculty and/or student information, data, writing, and research.
6) Some familiarity with student life and student organizations.
7) A factual and visual sense of the community, facilities, and diversity of people.
8) Direct contact with staff or perhaps a student or alumni representative (especially important for ensuring that you get the inside scoop about the school) and access to its recruitment officer or other administrative contact.
9) And, of course, a way to request an application or download one online.

Do not hesitate to contact the schools through their Web pages. If you are a doctoral applicant, it is probably especially important to communicate with those faculty you think you might want to have as mentors. Feel free to e-mail them and engage them in discussions about their work. If possible, contact current students and find out their opinions. This can give you an "inside scoop" on the school's strengths and weaknesses. Contact staff to learn about the support they provide.

In short, Internet sites are not just online brochures. They are usually meant to be interactive and to serve as the next best thing to being there. Treat e-mail as you would verbal communication, not as an imposition on the recipient. Ask questions liberally, at least until you start getting particularly terse replies.

It is best to consider the Internet a supplement to other research tools. The mere existence of even a complete Web site does not necessarily mean that you won't need or want a printed brochure or other information.

Other Online Resources for Those Applying to Schools of Social Work

Your Social Work Advisor (http://www.socialworkadvisor.com/) is a commercial service for applicants to social work schools, offering help in identifying the right fit for the applicant and other related services. Don't hesitate to contact and ask questions. You won't be charged without agreeing to pay for charged services.

The *Council on Social Work Education (http://www.cswe.org/)* is the accrediting body for bachelor's and master's programs in social work. Here you can find information about what is happening in social work education in the United States or explore the standards and policies by which schools are accredited.

BPD's List of Internet Discussion Lists for Social Workers (http://www.rit.edu/~694www/lists.htm) Most school mailing lists are probably private, but if you are allowed to participate, it could be a helpful way to investigate schools by conversing with current students or "lurking" to hear what students or faculty at particular schools discuss.

U.S. News and World Report's Ranking of Schools of Social Work (http://www4.usnews.com/usnews/ edu/beyond/gsocwork.htm) Here, you can find the magazine's ranking of schools.

Using the Internet in Your Social Work Studies

Of all the professions, social work, perhaps more than any other, stands to benefit from the educational and research opportunities on the Internet. Law students, medical students, and most others can find just about all they need in their own specific libraries or sections of their libraries. But social work students must often depend on material found in all of these places, as well as in a social work library. The ability to find information in one centralized place is of particular benefit for social work students.

Social workers also need current information. Many courses in social work, especially those teaching social policy, relate to events that change daily. Access to up-to-the-minute national news and information will benefit social work students greatly.

Perhaps equally as important is the fact that uses of the Internet in the profession are likely to be driven largely by the students who become proficient with it in school and bring this skill into the workforce. Knowledge of how to best use the Internet in social work is likely to be a premium skill, and those with such abilities are likely to be more competitive and attractive to employers.

Relying *only* on the Internet or allowing exploration of the Internet to dominate your research activities is a risky idea. Until you are sufficiently confident that information you want exists on the Internet, and that you know how to get to it, you should continue to center your efforts on the more traditional approaches. We are not at all ready to abandon our libraries (nor will we likely ever want to do this).

It is important to look at each Web site and Internet resource critically. What is its source? Is it based on research or is it one person's (or one group's) opinion? Does the provider have a hidden agenda? An editorial in the April 16, 1997, issue of the *Journal of the American Medical Association* (JAMA) addressed the issue of quality of medical information on the Internet. The recommendations in this article can apply to non-medical information, as well. The authors identified four core standards relating to authorship, attribution of references and sources, disclosure of Web site ownership, and currency of the site's content, suggesting that at least three of the four standards should be met. For the full text of the article, including the four standards, see *http://www.ama-assn.org/ sci-pubs/journals/archive/jama/vol_277/no_15/ed7016x.htm.*

When to Use the Internet

Knowing when to use the Internet to answer a question is largely going to be learned by experience, but there are a few tips we can offer:

1. *For quick inquiries before you get started on your research.*
   It is often good to make a brief inquiry of the Internet as you start out. If some answers are there, you can save yourself some time. In other cases, you can expand your research based on what you find, such as references to printed materials.

2. *For inquiries that might involve asking a person.*
   Another good time to "ask the Internet" is when you think you might be able to refer the question to a person. Library books do not usually offer and encourage contact with the author. The Internet, however, does. Often, online text includes an e-mail link to the person who provided it. Thus, if your question is too specific and not covered by what is presented, you can contact a real person and ask your question. In other cases, you can go right to organizations, groups, and individuals seeking answers. Do not hesitate to ask more than one possible source, since there is no way of knowing how often people answer their e-mail. One example might be an assignment in which you are seeking other social workers' opinions about a controversial topic. If you post a request for these opinions on a mailing list, you will probably get at least a few usable responses. However, be aware that you may also get some negative reactions from list members who find your request inappropriate. As long as you're prepared for this possibility, you should not be too alarmed.

3. *For natural Internet questions.*
   There is really no way to teach this, but you will, by experience, start to get a sense of those questions that are most natural for the Internet. Usually the first question to ask in using the Internet for basic research is, "Who might make this information available?" Once you have thought about this, you will have some direction in your Internet search.

4. *When all other options you can think of have been exhausted.*
   The Internet is a great "last-ditch" place to look for information you need and can't find anywhere else. Some search engines now allow plain English phrasing, which means you can treat the Internet like an oracle and ask a question. Some questions will be long shots for the Internet, some will be difficult to find, and some will just come right up.

Examples

There are many kinds of questions social work students might ask on the Internet. Here are a few examples:

Questions about the structure of federal and state government—facts and figures provided by agency and departmental sites and politicians.

Many organizations and institutions have a vested interest in providing useful government information for students. Some that have Web sites are the Library of Congress *(http://lcweb.loc.gov/)* and Thomas *(http://thomas.loc.gov/)*, the House of Representatives *(http:// www.house.gov/)*, the Senate *(http://www.senate.gov/)*, and the White House *(http://www.whitehouse.gov/)*.

You can also search government resources using a directory such as *Yahoo! (http://www.yahoo.com/ Government/)*.

Using the above governmental tools one can answer some of the following questions:

Q) *What is the federal budget for each agency?*
A) Navigating through some of the above sites to the *Office of Management and Budget (http:// www.access.gpo.gov/omb/index.html)* provides the answer if you have Acrobat Reader to view it. [Note: Acrobat Reader is available online for free downloading and can be easily found through most search engines, although it may not function on some older computers].

Up Close: BPD on the Internet
http://www.rit.edu/~694www/bpd.htm

The Association of Baccalaureate Social Work Program Directors (BPD) has taken the lead in introducing the Internet into social work education. Marshall Smith maintains the BPD Web site from his office at the Rochester Institute of Technology, where he is a professor of social work. As chair of the BPD Committee on Information Technology and Social Work Education, he also manages the BPD mailing list and the BSWSTUDENT mailing list, both projects of BPD.

The BPD mailing list differs from others, like SOCWORK, says Smith, because it is meant to be a vehicle for information exchange, rather than general discussion. "Some people make the assumption that using Usenet and chat rooms are what people want...that they want to be virtually together," says Smith. "Well, that's fine occasionally, when you have a guest, and have an opportunity to have a conversation with someone you wouldn't have access to ordinarily." But, overall, he has found that most social workers are more interested in having access to information, "to be able to post something and have 3-4 e-mail messages by the next day with an answer." He compares it to having "your own personal librarian...instant access to your colleagues." And BPD members are taking advantage of this information access in large numbers. As of mid-January 1998, the BPD mailing list had 297 subscribers—representing 33.9% of BPD's 875 members, and 45.9% of the 646 members who reported having e-mail addresses.

The BPD Web site's first goal was to provide links to BSW programs and MSW programs. "We have the only up-to-date list of accredited BSW programs and in-candidacy programs with links to the programs," says Smith of the BPD site.

Lately, BPD has joined with other organizations to form a new "social work web"—a network of links and sites that are "peer-reviewed." Smith explains that to be connected to this network, a site must have "serious information" that is based on solid research, and not link to sites with "transient quality." Linking to sites from this Web or network would assure the researcher that he or she is linking to sites that have been reviewed by someone who is an expert in the area. "You may not have access to that person, but you have access to that person's judgment of the links that are provided. So, you can be assured as a teacher or practitioner that you can get some pretty good basic information," he explains.

Smith has presented numerous workshops at BPD, NASW, and CSWE conferences on using the Internet. "There doesn't seem to be as much demand for basic [Internet] literacy anymore," he observes. Now that most people who are interested in connecting to the Internet have already learned how to connect, they want to know how to use it professionally and how to get good quality information. They're getting more advanced in their uses of the Internet and in their needs for information. So, Smith doesn't see an end to the need for these workshops.

And what's in the future? "We're talking about influencing CSWE to do a pilot experiment with accreditation on the Web," says Smith.

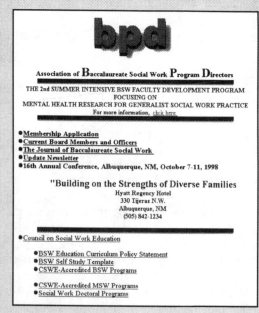

Association of Baccalaureate Social Work Program Directors (BPD) home page. Reprinted with permission.

Q) What legislation was proposed during the 104th Congress that affected women?

A) Using *Thomas*, you can easily check by topic to find that the Newborns' and Mothers' Health Protection Act of 1996 (S.969) was proposed by Senator Bradley to require that health plans provide coverage for a minimum hospital stay for a mother and child following the birth of the child, and for other purposes.

Q) How effective are community anti-drug efforts?

A) Looking for documents through the *Office of National Drug Control Policy's Clearinghouse*, you can find several articles and research reports on the topic. For example, a report on 13 community-based anti-drug efforts found that statistical data is too often unavailable or inconclusive to say for certain whether community anti-drug efforts reduce crime and drug use, although evaluators sometimes do cite other measures indicating their success.

Q) How many families in the U.S. have to pay for child care because both parents work, and what is the cost to these families?

A) Using the *U.S. Census Bureau's Page (http://www.census.gov/)* you can find a wealth of statistical information available online. In this particular case, searching the topical directory into "child care" reveals a report on the cost of care for pre-schoolers. The report indicates that in 1993, there were 8.1 million families who required day care for their pre-schoolers and that the average cost was $74 per week. For families below the poverty line, the percentage of income was about 18%.

Other Sources for Research and Data

Particular organizations, schools of social work, institutes, and others publish research and data online. HandsNet is one source for finding these resources or for contacting individuals at places that might have data not yet available online. Yahoo!'s Directory *(http://www.yahoo.com/ Social_Science/Data_Collections/)*, for example, can be a good place to start.

A good guide to state public opinion research centers is available at the *Worldwide Listing of Online Survey Research/Public Opinion Centers (http://www.ukans.edu/cwis/units/coms2/po/index.html)* from the University of Kansas. Another good source for opinion research and a broad range of other data is the comprehensive meta-list of research sources at the University of Michigan's *Documents Center (http://www.lib.umich.edu/libhome/Documents.center/stats.html)*.

Articles that are available online can be an important supplement to your research. Searching search engines by terms will uncover some articles authors have made available online, as will searching online journals. Another way to search for these articles is through the *Electric Library (http://www3.elibrary.com/)*, which is one of the few sites that require a membership fee. For $60 a year, you will have access to the full text of hundreds of magazines from popular ones like *Time* and *USA Today* to more specific ones like *Administration and Society, Research on Social Work Practice, Journal of Social Psychology*, and *Youth and Society*. The *Electric Library* also contains over 1.6 million newspaper articles from international, national, and local papers. Over 32,000 radio and television program transcripts are contained in its database, as are 162,000 book chapters from various works of fiction and nonfiction, and almanacs, dictionaries, and encyclopedia sources. Even the complete works of Shakespeare can be read through the *Electric Library*.

There are also a few sites where you can find links specifically to social work journals. One example is the social work journals page at University of North Carolina-Pembroke *(http://www.uncp.edu/ sw/swjournl.html)*. This page contains links to over 40 social work journals.

Questions about Model Programs, Innovative Agencies, Successful Approaches to Social Work

Another approach you may take is to use the Internet to explore innovative, successful, model programs in social services. The Internet is an excellent way to explore the practice of social work as it is happening in agencies and organizations.

Up Close: A Social Work Student Uses the Internet

Deborah Smyre, a 1997 BSW graduate, found the Internet useful in researching social justice topics for class assignments as an undergraduate student. She also found "a wealth of information" on ethnic communities when doing research for classes in her program, which focused on cultural competence.

Now that she's in graduate school, "it's become even more essential to have the power of Internet searches for professional journal articles, policy updates, and news reports," she says. "I've discovered a large community of online social workers from every part of the country in a wide variety of practice settings. This community meets in many different forums, including weekly live chat sessions on America Online, plus several mailing lists with specific topics such as mental health policy and managed care issues. I think of it as networking '90s style."

Besides working toward her MSW, Smyre works as a Women's Advocate at a battered women's shelter. "I believe the Internet is very important to my work. It's a necessary tool for keeping up-to-date on legislative issues related to violence against women, as well as for keeping in contact with other professionals engaged in similar work. Knowledge is power, and I know of no better, faster way to share knowledge among peers than via the Internet."

She has used the Internet to share her knowledge by developing her own Web site while she was still an undergraduate student.

Her Web pages include sections devoted to social work, diversity, adoption, public health, HIV/AIDS resources, her hobbies of genealogy and gardening, and a family members' page. The social work section began as a list of convenient links to research sites for students. Now it also serves as a stepping-off point for professionals, with links to NASW, CSWE and local universities.

Smyre's home page *(http://www.primenet.com/~dsmyre)* will lead to other pages on the site. The diversity page *(http://www.primenet.com/~dsmyre/diverse.htm)* was created from her involvement with multiracial identity issues and her interest in connecting with other interracial families and individuals. It has become a clearinghouse for hard-to-find links on this topic. The adoption page *(http://www.primenet.com/~dsmyre/adoption.htm)* was built as a result of Smyre's personal interest in the subject, as an adult adoptee, and also includes links to non-custodial mothers' Web sites and mailing lists. The broader issues of parent-child separation come together on this site.

As a result of these Web pages, she has received e-mail from social workers and students from across the U.S. The diversity page, she says, has been the most useful site for researchers. She sees cultural competence as a growing focus among social workers, and has tried to provide links to sites with a wide variety of information on the subject.

Suppose, for example, you are researching the effectiveness of programs dealing with homelessness. *Project H.O.M.E. (http://members.aol.com/prjhome/index.html)*, a program in Philadelphia, has a Web site that provides a substantial amount of information about its organization, structure, mission, and philosophy. What you don't learn online about this agency, you can learn by sending a request for information to its project coordinator. Successful programs usually hope to be replicated. The Internet helps to disseminate success stories. Not only will such explorations open entirely new possibilities for students of social work, but the process itself will be an important

"Social workers can benefit greatly by the ease of networking via the Internet. When it's time to gather data about social justice issues, the Internet is my first stop," she says. "The social work mailing lists are populated by both experienced professionals and fledgling students, so there's a comfort level to be found for everyone."

"It's a rare luxury we have with the Internet. We're able to write out our questions and receive back helpful answers from our peers," she continues. "We're able to share our frustrations as well as our triumphs, knowing we'll receive thoughtful, supportive responses in return. My undergrad professors always urged students to process our experiences in the field with one another. I believe the Internet offers us yet another way to process our experiences with fellow professionals."

She warns, however, that the Internet is a public forum. "Occasionally, I've read posts describing client contacts with a bit too much detail. There are still privacy issues to keep in mind when communicating over the Internet," she maintains.

She hopes that social work students will be presented with more opportunities to use the Internet as an academic and professional tool. "I've discovered a great deal of information and a number of friendly, supportive professionals online," she says. "I'd like to share that experience with as many other social workers as possible."

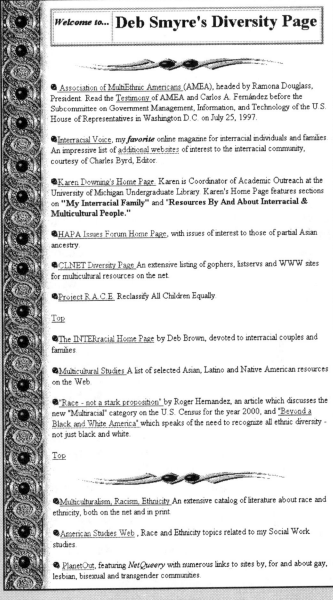

Deb Smyre's Diversity Page. Reprinted with permission.

learning experience as you gain a sense of how the Internet community can help to spread successful and well-designed model programs.

The possibilities for social work students to perform research on the Internet are by no means exhausted by the above examples. In fact, the possibilities are so many and so great that the hard part is making sure the choices don't paralyze you.

Faculty may provide some help in focusing students' efforts by providing lists or "bookmarks" of sites relevant to a particular course, but it is also important for students to learn to find such sites on their own.

Non-Academic Benefits for Students

Social work students have been known to be particularly active in a variety of public interest endeavors, advocacy efforts, and educational programs. Perhaps the Internet can serve as a way to expand on such activities conveniently. Look to Chapter 17 to see some of the online opportunities in this area. The possibilities are endless, although the realities right now may be somewhat limited. But to be sure, you can engage in e-mail writing campaigns, you can educate and tutor online, you can share ideas, and you can treat the Internet as a meeting room for discussing projects that you will carry out in other forums.

Some students wonder about job search opportunities offered by the Internet. Students interested in international social work or in practicing in another state after graduation might begin to "network" with relevant agencies through their online sites. Look at Chapter 18, and you will likely find that the opportunities are more easily accessed than you think. Internet job search resources for social workers typically divide into three categories; *general job search resources*, which are sites that post available positions in any field, and often contain listings relevant for social workers across the nation; *social work-specific sites*, which are those that do the same, but serve narrowly for social work or even more specific jobs within social work, and *regional job search sources*, which are those that offer job postings only for a particular city or area—often listed in local newspapers.

A good rule of thumb for students who are job-searching is to try the social-work specific sites first, since they will likely be the least time-consuming to review.

Social Work Student Interactions

Through the Internet, students and student groups can begin to reach out to one another across the nation and the globe. Some professors have, for example, set up Internet "pen pal" programs between their students and those at other schools. The opportunity to discuss social work related issues with students in other cities or nations can be a very broadening experience and can give students a new perspective on topics being addressed in their classes. It may also help form new networks of friends and colleagues. Students may be able to recruit well-known educators, writers, and practitioners to make online "presentations" or "discussions" for groups of students. The Internet opens a whole world of possibilities for bringing together people for the sake of valuable and educational discussions.

The idea of linking social work students has begun to take shape in the fledgling project called the Social Work Student Nexus *(http://www.chas.uchicago.edu/ssa/swsn/)*. The goal of this project is to provide a place for organizing any site that is specifically relevant to social work students. Visitors to this site can register in the Social Work Cafe *(http://www.geocities.com/Heartland/4862/swcafe.html)*, which is maintained by social work student Tobi Shane. This will ensure that they receive notice of updates and events.

The Nexus also featured its first Net event in December 1997, with an e-mail conference on ethics in social work. Some 40 or 50 students and faculty globally joined in this discussion. The Nexus also includes links to student groups at schools that have an online presence, links to student writings and journals relevant to students, a bookstore, and both ongoing and time-limited discussions.

The Nexus encourages students to create resources and to organize activities for the benefit of all social work students. As a volunteer-driven site, it hopes to see more students take the initiative to reach out to one another. The student organizers of the site plan to develop educational material about how to use the Internet and how to organize advocacy efforts, educational tools, and communication networks online.

Another example of social work student interaction on the Internet is the BSWSTUDENT mailing list *(bswstudent@listserver.isc.rit.edu)*. This mailing list, a project of the Association of Baccalaureate Social Work Program Directors (BPD), allows undergraduate social work students to discuss among each other such topics as field placements, graduate school applications, coursework, and the like.

Student groups around the country are developing Web sites that will allow them to share ideas with each other. Many schools have student social work clubs or organizations. If you are involved in such an organization, you can look at the Web sites of similar groups to get ideas for new projects. Similarly, your group may want to develop a site of its own.

Doctoral Students

Doctoral students may be particularly interested in finding funding sources for dissertations or support for study abroad. More detailed information about funding sources is found in Chapter 16, but social work doctoral students may want to pay particular attention to the *Online Study Abroad Directory*, the *Social Science Research Council*, the *Federal Information Exchange*, the *Illinois Researcher Information Service*, the *Graduate Fellowships Newsletter*, the *Student Guide to Financial Aid*, and *CSWE Doctoral Student Funding Programs*, all of which have Web sites (see reviews in Part 3).

Doctoral students will also be interested in accessing the announcements of teaching positions available at the various schools. One helpful site is the Academic Position Network *(http://www.umn.edu/apn/)*. Doctoral students may also want to look at the Council on Social Work Education site to find information about this organization's Teacher's Registry *(http://www.cswe.org)*.

There are other uses of the Internet that doctoral students are beginning to explore. For example, some are beginning to use the Internet in search of research subjects. For example, one student we spoke with who was studying interracial marriages used the Internet to find and recruit interracial couples. Each couple invited to participate was e-mailed a survey and consent form, to be printed and mailed back. The benefits to the student included saving time, reducing costs, and finding subjects she would not have been likely to locate without the Internet.

A number of dissertations have been made accessible on the Internet. Electronic versions of dissertations offer the opportunity for many more to benefit from access to research, and they offer the researchers possibilities for gaining feedback from a broader audience of academicians and others in and out of their fields. An online document also gives the ability to use hypertext links, graphics, and even sound and video to enhance the quality and nature of the presentation of the substantive material. On the other hand, such a publication format presents a greater risk of plagiarism or misuse. Currently, this is a source for more thinking and consideration. A good place to learn more about this topic is *Electronic Theses and Dissertations in the Humanities* at *http://etext.lib.virginia.edu/ETD/ETD.html.*

Finally, we know of at least a few social work doctoral students who are writing dissertations on the use of the Internet in social work, so this in itself is emerging as a topic for exploration and research.

For Faculty: Using the Internet for Teaching, Scholarship, and Breaching the Ivory Towers

Faculty, too, are increasingly using the Internet in their teaching and research. Most faculty already use e-mail to a great extent to communicate with colleagues in other institutions—a function that represents one of the earliest uses of the Internet and part of its historical development toward mainstream popularity.

Faculty research investigators may want to use the Internet, specifically the Web, for the dissemination of research projects to a broader audience of practitioners, policy-makers, academics in their own and other fields, and others. Funders are particularly excited about the ability to disseminate research online, both for the additional recognition it provides them and the broader reach and impact it gives the research. The breadth of dissemination now possible, the almost universal accessibility for little or no cost, and the ability to provide detailed information all could have an impact on the way research is used in the future. For example, what researcher has not been disappointed by the media's simplifying presentation of study findings? How often have you wished you could know more about the methodology used in a study? Creating a project Web site can help researchers to control the information and the way it is conveyed and provide the external audience with more detailed information than might otherwise be so conveniently available about their research.

Faculty are also integrating the Internet into the courses they teach. Many include substantive readings that are on the Internet, and many use communication tools (such as e-mail) to assist in teaching and administering their classes.

Faculty should be aware, though, that while some students may be Internet-savvy, others will be wary of this technology and may need some coaxing and support. Students will need to be shown the Internet's relevance to social work if they are to overcome this resistance.

We will now look more closely at applications of the Internet relevant for faculty.

Using Mailing Lists and Usenet Groups

Mailing lists and Usenet newsgroups can help facilitate discussion outside of class. Under traditional methods of teaching, students often organize themselves for discussion among one another or seek out faculty individually to expand upon their thinking. Faculty bear the burden of ensuring continuity from class session to class session. Discussion by e-mail can help to keep the class on course during the week and can help facilitate a higher level of discussion during the class.

Faculty have new opportunities to be innovative and creative with this. Elizabeth Durkin, for example, teaches a course on the Evaluation of Social Welfare Programs and Policies at the University of Chicago School of Social Service Administration. She organized a mailing list that included not only 11 students in the class, but also 20 professionals in the field she recruited to participate and to share in the discussion. Such an integrated level of participation, which would have been impractical without the Internet, is now convenient, fun, and probably educational for the professionals who participate.

Online Readings: The Class Home Page

As a faculty member, you might start by developing a simple class home page that provides links to relevant sites. Some faculty have found that the students themselves will help in discovering new information online that will help their sites grow over time. Class Web sites are becoming increasingly popular, and faculty at social work schools are using them to post the class syllabus, description, reading list, and more.

For example, Dr. Charles Figley (*http://www.fsu.edu/~social/figley/sow5367.html*) at Florida State University, has used a Web site for a class on Theory and Practice of Crisis Intervention and Brief Treatment, SOW 5367-1. The site includes outlines and lecture notes for each class. It contains relevant information on the expectations for class, course description, objectives, grading, and other information. While material of this kind is typically handed out to students, by making it available online, it is all in one place, easily updated, and students can print it out if they have lost their original handouts.

Dr. Wendy Crook *(http://www.fsu.edu/~social/fac/crook/index.html)*, also of Florida State University, uses a Web site as a teaching tool for master's level classes. The Web site is used extensively for class activities. The class meets regularly, but the following activities take place online:

People: The Web site is a place where students in the class can get to know one another. Students have their own information pages on which they can introduce themselves, share their interests and hobbies, and so on. E-mail can be sent to the individual students from here. The "people" area also organizes the students into such groups as those interested in children, homelessness, or mental health. From the list of the students within each group, one can send e-mail to everyone or to individuals.

Articles: Students can open assigned articles online, read them, and then respond to them on the Web site. The student responses appear immediately and can be read by the other students and by the professor. Articles posted at the site were granted copyright permissions in the same manner as would be done for printing course packets. For more information on copyrights, see the *U.S. Copyright Office (http://lcweb.loc.gov/copyright/)*.

Concepts: One section of the class site organizes concepts that students can learn about and discuss. For example, the working definition of the word "community" can be found here.

Reports: Students execute class assignments online. For example, Dr. Crook asked students to find a social service organization online and report about it based on what was learned at its Web site. The report is submitted online and becomes part of the class Web site.

Logs: Students submit a weekly log online containing descriptions of their group meetings and progress on their projects. A group reporter is responsible for collecting individual logs and writing a group report for all to read.

How much time does it take for this level of administration of a class online? Dr. Crook notes that there is an investment of time in the set-up during the first year, learning the system, and working out the necessary bugs, but states that it was "so interesting that I didn't mind doing it." Also, it takes some time to help students get acquainted with the Internet, if they are not already experienced with it, and teaching them how the course Web site works. However, students who were anxious about the online class format at first quickly became less apprehensive. Over the first several weeks, the quality of their work online improved and the students often expressed how helpful the experience was in giving them a new skill applicable in other classes, as well as in other areas of their professional and personal lives.

Dr. Crook says that any extra time it took (reading the additional student writing, participating in online discussions, and so on) was, for the most part, offset by the savings in time from the traditional routines of mailing appointments, grading papers, and the like. While the Internet site does not make teaching easier or less time-consuming, it does help to shift activities in ways that are more productive and enhance the quality of the learning experience for the students, according to Dr. Crook. She feels, for example, that the online format allowed for greater continuity in discussions than a traditional class setting. Students could continue outside of class to expand upon thoughts developed in class. New ideas could be generated that did not have time to gel in class and when, ultimately, students returned to class, they did not need to be reminded of where they left off the previous week. All of this may promote a deeper level of discourse throughout the class.

Dr. Crook finds the combination of the Web site with the classroom creates a "community of learners." "You can't hear *all* their ideas in class," she notes, but the online forum gives everyone a chance to respond to what is said in the class. Some quiet students participate in class discussions more online than in class. Students have more time to think through their comments, and to phrase them carefully. Dr. Crook has observed differences between what students say in class and what they write online. As a community of learners, students benefit from one another more than in a traditional class. Even the professor has learned new things through the discussion, such as new Internet resources found by the students.

The Internet site for the course makes use of a "shell" application (a program within which the site was created and is maintained). For more information about this, contact Walt Wager at wagerw@cet.fsu.edu.

Some other examples of social work education on the Internet can be found at the following sites:

Social Work Education on the Internet *(http://www.ssc.msu.edu/~sw/webcrse/intcrse.html)*

Professor Gerald Gross's Foundations in Social Work Research and Applied Research in Social Work sites *(http://www.social.syr.edu/People/Gross.htm)*

Is the Content of Your Class Affected by the Internet?

Another factor you might want to consider as a faculty member is whether your curriculum content is (or may soon be) in any way affected by the existence of the Internet. In a course on community organizing, should you spend some class time considering uses of computers and Internet technology for empowering communities? In courses on services for the elderly, what role might the Internet play in such programs? SeniorNet *(http://www.seniornet.org)*, for example, is making a big impact on this population, and students in these courses would be served well by learning about such innovative programs.

Faculty might visit the *World Lecture Hall (http://www.utexas.edu/world/lecture/)* to see how faculty in any particular field use the Internet. Under Social Work, there are ten examples, including:

(1) *Holistic Family Practice* by Gerald W. Vest, New Mexico State University. A course syllabus and reference page.

(2) *Homelessness: Issues and Action* by David T. Stewart, University of California, Berkeley.

(3) *Social Work Research* by Glenn Stone, Indiana University.

(4) *Social Work Statistics* by Lee Gustafson, University of Texas at Austin.

(5) *Social Work Statistics* by Susan L. Schoppelrey, The University of Texas at Austin.

Ideally, over time, a site such as this can be a point for faculty to share material with one another for use in their classes. For example, faculty teaching statistics could presumably utilize such online material as *UCLA's Statistics Textbook (http://www.stat.ucla.edu/textbook/) and Case Studies (http://www.stat.ucla.edu/cases/).*

Faculty can continue to explore the use of educational MUDs, MOOs and MUSHs. (These terms are defined in the Glossary on page 224.) These provide a virtual reality forum in which real-time interaction can take place online. (For an example of a MOO with significant social work content, see Diversity University at *http://www.du.org.* DU was started by a social worker, as well.) They may also consider the use of interactive books published on the Internet. Increasingly, the Internet is seeing the development of published works online.

The Social Work School Administrator: Connectivity to Colleagues

Just as Web sites, e-mail, mailing lists, and such are helpful in creating the possibility of a larger community of social work students and faculty, so too might administrators in any area benefit from access to one another. Sharing information becomes easier, and institutional methods of doing things can be shared with one another, so that individual professionals are not working in as isolated an environment as they might have in the past. The ability to form a network online should help all administrators to learn from one another. For example, there is a mailing list for field placement officers, used to discuss issues and ideas relating to their work.

Administrators are also beginning to make use of e-mail for communicating with people in their schools. This not only provides them with a convenient way to disseminate information quickly, and in a format that may be easier for others to use and to digest, but it also encourages the school community to uniformly use the Internet.

Whether your office or department should maintain a home page may depend on various factors, but very often the answer is "yes." Even a home page helpful only internally may be worth the time to establish. Field placement offices, alumni offices, development offices, career placement centers, and others are increasingly developing sites helpful to their students or other audiences.

Ball State University School of Social Work provides students with basic information about available field placement sites at the Web page, *Practicum Sites (http://www.socwk.bsu.edu/prac.htm)*, for example. Florida State University School of Social Work uses its site at *The Office of Field Instruction (http://ssw.fsu.edu/field/index.html)* to provide announcements and detail policies and procedures. Similarly, *The Field Site Locator (http://www.social.syr.edu/fieldsearch/)* of Syracuse University School of Social Work allows students to enter the desired location/county and kind of field agency they wish, and an appropriate list is generated.

Syracuse's Web site also provides a useful "pegboard," updated to indicate at any time of the day which faculty members are in the building. Students can use the Web site to schedule appointments with their advisors and to read training material on using the computer lab.

Computer labs, student services, and even photocopying rooms have created Web sites, enabling students to interact with the school more conveniently.

The Social Work Graduate

What should a social work graduate expect from his or her alma mater? Alumni offices have been among the most prolific Web site makers in schools of social work. Some schools offer their alumni journals online, provide alumni with an easy way to share news and address changes, and detail alumni events and programs. Career planning and placement centers often have Web sites, as well, which offer job search assistance to students and graduates.

For example, Columbia University School of Social Work has an alumni site *(http://www.columbia.edu/cu/ssw/alumni/home.html)*, which provides a calendar of events, career services, a change of address form, an online alumni newsletter, and other information for CUSSW graduates. Similarly, the University of Michigan School of Social Work Alumni Society has a Web site at *http://www.umich.edu/~socwork/alumni/*. On this site, you (if you graduated from the University of Michigan) can look to find news of your classmates from a particular year, fill out a form to update the alumni office about your recent accomplishments, find a listing of continuing education offerings at the school, or learn how to make a gift to the school.

As a graduate, you should get in touch with your school and encourage its staff to provide useful content, services, and ways to access the school and other graduates. Schools can offer alumni directories, can use the Internet for linking students with alumni for mentoring purposes, can provide access to faculty, and can offer continuing education programs. In short, the Internet can be a good tool for maintaining a strong relationship between graduates and their schools.

Chapter 20

Publishing on the Web

At some point you may say to yourself, "I'd like to contribute something to this phenomenon called the Web." Maybe you have an area of special expertise or interest you want to share with others. Or maybe the role of agency "Webmaster" has just been added to your job responsibilities under the all-encompassing "other duties as assigned."

Print publications reach a limited audience and are circulated, in general, for a limited amount of time. The World Wide Web, on the other hand, allows anyone to publish and to reach a world-wide audience. The Web allows the publisher to provide content (information) as well as to solicit inter-action/information with and from the audience.

With widespread use of and access to the World Wide Web, anyone can now become a publisher. Should you?

This is only one of many questions to ask yourself before publishing a Web page, an article, or a full-fledged Web site. Even if you've learned HTML (hypertext markup language) and have the technical know-how (or have access to someone who does, or software that does it all for you), think about the following questions before writing a single word or HTML tag:

1. What is the purpose of my site? Why do I need it?
2. What information do I want to include?
3. Who is the audience? Other professionals? Consumers/clients? Members of my organization? The general public?
4. Where will I publish it? On my own/my agency's server, or on a remote server?
5. How much will it cost to start up and maintain?
6. Who will maintain it?
7. How much time will it take?
8. Will it include forms, chat, a searchable database, a method for readers to post information on the site, or other interactive features?
9. Do I need detailed statistics on the site's activity?
10. Do I need a secure server for transfer of sensitive information (such as credit card numbers for online ordering or other confidential information)?
11. What kind of image should my site project? Do I want to use lots of fancy graphics or just convey a simple message with words and a simple layout?

Up Close: National Association of Social Workers (NASW)
http://www.socialworkers.org/

In late 1996, NASW, the largest professional association for social workers, developed a Web site, and in early 1997, NASW staffer Rita Vandivort-Warren took over the role of "Webmistress" for the organization.

Vandivort-Warren uses Microsoft® FrontPage 97 software to regularly update the site, which is housed on an in-house server at the NASW national office. "Learning how to manipulate the graphics is the hardest part for social workers trying to do a Web page," she observes.

The NASW Web site is a one-stop online source of materials that could previously only be obtained in print or by calling NASW. The entire text of the *NASW Code of Ethics*, which took effect in January 1997, is available at the site, for example. The NASW Joblink listing of job opportunities is very popular, and the Register of Clinical Social Workers can be searched by area, specialty, or name. Current government relations updates are also found there, as is information on upcoming national and chapter conferences and calls for papers, a comprehensive listing of other social work membership organizations, and a listing of contact information for all 55 NASW chapters. "Right now we're primarily looking at new documents [to put online]... It would be nice to have all of our standards online. It takes time to build," says Vandivort-Warren.

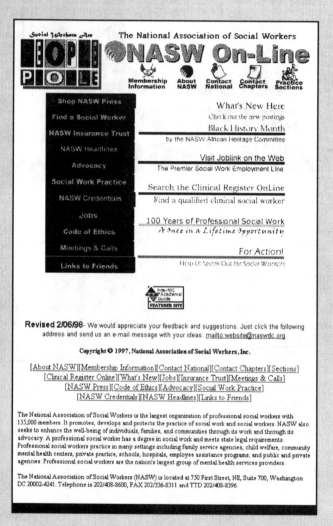

National Association of Social Workers (NASW) home page. Reprinted with permission.

"Web sites are publishing online," she explains. "People tend to think of it as a technology rather than a publishing tool. What that means is they tend to think of it more statically. [In] publishing, everything changes—you have to keep doing it all over again. I don't think people realize the extent of change that's required." Some of the planned changes are to have a members only section, include more of the standards and other reference documents, to have online membership and sections applications (currently there are forms online that can be printed out, but one cannot apply or register online), a chat, forums for threaded comments, and a search engine.

Individual NASW chapters have been developing their own sites, too. California, Illinois, Kentucky, Louisiana, New Jersey, New Mexico, Nevada, New York City, New York State, North Carolina, Oklahoma, Oregon, Texas, and West Virginia have sites of their own, with more in the planning stages. These range from simple contact information for the chapter to full-fledged sites with online chat and other advanced capabilities.

Advantages of Publishing on the Web

Publishing on the Web is timely—information can be published with virtually no lead time. Even a daily newspaper takes several hours to get a late-breaking story out to its readers. A Web publisher can receive a news release by fax or e-mail at 2:00 p.m., write the HTML code by 2:15, and have the information "published" by 2:30. Of course, people have to go to the Web page to access the information, but if they do, it will be there.

Web pages can expand the audience of a print publication, or make available information that will not be published in print form.

A high-quality Web page can be created at little cost. The Web gives smaller publishers (or social services agencies publishing a brochure on the Web, for example) the ability to compete in quality with larger publishers. A smaller publisher can use color, text, and graphics, in the same ways that a larger one can, without spending an arm and a leg. There are even companies that will offer free Web space to individuals or non-profits, and low-cost Web page creation software is available.

Publishing on the Web can be very inexpensive for an individual or small organization publishing on his or her own, although commercially designed Web sites can be quite expensive.

Potential Uses of Web Publishing

The Web can be used to provide an online version of an existing print publication. This might be a magazine, such as *THE NEW SOCIAL WORKER*, or a journal. It might also be an agency newsletter, brochure, fee schedule, handouts on client issues, or other materials that are available through an agency in printed form.

It can also be used to publish information on an issue or client population, such as that served by your agency, as a public service.

Many agencies publish Web sites that market their services. These sites might include information about the services provided, who provides these services, hours of operation, how to make a referral, and so forth.

Individual social workers can publish Web pages about topics of interest to them as social workers, or they can post their résumés online.

Regardless of the purpose of your Web publication, the approach needs to be different from that of a print publication, keeping in mind the interactive nature and capabilities of the Web.

Disadvantages of Web Publishing

Maintaining a Web site or page can be time-consuming. Some treat a Web page as a one-shot deal—write the page, put it on the Web, and forget about it. This is a mistake. If you want people to come back to your page—if you want it to have an impact—you'll need to update it frequently. Think about whether you have the time to do what's necessary, or whether your agency has the staff to perform this function.

Another concern about Web publishing is that documents do not "exist" permanently. Unlike an article that appears in print in a magazine, journal, or newspaper, an article that is posted for a limited time on the Web and then removed or revised, actually doesn't "exist" any longer in its original form. For researchers or students who are citing Web documents in scholarly papers, this can be a concern, and it presents a good reason for them to print out documents they plan to cite.

HTML? What's That?

Hypertext Markup Language is the computer language that tells Web browsers how a Web page should look. It's pretty simple; in fact, until recent commands were added to the language, many complained that it was too limited. It is based on the concept of adding tags before and after a piece of content, telling that the content should be bold or italic or a certain size, among other features.

In order to write a Web page, you need to either know the basics of this language, which we cover briefly on page 143, or use software that puts the HTML tags in the document for you.

It is also possible to create a Web page without knowing HTML. There are several popular software packages that operate on a WYSIWYG (what you see is what you get) basis. This is similar to a desktop publishing or word processing program, in which you see on your computer monitor what the actual page will look like, but you don't need to worry about the technical details of how the computer reads or writes the file. Some examples of this software are Microsoft® FrontPage and Adobe Pagemill. You may be able to download trial versions of some of these packages from the companies' Web sites, so you can try them before you buy.

If you want to learn HTML, just go to any bookstore and look in the computer section. There is a large selection of instructional books to choose from, with titles like *Teach Yourself HTML in 24 Hours*.

If You Build It, Will They Come?

Once you have a Web site, you need to let people know about it, so it will be used to its fullest. There are several ways to announce a Web site. The ways we have found most successful are:

(1) Send a brief announcement to any online mailing lists to which you subscribe that are related to the site's content, as well as to the administrators of Web sites that link to sites like yours.
(2) Submit your site's URL and a brief description to as many directories and search engines as possible. You can submit it to each one individually yourself, or you can submit it to a company (such as Submit It) that will, for a fee, submit it to many at one time for you.
(3) Send a brief press release to print publications that go to the audience you want to reach.
(4) If you significantly update or revise your site, send another announcement to the above groups.

Once They Come, Will They Come Again?

A Web site's success is often measured not by how many people visit it, but by how many return again and again. (However, this is not always the case. For example, if you post an article on the Web, you may be satisfied that a visitor has found and read it once. You may not expect the same person to return to the same article repeatedly.) There are several tips for getting people to return to your site.

(1) Ask visitors to "bookmark" your site. This means to put it in their browser's list of favorites, so they can return with a push of a button, rather than having to retype the URL.
(2) Update the site frequently. If readers know there will be new information at your site, they will find it valuable enough to return.
(3) Offer an e-mail newsletter that visitors can subscribe to from your site. Then send them some useful information every week or month, or just let them know when there's something new on the site.
(4) Have an on-site bulletin board or chat room. Web sites that offer these kinds of interactive features have the added value of becoming a real online "community."

Up Close: Nate Prentice's Social Work Jokes Page
http://dolphin.upenn.edu/~prentice/swjokes.html

Nate Prentice, a University of Pennsylvania social work doctoral student, has gained considerable notoriety for his Social Work Jokes page. "It is comprised of a variety of different types of social work jokes beyond, 'How many social workers does it take to screw in a light bulb? It depends on whether or not the bulb wants to be changed,' " says Prentice.

Prentice has organized the jokes into the categories of light bulbs, stories from the field, quickies, social workese, social work sayings, and social work jokes N.O.S. (not otherwise specified).

He adds, "Social work is a profession which takes itself far, far too seriously. My purpose is to provide a forum for social workers to come together and help each other to find the humor in front of us every day as social workers. It is also to make sure that we can give lawyers a run for their money."

Prentice began learning HTML in 1994 and wanted to make a "significant contribution," so he looked for a "niche" idea. He came up with the idea for the Jokes Page.

Nate Prentice's Social Work Jokes Page.
Reprinted with permission.

Interestingly, Prentice has met with some objections from social workers who don't find his humor—well...humorous.

"When I first started the site, I accepted any jokes. After a while, though, I received a couple of posts from people who protested a couple of jokes which could be interpreted as racist. I took a look at the jokes and decided to remove them. Others, however, protested jokes that made fun of clients," Prentice explains. "With these, I had to begin to set limits. I put a request out on the page for people who browsed it to submit what they thought about these types of jokes. The overwhelming response was that in a case conference, gallows humor comes out as a way of releasing steam. Therefore, they approved of those kinds of jokes. I compromised by putting in a blurb explaining this rationale for inclusion of these jokes. I haven't heard any complaints since."

If you're feeling burnt out, maybe a social work light bulb joke is just the thing to brighten your day. Take a look at Nate Prentice's page.

Going Online

Step 1. Identify your server.

Before setting up a Web page, it is helpful to decide which server to use. The server is the computer where your Web site files physically reside. It should be accessible 24 hours a day. There are several choices:

1. *In-house server.* If you work at a university, there will likely be a server available for you to use through the campus computing center. Likewise, if you work for a large agency or organization, there may be resources to set up an in-house computer as a Web server.

2. *An online service.* Most commercial services, such as America Online (AOL), now offer their subscribers space for a small Web site, included in the subscription price.

3. *Internet Service Provider.* Many local and national Internet Service Providers offer their subscribers space for a Web site. The cost of the Web space may be included in the Internet access account fee, or there may be an additional charge. One advantage of using an ISP's Web space, even if it costs more than another option, is that it may allow you to use your own domain name.

4. *Web-hosting services.* These are companies that specialize in "renting" Web space on their servers, often at reasonable prices. Many of these companies advertise in the back of *Windows* and other computer magazines. Some commercial (and non-commercial) Web hosts offer non-profit organizations free or reduced-fee space for home pages. Most of these companies will allow you to use your own domain name, as part of a "virtual domain" hosting plan.

Some of the issues you need to resolve include the cost, limits on how many bytes are allowed for the Web site files, the process by which the files are updated (can you do this yourself from a remote computer, or do you upload the file to your ISP and the ISP puts it online when he or she gets around to it?), and whether the server provides you with a way to determine the number of "hits" and other statistics.

Some of the other issues you should consider when choosing a server include limits on commercial use, whether the server supports encryption software, whether access and availability is reasonable, extras offered such as site counters and site search engines, and the availability of experienced technical support.

There are many organizations that provide free space for non-profit organizations, or do so for a modest charge. There are directories available on the Internet that list hundreds of these. One of these can be found at the Freenets and Community Networks site at *http://www.lights.com/freenet.*

Step 2. Determine the Content and WWW Design

What are you trying to communicate, and who is your audience? What is the purpose of the site? To attract clients or members? To get new donors? To recruit volunteers? To provide a public service? All of the above?

Flashy graphics, animation, sound, and visual effects may attract visitors, but some may be frustrated by the time these take to view. You will need to balance the speed of pure text content with the need for visual effects. Take into consideration those who use less advanced computers or slower modems than you do.

If you create a site, consider whether others would want to visit it and why. Are you creating a site to ask for donations for your organization? If that is all, then do not be too surprised if you get few visitors. This is not to say that you cannot and should not seek donations on your Web site. You have to be a bit subtle about it. You perhaps need to include information resources that are beneficial to the visitor.

Typically, you will start with a home page that serves as a table of contents, with links to other pages within your site. To give you a head start on a constructive and efficient design, look at the pages of other organizations that you find attractive and effective. Then look at the source code, or HTML code, of those pages to see how they achieved the effect that you liked. Software, such as Web Fetch or Wing Flyer, is designed to capture all of the HTML source code that created a page (but beware, these files may be copyrighted). Even without this software, the HTML file of every page you view with your browser is captured byte for byte in a file in the caché subdirectory of your communications program's directory. Since HTML is compatible with ASCII (which is the basis for text files), you can view these files in Windows® Notepad or any word processing program. Simply open up the file in either of these programs.

If you are using Netscape Navigator as your browser, you can open the View menu and click on "Document Source" to see the coding for any page.

Step 3. Convert your files to HTML.

Inexpensive (or even free) software is available to convert conventional document files to HTML format. You also can do it manually by placing HTML codes where they belong.

Each HTML file should include the following:

```
<HTML>
<HEAD><TITLE>Insert title here</TITLE></HEAD>
<BODY>insert rest of page here</BODY>
</HTML>
```

As you can see, HTML codes often are in pairs. There is a code at the beginning and a code at the end of words to which the code is applied. The beginning code is enclosed by an open caret and closed caret. The code at the end is enclosed by an open caret followed by a forward slash, and ends with a closed caret.

Background colors can be changed from the default white by placing codes within the <body> code. For example, using Body Bgcolor=A5 2A 2A will make the background brown.

Headings can be sized by adding the tag <hx>insert text here</hx>, where x is a positive whole number from 1 to 6 (small to large).

Paragraph/line breaks. A line break code (<br>) will start the text that follows on a new line without adding space above or below the line. A paragraph break code (<p>) will place the text that follows this code on a new line, with a space between the previous line and the new line, making a new paragraph. There is no need to put a line break at the end of each line within a paragraph—the lines will automatically wrap. The line break is used when you need a "hard return" after a partial line, such as in an address or a poem.

Other commonly used text codes include:

```
<center>insert text to be centered </center>
<b>insert text to be made bold</b>
<i>insert text to be italicized</i>
<font color="RGB" Size=n>insert text to have a font or color change </Font> where RGB is the
color code and n is a number between -7 and 7 which is greater or less than the baseline font
size.
<blockquote>insert text here to be indented from both margins</blockquote>
<HR> creates a horizontal line
<HR WIDTH=X% Align=Y SIZE=Z> creates a line where x is the % proportion of page width, Y is
the position (left, center or right), and Z is the thickness of the line.
```

Ordered lists are sequentially numbered items. The list is begun and ended by <OL>insert items to be listed</OL>. Each item that is part of the list is preceded by the tag <LI>. Using this tag places a number in front of each item.

Unnumbered lists are bulleted items. The list is begun and ended by <UL>insert items to be bulleted</UL>. Each item that is to be preceded by a bullet is tagged in the same way as an ordered list.

Links

As we discussed before, there are several basic kinds of links that appear on Web pages. Here is how some of these look in HTML code:

Links to a local file. This is a link to a file within the same directory (and within the same Web site) being linked from. It appears on the browser in a different color than plain text. The tag for accomplishing this in the body of the page is:

<A HREF="name of file.html">the text that you want to appear on the page</A>

Links to other HTML pages:
<A HREF="http://fullURL">name of page</A>
This type of link sends the viewer to another Web page, which can be within the same Web site or part of another site.

Links to e-mail:
<A HREF="MAILTO:linda.grobman@paonline.com">Send mail to Linda</A>
This type of link provides a form for the viewer to send e-mail to you or someone else in your organization.

Insertion of graphics files:
<IMG SRC "nameofgraphicsfile.GIF" height=xxx width=yyy> where x and y are integers
This type of link puts a graphic on the Web page.

The tags may seem intimidating or confusing at first, but they can be learned quickly. You can put together an attractive Web page without being any more sophisticated than using the above tags. For the more adventurous, there are languages other than HTML, such as JAVA, which is used to provide advanced and interactive features on your page.

There are plenty of reference books on how to design and construct a WWW page, and there are also lots of Web sites that explain the basics, including:

The Contact Center: *http://www.contact.org/tools/computer.htm*

See pages 150-151 for a sample World Wide Web home page, and the HTML code that generated that page.

Domain Names

Every computer connected to the Internet has a unique Internet Protocol (IP) address. These addresses look like four numbers, separated by a period (207.44.25.233, for example). When you connect to another computer over the Internet, your computer needs to know the IP. However, IPs are too difficult to remember, for the most part. A system has been developed to provide more memorable addresses, called domain names. Once you get used to this system, domain names become easy to remember. In addition, you can tell a lot from the domain name—the type of organization, the geographical location, and often the name of the user. A domain name is the part of the Internet address after the "@" sign. For example, our personal e-mail addresses are: linda.grobman@paonline.com and g-grant@uchicago.edu. Paonline and the University of Chicago

CUSSN—Computer Use in Social Services Network
http://www.uta.edu/cussn/cussn.html

CUSSN is an example of yet another type of Web site that is useful to those in social work and the social services. It is an informal association of professionals interested in exchanging information and experiences on using computers in the human services, according to its founder Dick Schoech, and has been in existence in some form since 1981.

The CUSSN Web site began in February 1996, and is housed on the server in the University of Texas computing department. There was no cost to set up the site, other than Dr. Schoech's time. The site received 10,137 hits between February 1996 and September 1997. A unique feature of CUSSN is the availability of freeware, shareware, and demo software for download from the site. Software is available in the categories of clinical/therapeutic, health, welfare/child protection, aging, developmental disabilities, education/training, and others.

This site also includes information on the *Computers in Human Services* journal (edited by Dr. Schoech), humor and satire related to computers in human services, information on related conferences and courses, and more.

are our respective Internet Service Providers (ISPs), ".com" indicates that it is a commercial provider, and ".edu" indicates an academic provider. However, we could, for a fee, have one of these changed to: linda.grobman@socialworker.com, assuming no one else has taken the domain name "socialworker.com" already. (Actually, that *IS* the domain of this book's publisher.)

Most domain name suffixes tell you something about the type of organization, and the last extension often indicates the country code (see page 19).

Obtaining a Domain Name

Domain names make Web site addresses easy to read and remember. Let's say you are setting up a Web site, and your Web space is being provided by a company called "Yourweb." Yourweb is a reseller for space on a server at "Myweb." Your site's URL may look like this:

http://www.myweb.com/~yourweb/yourorganization/home.html

If Yourweb allows its customers to have "virtual domain" space, your site's URL could be shortened to the easier to remember and more distinctive:

http://www.yourorganization.org

There are registration fees for setting up virtual domains, in addition to the fee for connecting to the Internet charged by your Internet Service Provider. Many organizations find the cost well worth it. Domain names are registered through the Internet Information Center (InterNIC). There is an initial registration fee of $70 for the first two years and an annual fee of $35 after that, in addition to the fees charged by your provider(s).

Applications must be submitted electronically, by filling out a template on the World Wide Web site of InterNIC *(http://www.rs.internic.net)* or by FTP to the text version *(ftp.rs.internic.net)*. If you do the latter, log on as anonymous and use "guest" as the password. You will need your name and address, the domain name you want to use (e.g., yourname.org) and the primary and secondary server Internet protocol number, which you can obtain from your ISP or Web space provider. Names are assigned on a first-come, first-served basis and are checked for prior use and for whether they are in some way objectionable. If this sounds too complicated, check with your server; many will do all of this work for an additional fee.

Web Publishing in Action

There are several examples of Web publishing in action throughout this book. Let's take a look at the evolution of one social work site developed by Linda Grobman, co-author of this book.

THE NEW SOCIAL WORKER Online (http://www.socialworker.com) is an electronic version of an existing print publication. It includes information from the print publication, as well as original material not in print. Information provided includes articles from back issues, subscription infor- mation, an online career center with links to social work and job search resources, and timely announcements of news of social work happenings that occur between issues of the print magazine.

This site encourages interaction by conducting an online survey. Past survey questions related to religion and social work, confidentiality, and why people chose social work as a career. The site also invites readers to correspond with the editor, and a Social Work Careers Chat and message board were added in 1997.

This site is maintained by Linda Grobman, Editor/Publisher of *THE NEW SOCIAL WORKER* and co- author of this book, and is housed on a commercial Web hosting server.

Started in August 1995, this site was developed using *HTML Assistant Pro Lite*, a basic HTML editing software program. Linda taught herself HTML by reading the software's manual and the book *Web Publishing with HTML in a Week* by Laura Lemay. Actually, she devoured the book's pages in about two hours and was ready to go to work. The site was up and running in about a week.

Once she learned how to do the technical part, Linda decided on the content of the site. The challenge was to create an online companion to the print magazine that did more than just rehash what was already in print. And it needed to be more than just an online vehicle for selling subscrip- tions. Linda decided to include information about the magazine and full text articles from the magazine, to give people a flavor of what the print magazine was all about. But she also wanted the site to provide a separate career guidance service to social workers and social work students, so she added articles and links to career-related sites, as well as listings of job announcements. She also wanted the site to be a resource center for social workers in general, so she added a page of links to social work-related sites of all kinds.

All too often, Web site creators make the mistake of treating an online publication in the same way as a print one. This may result in coming across as too commercial—as simply an online copy of a print advertisement—or as pushing one person's agenda too much, or not being up-to-date or interactive enough. Linda's goal was to make *THE NEW SOCIAL WORKER ONLINE* an extension of a print publication (rather than an online copy), but also a new service, as well. Unlike a print publi- cation, which doesn't change once it's in print, the Web site changes regularly. (And now that this book has gone to press, the site has expanded, so that it is also a companion site to this book, providing links to many of the sites mentioned here.)

Once the content was in place and the site was designed, Linda looked for a way to publish it on the Web. Since she has her own small business (the publishing company that publishes *THE NEW SOCIAL WORKER* and this and other books), she did not have access to a university or social service agency Web server. She did some research, using the Web, and found a small company that rented Web space. All she needed to do was use FTP (file transfer protocol) to transfer her Web site files to the company's computer (the server) each time she wanted to add or change something on the site.

Once the site was up and running, Linda submitted the URL (the site's address) and description to the major search engines, such as Alta Vista, Lycos, Webcrawler, and others. She also contacted other social work Web site Webmasters to let them know about the site, and they linked to it from their pages. Additionally, Linda sent an announcement to several social work mailing lists online, letting their members know about the site. These were important steps, because they provided ways for people to find the site. Even with the greatest site in the world, no one will visit if they don't know about it!

In the summer of 1997, Linda redesigned the site using Adobe Pagemill 2.0 for Windows, adding graphics, an easier-to-follow layout, the ability to search the site by keywords, and other more advanced features than the original site had. When the site was redesigned, she researched Web hosting companies once again and moved it to one that offered virtual domain hosting, more Web space for a comparable price, and other more advanced features than the first company had to offer. Once she had uploaded the site files to the new address *(http://www.socialworker.com)*, she had to resubmit the site to the search engines and try to notify as many Webmasters as possible of the change, so they could update their links. While having your own domain name is better in the long run, changing URLs in midstream has its disadvantages. Some sites still link to the old URL, so Linda has maintained a presence there, for the sole purpose of providing a "We Have Moved" sign and a link to the new address.

Some Final Considerations

Before going online with your own Web page or site, decide what you want to accomplish with your electronic publication. Determine whether to focus more on content, "look" (graphics), or a combination of the two. Then decide on the content of your publication. Finally, design the format of your publication, and prepare to spend some time maintaining your site.

You will need to learn HTML language or how to use a software program such as Pagemill or Frontpage, which act like desktop publishing programs, putting the HTML code in for you "behind the scenes." Or you can collaborate with someone who has the technical know-how to put your content into a format that is compatible with the Web. Once your files are ready, contact a Web hosting service (unless your agency has its own server). Look in the advertising sections in several Internet-related magazines, and you will find many examples of ads for these companies. Go to their Web sites and see what they have to offer. If they list the sites of their customers, take a look at those sites and see how they look. Contact some of their current customers and ask them (1) Are you satisfied with the service? (2) Have you had any problems with the service? (3) Is there adequate technical support available? (4) Any other questions you have. Finally, once you have chosen a Web hosting company or other server, put it all online, announce it to the world, and count the hits!

Web Publishing Resources

One excellent resource for social workers who want to develop sites (or those who already have) is the HSWEB mailing list. To subscribe, send a message to *LISTSERV@listserv.uta.edu*. In the body of the message, type SUBSCRIBE HSWEB. This mailing list's members are all human services Webmasters, and they are more than willing to share ideas about what has worked (and not worked) in putting together a Web site.

Some general Web development resources are:

Nuthin' but Links
http://pages.prodigy.com/bombadil/

There are links to sites where you can find HTML tutorials, Web page graphics, animated GIFs, tools for determining colors, JAVA resources, CGI scripts, counters, guest books, and almost anything else you might need to build and enhance your Web site.

Barry's Clip Art Server
http://www.barrysclipart.com
This site has a searchable and indexed database of hundreds of downloadable, copyright-free images.

A+ Art
http://aplusart.simplenet.com/aplusart/index.html
Here, you can download copyright-free icons, bullets, animations, clip art, backgrounds, and bars.

More Web Page Design Tips

1. Frequently update the material on your site and make the content useful. Regardless of how "cool" your site looks, people won't return unless there is new information there on a regular basis.

2. Keep the design simple. People value their time. Graphics and special effects slow down browsers. Those who want to continually use your site don't want to have to search around each time because the design changes frequently.

3. Market what you are good at. If your organization's niche is in child advocacy, make your Web site the one-stop shopping place to find all of the information related to children, and don't stray too far from that.

4. If your organization depends on membership revenue, don't give out everything on your Web site. What is the incentive for individuals to become members if they receive the services for free just by logging in to your site?

5. Don't put information on the Web that you would be embarrassed to find on the front page of your local newspaper. For example, if you are calling for advocacy on a certain bill, you may not want to disclose the strategy of the legislative coalition with which you are working.

6. Don't be shy about providing plenty of links to related sites, including your statewide and national affiliates, and government sources of information. Make sure links are clear and made in such a way as to not imply that the content at another site is your own. It is a good idea to let Web masters know when you link to their sites. Most of them will be thrilled, and your notification will enable them to let you know if their sites move or if the URLs change.

7. If you are an individual Webmaster, rather than an organizational or agency one, you can use the Web as a sort of online portfolio to show off your talents. You can post your résumé, articles (or graduate school papers), and other original materials on your area of expertise/interest.

8. Don't put everything on your home page. Use it as a Table of Contents and introduction rather than as the body of the Web site. Use links to take your site's visitors to internal files, such as brochure, newsletter, message from the President, advocacy corner, board member list, and other files.

9. Place a text line on the home page letting viewers know when the page was last updated.

10. Place links at the bottom of each Web page to return to the home page and to send e-mail to the Webmaster.

11. If possible, provide a place on the home page for a link to a text-only version of your pages. If you are using sophisticated animations or frames, the page may be inaccessible to those using older browsers.

12. Simplify your domain name as much as you can.

13. Publicize your site on all of the popular directories and search engines. Point your browser to these search engines for information on how to register your site.

14. Make sure that you do not post material that is copyrighted by others without obtaining written permission, and be sure to place a copyright notice on your own material on your Web site.

15. Consider placing a link on your site to free translation services, such as the one offered by AltaVista *(http://www.altavista.digital.com)*. This service will translate your site (or a particular page of the visitor's choice) into several foreign languages, making it readable to a wider audience.

A Simple, Sample Web Page

There are many resources that will help you design a Web page as simple or as elaborate as you would like. To get you started, we have provided a sample, simple Web page. Our sample page—a personal home page for hypothethical social worker Nan Profit, is a simple listing of links to other Web sites. On page 150, you will find a picture of the page as it appears in a Web browser. On page 151, you can see the actual HTML code we used to create the page. You can use this code as a template for making your own Web page. Just type the code into an HTML editor or word processing program, change the text on the page to include your own content, substitute your own graphics, and change the URLs in the links to real ones that will work with your page.

Some of the features illustrated in this example are:

1.   Heading
2.   Horizontal rule
3.   Subheading
4.   Ordered (or numbered) list
5.   Links to Web pages
6.   Bulleted (or unordered) list
7.   Bold type
8.   Italicized type
9.   Link to an e-mail address

The circled numbers on pages 150 and 151 correspond to the list above.

Please note that we also included at the bottom of the page the date that it was last updated and the URL for the page. The date last updated helps the viewer determine how current the information is, and helps you let people know that the information on your page is up-to-date. The URL is useful to those who may want to print the page out and return to it later.

A Sample Web Page

① Nan Profit's Social Work Resource Page

②

Social Work Sites   ③

④

1. Marvin's Social Work Online: Particularly nice for finding individual social work sites around specific areas of practice.
2. NASW
3. The New Social Worker Online   ⑤
4. Social Work Online
5. The Social Work Student Nexus
6. SWAN
7. Tom Cleerman's Social Work Page

Health and Mental Health Sites

* Bazelon Center for Mental Health Law
* Healthgate   ⑥
* Medline: Search Medline (free).

Legislative and Research Information

* The Census Bureau
* Federal Register Online: Search by words and dates.
* Thomas

Online Journals

* Child Maltreatment
* Journal of Poverty

Other Organizations

* The Child Welfare League of America
* The Children's Defense Fund
* Children Now
* Kids Campaigns, by Benton Foundation

⑦ **Nan Profit**
Executive Director
Good Works Social Services Center
22 Twain Street, Lionel, NY 99999
⑧ nprofit@gwssc.org   ⑨

This page last updated February 20, 1998.

The URL for this page is http://www.nanprofit.org.

This is our sample Web page as it looks when viewed in a Web browser.

Circled numbers refer to features listed on page 149.

HTML Code for Nan Profit's Social Work Resource Page

```
<HTML>
<HEAD>
 <TITLE>Nan Profit's Social Work Resource Page</TITLE>
</HEAD>
<BODY BGCOLOR="#ffffff">
```

① `<P><CENTER><B><FONT SIZE=+4>Nan Profit's Social Work Resource Page</FONT></B></CENTER></P>`

② `<P><HR ALIGN=LEFT></P>`

③ `<H2>Social Work Sites</H2>`

④
```
<OL>
 <LI><A HREF="http://www.geocities.com/Athens/9050/socwork.html">Marvin's
 Social Work Online</A>: Particularly nice for finding individual social
 work sites around specific areas of practice.
 <LI><A HREF="http://www.naswdc.org/">NASW</A>
```
⑤
```
 <LI><A HREF="http://www.socialworker.com/">The New Social Worker Online</A>
 <LI><A HREF="http://www.geocities.com/Athens/9050/socwork.html">Social
 Work Online</A>
 <LI><A HREF="http://www.chas.uchicago.edu/ssa/swsn/">The Social Work Student
 Nexus</A>
 <LI><A HREF="http://www.sc.edu/swan/">SWAN</A>
 <LI><A HREF="http://www.sparknet.net/~tjcleer">Tom Cleerman's Social Work
 Page</A>
</OL>
```

```
<H2><HR ALIGN=LEFT>Health and Mental Health Sites</H2>
```

⑥
```
<UL>
 <LI><A HREF="http://www.bazelon.org/">Bazelon Center for Mental Health
 Law</A>
 <LI><A HREF="http://www.healthgate.com/HealthGate/home.html">Healthgate</A>
 <LI><A HREF="http://www.healthgate.com/HealthGate/MEDLINE/search.shtml">Medline</A>:
 Search Medline (free).

</UL>
```

```
<H2><HR ALIGN=LEFT>Legislative and Research Information</H2>

<UL>
 <LI><A HREF="http://www.census.gov/">The Census Bureau</A>
 <LI><A HREF="http://www.access.gpo.gov/su_docs/aces/aces140.html">Federal
 Register Online</A>: Search by words and dates.
 <LI><A HREF="http://thomas.loc.gov/home/thomas.html">Thomas</A>
</UL>
```

```
<H2><HR ALIGN=LEFT>Online Journals</H2>

<UL>
 <LI><A HREF="http://www.chas.uchicago.edu/ssa/advocates_forum.html%3EThe%20Advocate%27s%20Forum%3C/
a%3E%0A%3Cli%3E%3Ca%20href%3D">Child
 Maltreatment</A>
 <LI><A HREF="http://128.146.40.65/jpov/">Journal of Poverty</A>
</UL>
```

```
<H2><HR ALIGN=LEFT>Other Organizations</H2>

<UL>
 <LI><A HREF="http://www.handsnet.org/cwla/">The Child Welfare League of
 America</A>
 <LI><A HREF="http://www.childrensdefense.org/">The Children's Defense Fund</A>
 <LI><A HREF="http://www.childrennow.org/">Children Now</A>
 <LI><A HREF="http://www.kidscampaign.org/">Kids Campaigns, by Benton Foundation</A>
</UL>
```

⑦
```
<P><HR ALIGN=LEFT><B><FONT SIZE=-1>Nan Profit</FONT></B><FONT SIZE=-1><BR>
Executive Director<BR>
Good Works Social Services Center<BR>
22 Twain Street, Lionel, NY 99999<BR>
```
⑧ `<I><A HREF="mailto:nprofit@gwssc.org">nprofit@gwssc.org</A></I></FONT></P>`

⑨ `<P><I><FONT SIZE=-1>This page last updated February 20, 1998.</FONT></I></P>`

```
<P><B><FONT SIZE=-1>The URL for this page is http://www.nanprofit.org.</FONT></B>
</BODY>
</HTML>
```

This is how our sample Web page looks when you type it into your computer. When viewed in a Web browser, it looks like the picture on the previous page.

To publish this page on the Web, you would do the following:

1) Type the text as shown here.

2) Save it in a file with .htm or .html at the end (such as nanprofit.htm).

3) Upload (or copy) it to the computer that provides disk space for your Web site. This might be a server at your agency, or a remote Web hosting service.

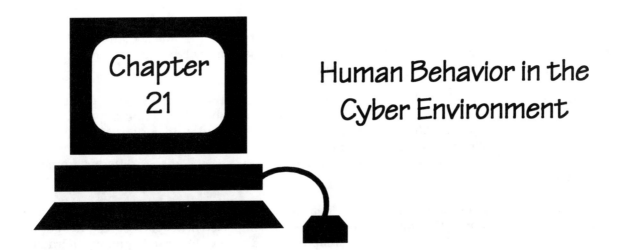

Chapter 21

Human Behavior in the Cyber Environment

Dominating public discourse about the Internet have been concerns about the risks and dangers involved in Internet use. Examples of the major issues articulated in newspaper editorials, talk shows, public policy forums, and legislative arenas are:

(1) Concerns about overuse of the Internet by children and adults spending hours online.
(2) Fears about Internet content such as pornography (especially access to this by children), dangerous information (e.g., instructions about making explosives), and Web sites promoting hate toward particular groups.
(3) Privacy issues, such as the use of cameras broadcasting images onto the Internet, confidentiality, and the fear of being identified and stalked by dangerous people.
(4) Fears about what the Internet means to traditional social skills, for example, the fear that people will lose their ability to interact face-to-face, and the concern that the socially naive will be preyed upon by disreputable and dishonest people online.

This chapter addresses some of these topics to help separate the myths from the realities, to clarify the issues, and set the context for understanding them better.

This chapter does not seek to convince you that the Internet poses no danger whatsoever. The fact is that some of these risks are real to one extent or another. On the other hand, do not expect an exposition on how the Internet threatens to tear down the fabric of our society. There are many reasons why it is easy for fears to become overblown in thinking about the Internet, and to forget that many of its downsides and dangers are balanced or outweighed by its corresponding benefits. Let us not forget that almost every technological advance has evoked fears of one kind or another about its overall impact on society.

What Barriers Are There to Objectively Evaluating the Risks of the Internet?

On one hand, it is easy for those who see vast potential for the Internet to focus only on its positive side and to dismiss the downsides. At the same time, our fears about the issues can become distorted or overblown by those who fear change in general or don't understand this new medium.

The Internet is new. It can be difficult to understand. While many attempt to understand the Internet by analogy to more familiar forms of communication, sources of information, and resources, these analogies are not perfect. Is it a library? Is it a television? Is it a video game? Is a chat room analogous to a coffee shop? Am I talking or writing when I am online? Often, these analogies raise as many questions as they do explanations.

We do know that the Internet will bring changes—a fact that can be most disturbing in itself. Knowing there will be changes, but being unclear exactly what they will be, causes excitement and anticipation for some and fear and anxiety in others.

In addition, the public holds widely divergent views about that segment of the population that "resides" online. For many, there is a strongly negative perception of the "kind of people" on the Internet. They may be at best different and at worst dangerous and uninviting. Those not online may feel that getting online means something more than just getting access to new resources. They may in fact feel that they are entering a new, perhaps cultish "society" that is different from what they are used to.

For some, this perception seems to involve the idea that the Internet is *not* representative of mainstream society. For example, they may see the Internet as comprised principally of "egg-heads" who enjoy and feel more comfortable with their computers than they do actual human interaction. Perhaps similarly, there is a perception that the Internet community contains a disproportionate number of anti-social, perhaps even psychopathic people, who use the Internet as an escape and who pose a threat to others.

Other people may believe that the Internet *is* representative of society, but may hold equally strong fears about what this means, worrying about the lack of protections from those who may threaten them. On the Internet, there are no gated communities, neighborhood watches, police, guard dogs, or burglar bars. How we view mainstream society may influence how we view the Internet community. Also, being online often means judging people by their writing alone and not being able to categorize them or pre-judge them according to their age, gender, or physical attributes, which often are unrevealed. For some, this is a great advantage, as we are left to judge others by the content of their characters, so to speak. But for others, this is more disconcerting since, ironically, it may mean they must distrust what they hear or read.

Thus, while many think of the Internet as comparable to a library and find it an exciting opportunity for children and adults alike, others see it as a redlight district where the unprepared may be stalked and victimized.

So What is the Internet Community Really Like?

Perhaps in its earlier incarnations, the Internet was largely the realm for a more tightly-knit community of people who shared a strong proficiency with computers. One can sometimes hear the lament in newsgroups about the number of "newbies" online. Nostalgically, they reminisce about the days when their smaller circle had these forums all to themselves. Some regret the newer developments that make the Internet more user-friendly and accessible to all. In days past, the difficulty getting connected served as a screening mechanism ensuring that those online were especially sophisticated with computers. Today, however, the Internet has become much more accessible, and the flood gates have opened for good or bad.

Not long ago, the Internet was disproportionately white and male. This, however, is changing rapidly, and the gender and race gaps are quickly disappearing. A deeper question, perhaps, is whether the economic gap will close. The Internet is not nearly as accessible for low-income individuals and communities, the obvious reason being the cost of computers and online services and the view that they are not essential for everyday life (unlike, for example, a car that may cost as much or more).

Whatever the facts may be regarding race, gender, and similar questions of equity, the Internet is so widely populated that just about anyone can find many others in his or her particular group online. Parents of children with autism can find other such parents in a matter of minutes at Web sites devoted to this topic. Similarly, there are sites for multiracial people, for women in science, even sites for those who are left-handed. There are newsgroups for elderly retired persons, those who enjoy folk dancing, or for just about every cultural group, from Albanians to Zimbabwenese.

The possible gaps that may exist in the proportions of particular groups online may have vital social signficance overall. But in terms of the people one encounters when online, the fullest possible range is already, for the most part, there and easily accessible for those who wish to seek them out. Moreover, one can limit connections to these groups, and there is no need to wander into open chat rooms. Simply viewing Web sites and reading discussion areas is like wandering through neighborhoods, invisible, until you choose to reveal yourself by participating. Whenever you wish, you can again disappear and move away.

How Do People "Meet" or Encounter One Another Online?

If one can find any group online, might we (or our children) still be at risk of being "approached" by someone dangerous? Many articulate their fears of child molestation online, as though being online means a physical presence. Is this warranted? Can one approach, captivate, and harm others through words and images?

There are several ways that people unknown to one another "meet" online. One way is for a person to build a Web page that lists an e-mail address or other method of contact. With little effort, anyone can obtain a Web page for little or no cost, and include in it comments, intended or not, to elicit response. This is not necessarily the most effective way to contact others. There are literally millions of Web pages, and the chances of someone running across yours are minimal without additional efforts to draw attention to it.

Another way to find people is to search for a particular forum or Web site that is indexed in search engines or directories as a place where people who share an interest or characteristic network with one another. Here, people can reach out to others who have elected to be listed or can announce their own Web sites to the particular group. Suppose for example, that one wished to find others interested in stamp collecting. It would take about five minutes of searching to find lists of philatelists and their e-mail addresses.

A third way to encounter people who share an interest topic is to become a participant in a newsgroup or mailing list discussion about that topic. In both of these cases, one may begin a dialogue with one person but must remember that the conversation can be read by anyone else participating, unless it is sent only to that person's e-mail address. When responding to the whole group, the message goes to every other participant. Any other participant can respond personally or in the public forum to the writer.

Finally, there are ways people can search directories of e-mail addresses or phone and address listings. Anyone with a phonebook listing may be listed in these sources, even if he or she is not online. Every New Year's Eve, Gary Grant receives an e-mail message from someone with his name who has decided to wish all the "Gary Grants" for whom he can find e-mail addresses a "Happy New Year." In 1996, this was 30 people. In 1997, the number grew to over 120. The person is obviously harmless, and the idea put a smile on Gary's face, but it shows how convenient the Internet can be for targeting people who could not have been targeted so easily in the past. Another example is the use of bulk e-mail advertisements. These can become bothersome and a serious pitfall to e-mail if they continue to grow beyond the handful one might get every week now.

But what does all of this say about the potential of someone reaching out to harm people online?

For the most part, people online are anonymous by the sheer numbers of people out there. The risk is minuscule of being randomly targeted just because of a presence online, whether through a Web site of one's own, listing in another's, or through participation in a discussion forum. This risk might rise to significance if one were to deliberately and repeatedly incite others, but even then, there are just far too many people online to fear random harassment will befall any single individual.

There may be some exceptions in which there is a legitimate reason to be cautious. Figuring out how to contact someone at home simply from his or her e-mail address would be tedious and difficult, if even possible. So it is probably wise to limit contact information to e-mail addresses and to never give out home information to those you don't know or trust online. The Internet's convenience for targeting members of a particular group so they can network with each other can just as easily be used by members of a hate organization to harm or intimidate members of a group they dislike.

Cautiously limiting the contact information provided will help ensure that if one is targeted, it is only through e-mail messages that can be ignored. An example might be a newsgroup for discussion about gay and lesbian issues. This group frequently will be visited by people who wish to provoke angry responses. While the best cure for this is to ignore hateful comments, the typical result is a major digression in which almost all the postings are angry banter in all capital letters and in language you would not want your children to read. This, of course, delights the provoker.

It is important to distinguish that the risks are unlikely to go beyond inappropriate online messages, the sender of which may live hundreds of miles away. Perhaps the worst that could happen is that the receiver of these messages would have to change e-mail addresses to get away from the hate mail. Even this would be rare for any person who is not a public figure and who persists in ignoring the efforts to provoke.

In short, while it is *possible* for someone to identify and target another online for offline harrassment or assault, the chances are probably far less than by other means. Physical threats would be much easier to implement among those one sees in public than among those one meets online. Of course, this still leaves the potential harm, especially to children, who may read profanity or threats from another. In this regard, many of the fears are legitimate. The newsgroups, in particular, are often a place where incivility and anger seem to breed. While many are perfectly harmless and productive communication forums, parents, teachers, and others should be watchful of them and prepared to deal with the possiblity of children reading something inappropriate. But once again, this is not a problem unique to the Internet. A parent at a baseball game might be in exactly the same position of having to explain inappropriate, rude, and obnoxious behavior. Few, however, would suggest that this should mean avoiding taking children to the ballpark.

Do People Take on Different Online Personas?

This discussion raises a question about how people behave online as compared to offline. Anonymity and the ability to avoid the consequences may mean that some people behave more rudely online than they would in real life. At a baseball game, one is limited to some extent in what one says or does by the risk of antagonizing the patrons around him or even being expelled from the stadium. There are typically no such limitations in online forums. Although there are cases of people being locked out of a mailing list or newsgroup because of inappropriate behavior, this usually only happens in the very worst cases, and people can often return under a new e-mail address or name.

Interestingly, the Internet can also have the reverse impact on people's personas. There are many examples in which people seem even friendlier online than they probably are in face-to-face interactions. A possible reason for this might be that the new environment makes them especially careful not to offend. They may be aware that there are rules of "netiquette" and an unfamiliar culture. In addition, it is easier to be misinterpreted online, and people may be more cautious in their wording when disagreeing with someone on the Internet. Thus, for many, there is an added effort to be deferential.

Also, one sees people being particularly open online, expressing more of themselves than they might in casual conversation in public. At the same time, for many, there is the reverse effect in which there is more of an effort to remain concealed.

The differences in people's behavior and tone online may become an interesting area of study in the future, and there seem to be many contradictions. It appears, however, that in many cases, people indeed act differently online than they do offline. What this may suggest for relationships that develop online—friendships, professional interactions, or romances—is not at all clear. It is likely that some—but not all—such relationships will become disappointments when people meet face-to-face. Will the Internet lead to a rash of bad relationships or will it instead help people with common interests to meet one another? If the Internet tends to bring people together who share common interests, will the diversity of peoples' friends diminish, or will it expand as people from different continents become more accessible to one another?

Overuse of the Internet

It is hard not to sympathize with the mother who worries that her child is spending too much time online or to agree that adults face a problem when they feel compelled to sit for hours deep into the night wandering Web sites or sitting in chat rooms. The fact that these are problematic seems so apparent that it does not need to be examined. Or does it? What is a healthy amount of time online? Are people getting addicted to the Internet, or are they simply spending extra time now learning their way around?

Overuse of television and video games has long been a topic of discussion and research. Many societal problems are attributed to these activities and their overuse. There has been a tendency to think of the Internet as the next wave in this line—the newest attraction on a video screen for people to sit and stare at. The Internet, it is feared, may further reduce the time our children spend in the outdoors playing sports or in the library reading books. It will further encroach on the social interaction necessary for their healthy development.

Much of this may be a legitimate concern. Consider, however, the differences between the Internet and either television or video games. While they appear similar in that the viewer watches a screen or monitor, the assumption that they are similar in every respect is false.

While television encourages people to passively view whatever program may be shown, the Internet requires users to determine their own direction. Microsoft® markets its Internet Explorer Web browser with the question "Where do you want to go today?" This speaks to the Internet's unlimited options.

While the television excites viewers with special effects and action, the Internet is much more text-based, with pictures and moving images as a supplement. Thus, children on the Internet are far more likely to be reading than they would watching television.

One feature of the Internet that television does not offer is interactivity. Through computer programs and communication with people, the Internet can serve as a teacher, answering questions. For example, there are popular sites at which children can ask questions relevant to their homework. There are also sites which, by computer program, allow for learning in much the same way as an educational program or CD-ROM.

Many interactive Web sites seek responses from their readers, encouraging them to think, formulate opinions, and articulate them in writing. Discussion forums involve dialogue with real people. In these ways, the Internet is more like a classroom or cafe than a video.

It is true that the Internet offers games and a fair share of frivolous entertainment, unrelated to educational objectives. For perhaps most children, this is the first lure of the Internet. Nevertheless, the quality of these games rarely competes with modern video games, and obtaining and enjoying them takes a higher level of sophistication. Again, children's online entertainment tends to involve reading.

Differences such as these demonstrate the problem trying to compare the Internet to our familiar forms of activities. We may be looking at a screen that resembles a television, but in doing so, we may be reading a book or talking to people. The only clear similarity is that the Internet does not involve much physical activity. However, there has been some research indicating that the time people are spending online is replacing time formerly spent watching television rather than the time spent in physical activities. If so, the Internet may pose less of a threat to children's time spent outdoors than feared. Instead of cumulatively adding to television and video games, the Internet is simply giving people a more productive activity to replace these.

The question then may not be "How much time is one spending online?" but rather, "Is it part of a balanced lifestyle?" If one is online so often as to exclude any other activity, if one neglects work, family, or physical health, then a problem exists. A good way to consider the question is to think about what one is doing online, since the activities there vary so widely. Is five hours a day a problem? Perhaps so, if the five hours is spent playing *Battleship (http://info.gte.com/gtel/fun/ battle/battle.htm)*. But if the time is spent reading news and literature, writing an online publication, playing a game of chess with an opponent on the other side of the world, exploring your interests and hobbies with others, learning about how to do a home repair, and then playing *Battleship* for 20 minutes, then perhaps it's not so bad after all.

Pornography and Other Controversial Content Available Online

Some of the strongest concerns about the Internet have formed around the topic of online pornography and, to a lesser extent, the access to other dangerous or harmful information online. Faced with the broad ability to publish text or photos, some have raised this as the greatest, or at least the most tangible, danger of the Internet.

In the months preceeding the Supreme Court's decision in *Reno v. the ACLU (96-511, June 26, 1997)*, the Internet community demonstrated its single greatest example of solidarity, as individual and organizational Web sites carried the familiar blue ribbon image proclaiming the site owner's stance against the infringement of the First Amendment by the Communications Decency Act. Perhaps it is not a surprise that those online so overwhelmingly opposed the legislation of Internet content.

In this decision, Justice Stephens spoke for the majority finding that the Internet should be afforded the same protections as printed publications and should not be censored. Much of the debate centered on drawing the right analogy. Printed text has traditionally been limited by the fact that any would-be publisher had to incur the costs of publishing material, and any would-be viewer had to incur the cost of purchasing it. With the Internet, the printed word could be made available to all for virtually nothing.

As Justice Stephens noted, the growth of the Internet has not been hampered by fears of this kind of content, but rather has grown at "phenomenal" rates despite it. It is probably true that, like the court, most people view this question as one of balancing the pros and the cons. Can we accept the incredible access to information for the good it brings people, knowing that there will be downsides when information is misused? The easiest solution to the issue would be to ban the Internet, to suppress information deemed dangerous to society. But most of us would find this unacceptable, and trying to limit the content would create a nightmare for policing efforts and for courts trying to discern pornography from art or educational material.

One of the most important reasons the Court may have ruled in favor of the opposite easy solution— to grant the Internet full freedoms of expression—was probably the fact that ways are being developed to limit access. Programs for parents to curtail access to unwanted sites exist now and can be expected to improve dramatically in the coming years. Contrary to the perception that one can accidentally stumble upon nude photos, sites containing pornography typically contain a warning at their gateway, a fact Justice Stephens emphasized.

In some ways, this problem, too, is not really brand new to the Internet. Children have often found ways to access magazines and other forms of pornography. The availability on computers, while easier to access, may be more difficult for young people to hide. An offshoot of the current debate has centered on those demanding that libraries utilize blocking software to prevent access to pornography. Libraries have, in most cases, refused to agree to this censorship. Few have considered, however, the impracticality of sitting in a public library viewing pornographic photos online while others stroll by.

There are other reasons why the problem may be overblown. To what extent will pornography be available for free online? Remember that the people creating such sites draw no income from them, unless they limit access to those who pay. To what extent will children be drawn to seek them out, or harmed if they do happen by one? But while these questions might reduce the fears, they cannot remove them entirely. No doubt, pornography and other content can be damaging to young viewers and some might be negatively affected by its presence online. Even if we agree on the other benefits of freedom of online expression, this could certainly create work for social workers and others in one form or another.

Privacy Online

A recent talk show featured another content-based fear of the Internet. It is possible to place a camera or video-cam and to broadcast an image to a Web site, updating it daily or even every few seconds, or to stream the video in. Audio can be similarly streamed in.

Many positive uses of this are apparent. For distance learning, it allows one to view a conference online. Video-cams along highways are allowing people to view traffic and to see weather relevant for their travel and driving.

Some uses are more creative and may be highly beneficial, or may raise entirely new issues of concern. One of the more creative is the use of such a camera in day care centers. Parents will no longer need to worry about the care their children receive when they can, using the Internet, peek in at any moment to see their children. This practice is being used in a number of day care centers already. Another creative use was Geocities' inventive and popular Hollywood bus stop camera. Broadcasting a bus stop bench where many stars pass, people could check in and hope to catch a glimpse of a favorite celebrity.

But then there are the misuses of this idea. One site, for example, was discovered to be linked to a camera placed in a public restroom. Will our tort laws protecting privacy be able to compensate for the potential personal damage this kind of publication can cause? In the past, there were practical limits to the extent of injury from the publication of words or images about an individual. The average person would find it difficult to publish on his or her own, and a publication with a large audience would tend to be in a better position to compensate the injury in a lawsuit. But now, any person has the ability to destroy another's reputation through online publication.

In addition, the increasing use of cameras online brings another development that will likely disconcert people. How will people feel knowing they are being broadcast to the Internet while they await a bus, even if the image is ordinary?

Conclusion

In surveying the risks and realities of the Internet, there are few easy answers. Certain things seem clear, however. First, the Internet will bring changes. Second, fear of the changes will not stop it from becoming an integral part of mainstream society. Equally certain is that the Internet will deliver immeasurable benefits to all people at the same time that it causes irreparable harm in other cases. One would like to say that time will tell how these balance against one another, but to be honest, even time will probably not be able to answer that question in the same way for everyone.

As different as the Internet is, in some ways it is quite the same as any other advance. Any technology can be misused. Since we can't avoid the risks by avoiding the technology, the better approach may be to dispassionately assess the real risks and dangers and to address, limit, and alleviate them to the extent possible. This will be an important issue for policy makers, social workers, and many others seeking to make the Internet as valuable as possible—increasing access to all who might benefit—and curtailing its harmful effects to children, to those whose privacy is violated, to those who experience damaging interrelations through Internet contact with others, and to any person who finds him or herself failing to balance healthy offline activities with Internet activities.

Afterword

Where Do We Go From Here?

You've gotten this far and you're ready to forge ahead. Good for you! As you can see, the Internet has much to offer, and at the same time it can offer too much. It can be frustrating, and it can be fascinating. It can be scary, and it can be fun. It can be isolating, and it can bring people together.

For social workers and their clients, it can be all this and much more. What you do with it, how you use it, is up to you. Try it one step at a time, or dive right in—whichever style fits you best—but don't be left behind.

We hope this book gives you some ideas and some inspiration. Your social work colleagues are already online and willing to help you learn as you go. Look at what they have done, join in the existing online opportunities to connect with them, and when you are ready, make your own contributions to the Internet's resources.

We hope this book calms some of your fears. One of the most commonly reported reasons for social workers' hesitance to join the online world is technophobia—fear of the technology. It is unlikely that you will break the computer if you hit the wrong button, and fear of the unknown can be alleviated by taking a course or reading a book (like this one!). Take it slowly, try some fun things, and with experience, you can change your status from newbie to 'Nethead.

We hope this book gives you some starting places to find social workers and social work information online. Use the reviews in the next section to find information on particular topics or categories. Use the suggested sites within the preceeding chapters to locate resources that can help you with specific uses of the Internet. Then, start to explore on your own. You'll be amazed at what you can find and how quickly you will learn to use the tools the Internet offers. And soon you'll wonder how you ever managed without it.

We invite you to let us know how you are using the Internet and what treasures you are finding. And we especially hope you'll let us know what new online resources you are developing that may be useful to other social workers.

Everything changes quickly on the 'Net, and we'll be on the constant lookout for updates to the information in this book. Feel free to contact us if you hear of anything we should know about!

See you on the 'Net!

Gary B. Grant (g-grant@uchicago.edu)
Linda M. Grobman (linda.grobman@paonline.com)

PART III:

Reviews of Web Sites
of Interest to Social Workers

Reviews

Reviews of Web Sites of Interest to Social Workers

Note: Unattributed quotes within these reviews that describe the purpose of organizations are taken from the organizations' Web sites.

Reviews are organized by categories. To find out if a specific site is included in these reviews, see the Review Index on page 232.

ADOPTION

Adoption From China
http://www.geocities.com/Tokyo/1771
This is a collection of sites developed by parents who have adopted from China. Sites include pictures and stories about the adoption.

AdoptionNetwork
http://www.adoption.org/
This is a major "volunteer-operated information resource for the adoption community." Using this "one-stop" resource, adoptees and birth parents can find supports (online and off, individual and organizational), contacts, reference material, current news, legislation, calendars of events, registries, and more. Adoptive parents and prospective parents can find information relevant to every stage of adoption, beginning with instructive content on where to start.

The Adoption Web Ring
http://www.plumsite.com/adoptionring/ring.shtml
The Adoption Ring is a ring of over 200 web pages devoted to the best interests of adoptees and those in the adoption triad. It includes sites for adoptees, birthparents, and adoptive parents. All those with educational or personal Web pages

regarding adoption and foster care are invited to submit their sites for inclusion.

Faces of Adoption: America's Waiting Children
http://nac.adopt.org/
"Welcome to Faces of Adoption: America's Waiting Children," a pleasant female voice greets you when you visit this site. Sponsored by the National Adoption Center and Children Awaiting Parents, this technologically advanced site includes photo listings of 306 children (as of January 5, 1998), an Adoption Quest section that includes articles on how to adopt and related issues, a 29-second audio clip of President Clinton on adoption, and more. Essential for anyone whose work involves adoption issues.

Reclaiming my Roots Reunion Registry
http://www.geocities.com/Heartland/Hills/2638/
This site was created by an individual who succeeded in a birth family search. It allows visitors to utilize existing registry database and information systems.

U.S. Adoption Search and Support Groups by State
http://www.webreflection.com/aiml/support.html
This is a large directory of regional adoption search and support groups.

AGING

Alzheimer's Association
http://www.alz.org
The site contains the organization's mission

statement, news releases, position statements, and a listing of chapters. Educational information for caregivers is provided (i.e., "10 Warning Signs"). Online advocacy efforts include public policy FAQs, current projects, and an online policy newsletter. There are links to related sites and the ability to search the site by key words. With few graphics other than a logo, the site loads quickly, a plus for those with slow browsers/computers.

Alzheimer's Disease Web Page
http://med-amsa.bu.edu/Alzheimer/home.html
This page is maintained by Bedford Geriatric Research Education Clinical Center in Bedford, MA. It includes resources for both family and professional caregivers and has won several awards, including MHNet 3 stars, Web Now 500 Top Web Sites, Web Pilot's Wings Award, and Look Smart Editor's Choice.

Association for Gerontology Education in Social Work (AGE-SW)
http://www.cs.umd.edu/users/connie/
This site includes large graphics, which may make loading slow. It includes contact information for AGE-SW, a membership application, newsletter highlights, gerontology resources, and an online "what's new" newsletter. Also includes member profiles and links to other Web sites and mailing lists related to gerontology.

Answers: The Magazine for Adult Children of Aging Parents
http://www.service.com/answers/cover.html
This is the Web site of a print magazine based in Birmingham, AL. It includes full text of three articles, table of contents from December 1993 issue, and a subscription form. It could use updating, but is a source of contact information for this magazine.

Eldercare Web
http://www.elderweb.com/
A wonderful online resource project by an individual, Karen Stevenson Brown. This well-rounded site provides an index to online literature, research, organizations, and directories dealing with health issues, housing, legal matters, social and financial concerns of the elderly and the people and families who provide supports for the frail elderly.

Family Caregiver Alliance
http://www.caregiver.org
This is the Web site of a support organization for caregivers of adults with Alzheimer's disease, stroke, traumatic brain injury, Parkinson's disease, ALS, and related brain disorders. It includes a clearinghouse with 30 fact sheets, a news bureau for reporters, an online support group (under construction at the time of this review), an "Ask FCA" section with questions and answers posted on the site, public policy positions and alerts, links to other sites, and a form to send requests for consultation.

Gerontological Society of America
http://www.geron.org
There is information about the organization, as well as news releases, career development information for students, job listings, legislative updates, information on grants and fellowships, and links to related sites.

GeroWeb
http://www.iog.wayne.edu/IOGlinks.html
"Brought to you by the Graduate Student Organization and the GeroInformatics Workgroup at the Wayne State University Institute of Gerontology, GeroWeb is designed as an online resource for researchers, educators, practitioners, and others interested in aging and older individuals." This site is a model for organizational structure, providing quick access to specific information sought. Links to outside sites are reviewed, and shortcuts to specific content are provided, along with descriptive text. Feedback from visitors, in the form of comments on each outside link, is used to improve the site.

The National Aging Information Center
http://www.aoa.dhhs.gov/naic/
A main feature of this site is the ability to search in three databases: (1) the Bibliographic Database for finding aging-related products, (2) the Database Reference System for finding aging-related data and statistics sources (also see the links to more online statistical resources on older persons), and (3) the Eldercare Locator for finding referral services for older persons in any particular locale (although this database is not yet searchable via the Web and requests must instead be telephoned). Publications produced by the agency are summarized (substantially) online and may be ordered in full by printing and mailing or faxing an online order form.

SeniorNet

http://www.seniornet.com/

"SeniorNet is a national nonprofit organization whose mission is to build a community of computer-using seniors," according to this site. The audience is anyone 55 years old or older. It was started as a research project at the University of San Francisco. There is an accompanying site on America Online (keyword: SeniorNet). Both sites offer message boards and online chats. There are more than 100 SeniorNet Learning Centers where older adults can take computer classes.

Third Age

http://www.thirdage.com/

"ThirdAge.com is the online home of a vibrant online society filled with ideas and interactions generated, hosted, and reflected by the views of its citizens—the Third Agers themselves. It is a Web-based community started by Third Age Media, Inc. where Third Agers can voice their opinions, recount experiences, and share advice with new friends through interactive technologies such as chat rooms and discussion boards. It presents the best the Web has to offer for active older adults." This "Web for grownups" features chats with such notables as Peter Max and Deepak Chopra, articles, shopping, and online forums.

AIDS

ACT UP NY

http://www.actupny.org

The AIDS Coalition to Unleash Power is known for its civil disobedience activities. This site of the New York Chapter of this organization includes a 29-minute audio or video civil disobedience training component. There are activist documents, such as manuals on how to be an activist, civil disobedience, and starting an ACT-UP chapter. The organization also offers t-shirts, buttons, and other items for sale, but does not have an online ordering mechanism. There is also information on donating to the cause.

AIDS Book Review Journal

http://www.library.ucsb.edu/journals/aids/

This site is a simple listing of each issue of this online journal published by the University of Illinois at Chicago, edited by H. Robert Malinowsky. The first issue was published in March 1993, and it continues every month or two until the most recent. It is only available in electronic form. A simple search engine is available for finding specific references. A typical issue includes reviews of videos, journals, and any other material on AIDS. The journal can also be subscribed to by e-mail list.

Children with AIDS Project

http://www.aidskids.org

A *USA Today* Hot Site. Included are stories of children with AIDS, adoption of such children, and links to AIDS and adoption resources. This site is published by the CWA project, which recruits families to adopt children with AIDS and provides AIDS education, training, advocacy, and legal services (relating to adoption). Also includes a "gift shop" featuring books, tapes, and other materials on AIDS.

HIV/AIDS Education in Social Work

http://www.geocities.com/CollegePark/7113/

Contains links to AIDS-related sites.

HIV Insite

http://hivinsite.ucsf.edu

This is one of the most comprehensive AIDS information sites we have found. The Medical section has case studies, treatment guidelines, a medical glossary, and clinical fact sheets. The Prevention section provides resources for prevention professionals and information on developing a community prevention Web page. The Social Issues section features an online AIDS Law Manual, policy and advocacy links, and reports. Resources has U.S. AIDS statistics, state AIDS information, and more. There is even a U.S. map that you can click on to find AIDS information and resources for your own state.

Marty Howard's HIV/AIDS Home Page

http://www.smartlink.net/~martinjh/

This site, maintained by a 55-year-old man who is HIV-positive, is heavy on information and contains very few graphics. There are links to Web sites, mailing lists, support groups, news, newsgroups, clinical trials/medication information, and alternative treatment information.

BOOKS/BOOKSTORES ONLINE

Amazon.com

http://www.amazon.com/

Amazon.com is currently not only the premier bookstore online, but is also one of the biggest Internet commerce success stories. Offering over 2.5 million book titles, amazon.com has gathered over 1 million registered customers. The site makes buying a book easy. All you need is the author's name or title of the book. You can also do a subject search to find books on a desired topic, view best seller lists, and use other browsing methods. Readers and authors can submit their comments and reviews of any book listed. Those interested in specific subject areas can sign up to get reviews by e-mail. Books are typically discounted and, in most cases, are shipped within 2-3 days (hard-to-find books will take significantly longer). Another feature is the ability for individuals or organizations to become amazon.com associates and generate income by placing specialized bookstores (linked to amazon.com) on their Web sites.

BarnesandNoble.com
http://www.barnesandnoble.com
While amazon.com "exists" only in cyberspace, BarnesandNoble.com is an online extension of the well-known Barnes and Noble chain of bookstores. Online customers can search the Barnes and Noble site by subject, title, or author and can order online using a secure form. There is also an online community, featuring live author chats; transcripts of these chats; and message boards on books, authors, and publishing. The Gift Match feature suggests books to order in different categories, such as mothers-to-be or friends. Visitors can also go to the Magazine Stand to order subscriptions to various periodicals. BarnesandNoble.com has an affiliate network (similar to Amazon's associate program), allowing Webmasters to set up online bookstores on their sites and earn commissions on book sales. The "Book Benefits Network" is an affiliate program set up specifically for non-profit organizations that want to earn non-dues revenue from online bookstores linking from their sites to BarnesandNoble.com.

BookZone
http://www.bookzone.com/
The Super Catalog presents hundreds of titles, excerpts, and author information for bound books, audiobooks, CDs, and diskettes. Another especially nice feature is information from over 600 publishers, from which the user can gain insight into what they need to do to become published authors. Check out BookZone's "Literary Leaps" section, which lists over 70 categories of book selections. The site also has a local search engine. BookZone's creators have made today's electronic literary information exchange system

both easy and fun! Join the over 180,000 people who visit the BookZone every month.

CHILDREN AND YOUTH

Big Brothers Big Sisters of America
http://www.bbbsa.org
The oldest mentoring organization in the U.S., BBBSA's Web site provides a directory of all the regional-level affiliated organizations and their contact staff. As these regional agencies also get online, their Web pages are incorporated into the national site. The site also gives directions and a form for making contributions, and provides current news about the organization, its mission/vision, and its impact.

Boys and Girls Clubs of America
http://www.bgca.org/index1.html
"The Boys and Girls Club Movement is a nationwide affiliation of local, autonomous organizations and Boys and Girls Clubs of America working to help youth of all backgrounds, with special concern for those from disadvantaged circumstances, develop the qualities needed to become responsible citizens and leaders." This frame-supported site includes video and audio clips of actor Denzel Washington speaking on behalf of the organization and a YouthWeb area of Web sites that have been built by Boys and Girls Clubs. There are pages devoted to the organization's programs, an entire page lauding the corporate sponsors of BGCA, and lots of interestingly designed pages.

Boy Scouts of America
http://www.bsa.scouting.org/
This site provides general information about scouting, with descriptions of various activities and programs of the BSA. The Local Council Locator allows you to type in your city and state and get the address and phone number of the closest Boy Scout Council. There are photographs and descriptions of official Boy Scout gear, with a toll-free number to call to receive a complete catalog. The Family Fun Page includes quizzes, a Morse code translator (type in a sentence, and it will be translated into Morse code), and other fun things.

The Child Welfare League of America
http://www.cwla.org
The Child Welfare League of America is "the nation's oldest and largest organization devoted

entirely to the well-being of America's vulnerable children and their families." CWLA uses the Web site to link member agencies—organizations that are part of its network of organizations supporting its mission. In doing so, the site provides, in effect, an online connection to many public and private child welfare agencies, as well as a practical communication network among the member agencies. There are links to the agency's publications, consulting services, membership, upcoming conferences, information on being a CWLA intern, and how to make donations and purchase the organization's products. The site also includes helpful advocacy tips and statistics on child welfare issues.

Children Now

http://www.childrennow.org

The mission of Children Now is to "promote pioneering solutions to improve the lives of America's children." This site includes poll data, child welfare data, briefings, articles, calls to action, and sample letters to policy makers. There is also a mailing list to receive regular updates from Children Now. Volunteer opportunities and state information are also available at this animated site.

Children's Defense Fund

http://www.tmn.com/cdf/

The Children's Defense Fund, founded in 1973, is perhaps the most visible and powerful national children's advocacy organization. The mission of the CDF is to "provide a strong and effective voice for all the children of America, who cannot vote, lobby, or speak for themselves." If you work with or on behalf of children, this is a must site to visit. The information is frequently updated. When you click on the "Issues" button, you see a page with five innocuous-sounding headings. Click on one (they relate to education, health care, welfare, crime/safety, and morality issues), and you are taken to a page that has up-to-date issue papers, bills of interest, and an FAQ that provides statistics and descriptions of the problems facing kids. There are great files such as "10 Things You Can Do to Help Children," which includes information about how to make donations to the organization. There is a chart depicting the cost of raising a child to the age of 18. There is information about internships, CDF publications for purchase, the text of articles by founder and president Marian Wright Edelman, and hundreds of other useful and interesting files. CDF's Web site is also used to teach actual

and potential child advocates about what they can do in their own communities and what actions are needed to protect children from violence, sickness, and the effects of poverty. This is a great site, with a professional and pleasant format and design.

Children's House in Cyberspace

http://childhouse.uio.no/

"Children's House is an interactive resource center—a meeting place for the exchange of information that serves the well being of children. Dedicated to supporting the generation and dissemination of knowledge about children's issues, Children's House facilitates the translation of the benefits of research and programming into policy and practice." The site gathers organizations serving children in various ways, from children's health to children's rights, to early childhood development. Each topic area is moderated by a particular organization that is charged with the role of gathering information relevant to that area. Thus, resources for advocacy, education, accessing research, and more can be found in this neatly organized community.

CityKids

http://www.child.net/citykids.htm

This site lists resources for kids in 27 major cities throughout the U.S.

Convomania

http://www.mania.apple.com/

A great site! "A place for seriously ill and disabled kids on the Internet," Convomania is sponsored by the Worldwide Disability Solutions Group at Apple Computer. There are scheduled and unscheduled chats, with the scheduled ones focusing on specific topics, such as what to do if you're suicidal. The "Maniax" mailing list is for kids only. An online "yearbook" features photos and bios of kids who visit the site, and an "exhibit hall" displays the kids' artwork depicting such things as hospital food.

Family Preservation & Child Welfare Network

http://hadm.sph.sc.edu/Students/KBelew/index.htm

Webmaster Kathy Belew, MSW, MPH, has compiled, in this model child welfare data site, information from 1996 to 1997 focusing on child and family services in South Carolina. The site contains links, essays, and statistical charts and graphs in the following areas: Child Abuse & Neglect; Foster Care, Adoptions, Childhood Disability, Child Welfare Services; Family Violence; Working Together Project; Region Statistics; and Adult Protective Services. Also, visit Kathy's chat room and an equally complete resource links page.

Girl Scouts of the USA

http://www.gsusa.org/
The Girl Scouts is the largest voluntary organization in the world for girls. Information is available at this site about affiliates, Girl Scout cookies, publications, awards, history of the organization, information about making donations, and how to become one of the 800,000 Girl Scout volunteers. The site includes an animated publications section and links to local affiliates that have Web pages of their own.

Illinois Department of Children and Family Services

http://www.state.il.us/dcfs
Includes information about the department and its services. There are online brochures on child protection, foster care, adoption, and day care, for example. An online DCFS library includes documents such as the history of social work in IL, the DCFS Code of Ethics, statistics, and a glossary. The department's Rules and Statutes can be downloaded. A popular feature is a photo listing of children awaiting adoption.

KidsCampaigns (Benton Foundation)

http://www.kidscampaign.org/
KidsCampaigns is "the information, knowledge and action center for adults who want to make their communities work for kids." There is a vast amount of information here relating to online advocacy. The principal interactive efforts carried out online include some of those found in Interact for Kids. Here you can sign the guestbook and begin receiving an e-mail newsletter informing you of breaking news. Augmenting these newsletters is an e-mail discussion group for people working on behalf of children. Even one-time visitors are urged to share their stories with Benton about their efforts relating to working for children. Article submissions are encouraged for possible inclusion on the Web site.

The National Assembly of National Voluntary Health and Social Welfare Organizations (National Assembly)

http://www.nassembly.org/html/search.html
This site has an online database of more than

2,000 paid and unpaid internships at youth development agencies such as Big Brothers/Big Sisters, Boy Scouts, Girl Scouts, YMCA, YWCA, and Volunteers of America. The database can be searched by state, city, and type of internship sought.

The National Association of Homes and Services for Children (NAHSC)

http://www.nahsc.org/
The National Association of Homes and Services for Children (NAHSC) "advocates for at-risk children and families and the private nonprofit organizations that serve them." This site links to member agencies and offers these agencies their own Web sites for assisting in their advocacy efforts. In doing this, NAHSC proactively creates an online community and network for advocacy. There are buttons to click to access files on advocacy, education, publications, links to member agencies, and more.

National Child Rights Alliance

http://linux.hartford.edu/~jerry/ncra.html
This is the only national organization directed entirely by youth and adult survivors of abuse and neglect. (Non-abused supporters are important to the work as well.) This site includes a number of articles on youth liberation, "divorces" between child and parent, civil rights, and health protection.

U.S. Administration for Children and Families

http://www.acf.dhhs.gov/
This site is well organized and easy to navigate. From the gateway, you can learn about the organization and find any person or department within the agency. The ACF Press Room section is a regularly updated news section with archived press releases, fact sheets, and statistical information, all very useful if you need to research the implementation of welfare reform across the states. Under programs and services, you can gather information about any particular office, division, committee, or sub–agency within the ACF. You can, for example, learn about TANF, JOBS, and AFDC through annual reports available online. Reports and statistical data are the bread and butter of all these sites, but some provide more. Through the Children's Bureau, for example, you can learn how to report incidents of child abuse, and those interested in becoming foster parents can find their state contact people. Funding announcements, policy guide-

lines, descriptions of initiatives, and details of events taking place are examples of the kind of information posted online. The Head Start pages provide a bulletin board restricted to those involved in or who use Head Start programs.

World Kids Network

http://wkn.org/

This site encourages children all over the world to "explore the possibilities of their world in the creative atmosphere of the Internet, to become computer literate, and to achieve their full potential in this dynamic new field." Kids can develop their own online projects through this network.

Youth Indicators

http://www.ed.gov/pubs/YouthIndicators/index.html

This is a publication of the Department of Education's Office of Educational Research and Improvement containing much information, and numerous tables and charts on trends on the well-being of America's youth. The office invites inquiries and suggestions on new data. Examples of data categories include home demographics and composition, family income, school descriptions, outcomes, out-of-school activities, health, citizenship and values, and future employment outcomes and aspirations of youth.

COMMUNITY

Alliance for National Renewal

http://www.ncl.org

This National Civic League program includes the participation of more than 180 community-building organizations, including the American Association of Retired Persons, Habitat for Humanity, and the Points of Light Foundation. The site includes an e-zine called *The Kitchen Table*, and a "Community Stories" index of articles about what is taking place in local communities, indexed by 10 different categories (such as children, youth, and families). The site is searchable, and there is information about publications.

CivicNet

http://www.tmn.com/civicnet/

This is a project of the Center for Civic Networking *(http://www.civic.net:2401/ccn.html)*, an organization providing civic networking services for other organizations. There was an online event scheduled for May 22 to June 30, 1997,

which aimed to help inspire participants and provide practical tools for community building, especially through the use of the Internet. The event was structured much the same as any traditional conference. Participation was restricted to registrants (at a $50 fee), and activities included exhibitions on products and services, discussion forums, speaker presentations, workshops, and breakout groups. Even posters and papers were available for participants.

CORRECTIONS

The Corrections Connection Network

http://www.corrections.com/

This is the most comprehensive site we have seen on just about any specific issue. It bills itself as "the largest online resource for news and information in corrections," and we believe it. The Corrections White Pages will help you find a corrections professional. Almost a dozen national corrections associations are associated with this site, including the American Correctional Association, American Correctional Food Services Association, American Correctional Health Services Association, American Jail Association, Correctional Industries Association, International Community Corrections, Jail Industries Association, MidAtlantic States Corrections Association, National Commission on Correctional Health Care, and more. These associations can be linked to from this site. There are also county, state, federal, and community corrections links; bulletin boards on numerous issues; a career center with job openings; a library; legislative center; statistics; salary surveys; scholarships; shopping; surplus sales; training; grants; and more. Employers can post job openings free of charge.

Family and Corrections Network (FCN)

http://www.fcnetwork.org

Published by FCN, the first national organization in the U.S. focused on families of offenders (since 1983), this site was developed in 1997. It includes information on programs serving families of offenders and related publications. There is a place to ask questions and get answers. Visitors to the site can post messages and poetry on "The Wall." There are related links, and the site is pleasantly designed.

Inmate Significant Others Support Page

http://www.geocities.com/Wellesley/2172/

Charolette L. Simmons, an MSW student at the University of Kansas, developed this site. It provides poetry (mostly by Simmons herself) and links for those who are close to someone who is in prison.

DEATH AND DYING

Bereavement Resource
http://www.funeral.net/info/brvres.html
This site, sponsored by Armstrong Funeral Home in Ontario, Canada, provides links to bereavement and grief-related sites, as well as a link to the funeral home's home page.

Crisis, Grief, and Healing Page
http://www.webhealing.com/
This site was developed by Tom Golden, LCSW, author of a book on the masculine side of healing. There is an "honor page" consisting of personal stories, as well as discussion boards for people who are grieving. You can find Golden's columns and excerpts from his book, as well as an order form for it.

DeathNet
http://www.IslandNet.com:80/~deathnet/
"Advancing the Art and Science of Dying Well." This site specializes in end-of-life issues and was created by John Hofsess, Executive Director of the Right to Die Society of Canada, in collaboration with Derek Humphrey, founder of the National Hemlock Society. This site includes information on the "right to die" and extensive information on Dr. Jack Kevorkian ("The Kevorkian File"), including how to contact him and criteria for assisted suicide. A restricted area called "The Art and Science of Suicide" asks readers to click a button to "verify that I am 21 years of age or older." When we clicked on it, we were taken to a page that lists various references for planning a "good death."

Growth House, Inc.
http://www.growthhouse.org/
Billing itself as "the Yahoo of Death and Dying," this award-winning site is an international gateway to resources on life-threatening illnesses and end-of-life issues. It boasts a search engine, online bookstore, and chat room. The chat room can be reserved for discussions on specific topics, and a regular chat is held on Monday nights with a pre-determined topic.

National Hospice Organization
http://www.nho.org
This organizational site has general information about hospice and the organization. There is a good links page, and a discussion forum. The NHO Store is an online catalog of resources available through the organization.

National Prison Hospice Association
http://www.npha.org
Here you will find information on hospice care for prisoners, an online newsletter, a very brief listing of links, staff contacts, and a registration form to receive a newsletter.

TLC Group
http://www.metronet.com/~tlc
Published by a private company that publishes books on transition, loss, and change, this site is a good resource for those who work with people dealing with grief. Besides information on its publications and how to order them, TLC Group provides on this site full-text articles, such as "Helping a Friend or Neighbor Cope with Loss," and "Beware the 5 Stages of Grief." There is an article on how to do a "loss history," and links to other grief resources. Readers are given permission to use the articles without compensation. There is no form for ordering online, but there is one that can be printed out and mailed in.

DISABILITIES

American Association on Mental Retardation
http://www.aamr.org
Here you can find organizational information (publications, education programs, membership), links to AAMR affiliates and other related sites, and some job listings.

The Arc Homepage
http://TheArc.org/welcome.html
The Association of Retarded Citizens is "the country's largest voluntary organization committed to the welfare of all children and adults with mental retardation and their families." Its site includes numerous fact sheets on mental retardation, position papers, and a discussion board for posting inquiries. The Arc's semi-monthly government affairs report is published online in full text, and the weekly *Capitol Insider* newsletter is a terrific source of legislative information. Point Survey rated this site among the top 5% of all social services sites. We agree.

The Disability Link Barn

http://www.accessunlimited.com/links.html
A listing of 1,213 disability-related links.

Disability Rights Activist

http://www.teleport.com/~abarhydt/
This is the place to go for advocacy information relating to disability issues. New action alerts are posted almost daily, and the latest court decisions, press releases, regulations, and news are posted here. This award-winning site does not have a lot of fancy graphics, icons, or maps, but has good, solid, and current information. When we reviewed the site, there were 13 current Action Alerts posted, giving a succinct summary of a public policy issue, the current status, what action was requested by the organization, and links to more information. This is how it should be done!

March of Dimes Birth Defects

http://www.modimes.org/
The March of Dimes is a non-profit organization dedicated to reducing birth defects and infant mortality. Established in 1938 by President Franklin Delano Roosevelt to put an end to polio, the organization accomplished this mission within 20 years with Dr. Jonas Salk's development of the polio vaccine. Among the documents that can be accessed from the home page are *March of Dimes history,* the *March of Dimes today, pregnancy and childbirth, birth defects, the March of Dimes chapter nearest you,* and *volunteering for the March of Dimes.* There is plenty of statistical information on this site, and files about birth defects, educational programs, and organizational press releases. An online form is provided for making donations via credit card (there does not seem to be a secure form at this time), and plenty of other files related to fundraising, donations, and volunteering to raise money. The site is searchable and has a wealth of information in both English and Spanish versions.

National Center to Improve Practice in Special Education

http://www.edc.org/FSC/NCIP/more_top.html
"The National Center to Improve Practice seeks to improve educational outcomes for students with disabilities by promoting the effective use of assistive and instructional technologies among educators and related personnel serving these students." Through this site, NCIP has created a national community of educators and leaders who promote and implement assistive and instructional technologies for students with disabilities. Among the site's features are a bulletin board where visitors can post conference information, calls for papers, and job announcements; an extensive page of links to sites related to technology and disabilities; information on joining NCIP's online mailing list; and an online library of documents pertaining to assistive technology.

National Easter Seal Society

http://www.seals.com
Founded in 1919, Easter Seals is a nationwide network of 109 affiliate societies operating programs to serve the disabled and their families. There are lots of links to disability-related sites.

Professionals with Disabilities

http://members.aol.com/rbde/profs.disability.html
A long list of links, some incorrectly formatted and/or outdated. The site, developed by social worker Rosemary B. DeCamp. MPA, MSW, LCSW, includes some statistics on professionals with disabilities.

Solutions @ disability.com

http://disability.com/index.html
This site provides information on a variety of products and services for people with disabilities and chronic health conditions. There is also information about the newspaper *One Step Ahead,* including articles, legal briefs, and links to other disability-related sites.

DISASTER/HUMANITARIAN RELIEF

American Red Cross

http://www.redcross.org/
This searchable site has the latest news concerning natural disasters and general/world news relating to natural and man-made disasters. Included in the site is a virtual museum giving the history of the agency. The colorful graphics, world-class design, and good information make it worthy of return visits. There is plenty of information concerning how to donate to the organization, including forms to make secure credit card transactions. This site sets the standard for charitable organization Web sites.

AmeriCares Foundation

http://www.americares.org/
AmeriCares is a private, international non-profit disaster relief and humanitarian aid organiza-

tion. The pages are simple, consisting of little about the organization, and including lots of links to other disaster/humanitarian relief agencies, categorized by children, hunger relief, education, medical care, refugees/disaster relief, and jobs/economic aid.

InterAction

http://www.interaction.org/

InterAction is the nation's largest coalition of private relief and development agencies. With 150 non-profit organizations, it advocates for humanitarian assistance to the world's needy. Its membership list is a Who's Who of international relief organizations, many of whom have their own Web sites, which are linked to Interaction's. *PC Computing* Magazine named this professionally designed, colorful site as one of the *Best 1001 Websites on the Internet* (among other awards bestowed on it). There is information about volunteer opportunities and, for a modest subscription fee, a newsletter detailing job opportunities at international organizations. You can find publications, information relating to advocacy with legislative alerts and updates on international aid issues, an events calendar, program links, and *A Guide to Appropriate Giving* with tips on how and what to donate to international relief organizations. There are lots of useful links, the information is frequently updated, the Web site is searchable, and it is one of the most well done Web sites we found.

ReliefNet

http://www.reliefnet.org/

"ReliefNet™ is a non-profit organization dedicated to helping humanitarian organizations raise global awareness and encourage support for relief efforts via the Internet." The site features an innovative "virtual relief concert" in support of humanitarian relief efforts.

Relief Web

http://www.reliefWeb.int/

Relief Web is organized by the United Nations Department of Humanitarian Affairs. Emergency areas around the world are monitored by the site, allowing individuals to focus aid where it may be most needed at any particular time. The site also gives data on the amount of humanitarian assistance that has been provided each year from each nation. The U.S., for example, provided $828,259,035 in 1996, according to figures reported to DHA. The site provides data on the humanitarian assistance provided in response to complex emergencies.

DISEASE-SPECIFIC ORGANIZATIONS

American Cancer Society

http://www.cancer.org

This site has frames and no-frames versions. It features the latest news on cancer and links to cancer-related sites. The site's FAQ is excellent. There is an entire section of the page devoted to a volunteer recruitment pilot program, involving four state chapters at the time this was written. Obviously, this is the place to start for information on what is perhaps America's most dreaded disease. Full-text articles, such as "Listen with Your Heart: Talking with the Cancer Patient," can be good for family and friends of clients/patients. Oncology social workers will find this a useful site to bookmark.

American Heart Association

http://www.amhrt.org/

Included on this searchable Web site is a button that links to the association's database of news media releases and advisories with Reuters Health Information Services. This is the site for information about cardiovascular disease, prevention, and clinical cardiology.

American Lung Association (ALA)

http://www.lungusa.org/

The American Lung Association is the largest organization in this country fighting lung disease, including asthma, emphysema, and lung cancer. Information can be found on the site about making donations and the tax advantages of doing so. There are plans to permit donations to be made online on secure forms. The home page has a cute animation of a pair of lungs in the process of breathing. The pages are searchable (the term "asthma" turned up matches in hundreds of files), and include information about important legislation pending on Capitol Hill, articles from associated medical journals that are edited to make them more understandable to the public, and association press releases. According to the site itself, "The ALA Web site contains 82 separate documents related to lung health, ALA news articles, medical and legislative updates, and more than 40 fact sheets." Knowing that all this information was available with just the click of a mouse made us breathe easier.

Cancer Care

http://www.cancercareinc.org

This impressive Web site has an abundance of useful information on its pages. Even so, it is well-organized in small chunks, so as not to be overwhelming. It can be easily read and absorbed and navigated. Visitors can download numerous information sheets for themselves or for clients, find out about Cancer Care programs nationwide, teleconference, or join a support group online or offline. All such groups are led, the site says, by a "professional oncology social worker." The "For Professionals" section contains articles written by social workers and others on how to develop various support groups for cancer patients. The site contains numerous links to other health care sources and has a special page on how to use the Internet to find more information, even if you are a beginner. The site is clearly written and very user-friendly, but the numerous graphics make it slow to download.

SIDS Network

http://sids-network.org/

This site gets 2,600 visits per day on average. There is a section for parents and siblings to share with others, articles on Sudden Infant Death Syndrome (SIDS), information on SIDS-related chats on IRC and AOL, and the opportunity to subscribe to an e-mail list. The "Pictures of Love" section includes photos of and stories about children who died of SIDS.

EMPLOYMENT

America's Job Bank

http://www.ajb.dni.us/index.html

"A product of the public employment service." This site was accessed 209,844,230 times in the six-month period preceding this review. It includes information for employers, job seekers, job market information, and job search tips. Employers can post job openings online and submit their URLs to be linked to from AJB. Job seekers can access a searchable database of jobs. We searched for the key words "social worker nationwide" and received a listing of 201 jobs. This site links to every State Employment Service that has a Web site, 2,608 employers' Web sites, and 654 private placement agencies. It also has a section of information about the job market, where we found social work listed as the 8th highest of the fastest-growing occupations. Internet job search tips are also provided.

Bureau of Labor Statistics—Occupational Outlook Handbook

http://stats.bls.gov/oco/ocos060.htm

This URL takes you to the page on social workers. The listing describes the nature of social work, working conditions, employment statistics, training information, job outlook, and salaries. The BLS Home Page (*http://stats.bls.gov/ocohome.htm*) provides more general information on getting a job, evaluating, job offers, and other helpful tips.

CareerPath

http://www.careerpath.com/

This is a great site for someone who is open to relocating, or who is looking for a job in a particular city. It lists the Sunday job classifieds from 49 newspapers (at the time of this review), including the *New York Times, Washington Post, Orlando Sun, Atlanta Constitution/Journal*, and others. A very popular site, it also offers articles on job search and enhanced features for registered users (there is no cost to register). We searched under the "social services" category for the key words "social worker" and found 141 matches, including 21 in the *Washington Post* and 27 in the *New York Times*. Saves many trips to the library or to newsstands trying to locate hard-to-find out-of-town newspapers.

E-SPAN

http://www.espan.com

E-Span offers employment and job-search information, as well as job listings.

JobWeb

http://www.jobweb.org/

The National Association of Colleges and Employers (NACE) sponsors this site "linking jobs, job seekers, and job-search information." Includes a searchable job listing. We searched for "social work" and got 5 matches nationwide. While the job database itself may not offer too much for social workers, the rest of the site is impressive. It has links to general career planning sites and extensive information for job seekers and for career planning professionals. Full-text articles on résumé-writing, interviewing, and other job search issues can be found on this site. Plan to spend some time here.

Monster Board

http://www.monster.com

This site offers a variety of links to job-search resources and connections to job listings.

National Association of Social Workers (NASW) Joblink
http://www.socialworkers.org/JOB.HTM
This is a searchable, online version of NASW's telephone job line. It lists current social work job listings nationwide.

National Opportunity NOCS
http://www.opportunitynocs.org
This weekly print publication of non-profit jobs was launched in 1986 by The Management Center of San Francisco. It became the most comprehensive listing of jobs in California's health, education, environment, arts, and social services fields, and was then replicated in several other cities. The online database project of this organization was launched in 1998. For a fee (less than it costs for most job posting forums), employers can enter their positions available in either the online database, the printed version, or both. Those seeking jobs can employ an easy-to-use and versatile search engine or can browse by state. The site also includes a number of outstanding resources—such as a career center with résumé advice, and a section of career management resources. Also, there are links to other non-profit resources and a non-profit library.

The New Social Worker Online Career Center
http://www.socialworker.com/career.htm
This sub-site of *The New Social Worker's* larger site offers articles related to social work careers and employment, links to sites for social work job seekers, and current social work job listings. For a small fee, employers can list job openings here.

On-line Career Center
http://www.occ.com/
A non-profit job search home page sponsored by employer organizations. It includes information on companies and job listings.

The Riley Guide
http://www.dbm.com/jobguide
This excellent online book includes everything you need to know to conduct a job search online. It provides extensive guidelines for this method of job searching and *must* be read by anyone considering using the Internet in his or her job search. Also includes links for various career areas.

Social Work and Social Services Jobs Online
http://gwbweb.wustl.edu/jobs/
This is probably the most extensive social work career/job site available. It includes a searchable job listing by location, U.S. and international. Also includes job resource links and career resource links. Employers can submit job postings at no cost through an online submission form. The job is posted within 3 days and stays on the site for 4 weeks. Excellent site for social work job seekers and employers.

USA Jobs
http://www.usajobs.opm.gov/
The United States Office of Personnel Management manages this site on federal jobs. There is a searchable database, which allows searching by educational level, desired salary, and other factors. There is general information about applying for federal jobs, salaries, student employment, federal job scams, a list of jobs by college major (8 job titles listed for social workers), information on various student employment opportunities (i.e., Outstanding Scholars Program, Volunteer Service, Summer Employment, and AmeriCorps). Federal job seekers will find the online application form most helpful.

FAMILIES

American Association for Marriage and Family Therapy
http://www.aamft.org
The AAMFT site includes the full text of the organization's Code of Ethics, articles about ethics, a student resources page, professional development page, and membership application. There's an interesting article comparing marriage and family therapists to those in other related disciplines.

The Baby Center
http://www.babycenter.com/
Business Week chose this site as the one to watch in 1998 and James Coates of the *Chicago Tribune* hailed it "an electronic exemplar of what the binary beat's best and brightest can do to exploit the web to its fullest." The Baby Center brings to a parent's computer screen and home access to the knowledge of leading experts, the support and experience of other parents, current news and resources and even an interactive shopping area—the Internet Baby Store. Even diapers can be ordered and delivered to a parent's door. The "Ask the Experts" section

utilizes people in a variety of fields, a lactation consultant, a family doctor, obstetricians, pediatricians, psychotherapists, and more. One can ask a new question of these experts, or read the answers to questions asked by others. Registered users can personalize their Baby Center Web pages to their own tailored needs.

Blended Family Resource Guide

http://www.blendedfamily.com/blendedfamily/ firstpage.html

This site speaks to the diversity of family groups as we approach the new millennium. Webmaster WooBerry brings stories of personal endeavors to blend children from a previous marriage into a new family setting, while empowering the user with hundreds of useful links to other helpful resources on the web. One of her award winning attractions is her page of Family/Parenting Web rings: Attachment Parenting and the Working Mother, The Ring of Blended Families, The Parent Education Ring, Gay and Lesbian Family Values Webring, The United Families Webring, The Ring of Single Parents, The Ring of Grandparents, Father's World Ring, Parent Soup, Parents Ring, and WorldVillage Citizens Web ring.

Divorce Central

http://www.divorcecentral.com/

This online "service and support center" for the divorced and divorcing, run by the authors of *The Complete Idiot's Guide to Surviving Divorce*, offers legal, financial, and parenting information. A resource room has information on various organizations to help the divorced and divorcing. The Divorce Central Lifeline features a support bulletin board, chat rooms, and FAQ. There are personals ads, e-cafes (chat rooms), singles travel information, an e-mail newsletter, and an online bookstore. The site also includes links to family law statutes by state.

Families Under Construction

http://www.famucon.com

Parent educator and certified marriage and family therapist, Dr. Carolyn Waterbury-Tieman, brings private practice theory to the Internet community from the Kentucky Association for Marriage and Family Therapy. Parental advice columns from a local newspaper and a church newsletter about parenting set the stage for Dr. Waterbury-Tieman's editorial debate of today's therapeutic philosophies. She also encourages visitors to ask questions regarding particular aspects of family life, and displays responses in a "Dear Abby" format.

Federal Office of Child Support Enforcement Home Page

http://www.acf.dhhs.gov/programs/cse

Current information on federal and state reports, policies, and related web sites concerning the collection of child support.

Foster Parents Home Page

http://fostercare.org/FPHP/

This site is designed both as a foster parent online community and as a source of information for actual or potential foster parents. It includes chat areas and bulletin boards, news and articles on various issues in foster parenting, surveys, mentorship opportunities and networking, and a great deal of information on resources both on and offline. There is a section for special needs information. This site is the project of an individual foster parent.

FSANet

http://www.fsanet.org

If you need to find a family service agency in a faraway city, look no further than Family Service America Network's online agency directory, where you can search by agency name, telephone number, service, city, or state. The *FSA News* is updated every Monday, and public policy action alerts and summaries are posted on this site. There is an online catalog of publications, a chat room, and a technology center where FSA members can get two free e-mail addresses. There is also a searchable library service. Several areas of this site can only be accessed by members, and the site's users are required to log in with an ID and password. Non-members can use a visitor ID to view public areas of the site.

National Association of Family Based Services

http://www.nafbs.org

Visitors to this site can post news, announcements, and job opportunities related to family based services. The full text of the organization's newsletter is online. A membership application can be printed out from the site, and there are chat rooms and message boards for board members and other professionals. The NAFBS annual conference announcement is on the site, although it was outdated when we visited.

Parent's Place

http://www.ParentsPlace.com/

This is a major resource for parents offering "ask an expert," live chats with other parents and professionals, resource links, timely news, and more.

Parents Soup

http://www.parentsoup.com/

This is another major parental site. This one emphasizes chats and the online community among members. For example, parents participate in specialized discussions with other parents of similarly-aged children.

Partnership For Family Involvement in Education

http://www.ed.gov/PFIE/

Part of the U.S. Department of Education's home page, this project seeks to "promote children's learning through the development of family-school-community Partnerships." The site includes listings of the thousands of partners sharing information on best practices and how to join. There are articles on timely topics, a calendar of events, and explanations of initiatives. The site offers a framework of shared responsibilities, forums for discussion, and wonderful links to federal publications and programs. Use the site map to locate site documents with ease!

Whole Family Center

http://www.wholefamily.com/

This inviting and unique site with great graphics and cartoons is divided into three "centers"—marriage center, parenting center, and kids and teens center. Real-life dramas are presented in RealAudio, and there is an online soap opera featuring a blended family. Additionally, visitors will find an online magazine, a referral center, self-evaluation tools, a bookstore, and the opportunity to receive a free newsletter. The people who run this site offer e-mail counseling and online courses for a fee. A must see for those working with families!

FUNDING

CASE Fund Raising: Prospect Research

http://192.203.212.6/256/frprspct.htm

This Council for Advancement and Support of Education (CASE) page provides annotated links to sites of interest to fund-raisers who want to do prospect research online.

Foundation Center

http://fdncenter.org/

The Foundation Center online is a comprehensive site offering a variety of services and resources. Answers to questions about corporate fund-raising, non-profit management, and the grantseeking process can be found here. An online librarian is available to answer questions. The site also links to specific resources online for fund-raisers. The Center's annual reports, research, and press releases are posted online as well as a newsletter, *Philanthropy News Digest,* posted weekly. Information about and order forms for books, CD-ROMs, and other material published by the Center are available online. Job openings at the Center are posted, as well as a description of the regular services offered offline. Links are available for grantmakers online. Educational material in full-text at the site include a short course in proposal writing, sample prospect forms, and a *User-Friendly Guide to Funding Research and Education.* The site map and search tools make this site easy to navigate.

Fund-Raising.com

http://www.fund-raising.com/frindex

There are links at this site to organizations and companies that offer products sold as fund-raisers or used as promotional goods for fund-raising campaigns. The site also features an "idea bank" in which visitors can post their ideas for fund-raisers or provide a summary of what has worked for their organizations.

Grants Web

http://Web.fie.com/cws/sra/resource.htm

Grants Web provides an excellent and comprehensive listing of sites announcing grants available in the U.S., Canada, and around the world.

GAY/LESBIAN

The Human Rights Campaign

http://www.hrc.org

The Human Rights Campaign is the nation's largest organization fighting for equal civil rights for lesbians and gay men. HRC's was one of the first sites on the Web to allow readers to find their members of Congress and send them e-mail by simply entering their ZIP codes. HRC goes one step further and gives you the members' biographical information and their voting records on gay and lesbian issues, thus making it easy to tailor your e-mail message for the individual member of Congress. The site also contains other "hands on" resources to make it easy for advocates to get involved, including: an extensive list of events that can be held on "National Coming Out Day" and, in 1997, a Web form to order online an "Ellen" house party kit (to watch the coming out of television comedienne Ellen DeGeneres' sitcom character, and raise money for HRC). HRC reported that the number of house parties registered via the Web equaled the number received from all of its field organizers combined; the Web ended up being an easier and quicker method for reaching advocates nationwide.

The National Gay and Lesbian Task Force
http://www.ngltf.org
The National Gay and Lesbian Task Force is "a leading progressive civil rights organization that has supported grassroots organizing and advocacy since 1973." Its professionally designed site offers a comprehensive online database of state-by-state legislation affecting the gay community. The database can be searched by state, type of legislation (civil rights, hate crimes, health), or by disposition (signed into law, vetoed by governor, died in committee). This is a good example of an organization taking advantage of the Web to provide local advocates with improved access to resources that were previously available only in a more cumbersome paper version.

GOVERNMENT SITES

CapWeb
http://www.capweb.net/
While not an official government site, Capweb was created by two Capitol Hill staffers, and is hosted by Net.Capitol, Inc., a private firm. This is a terrific site for finding out what is happening each day in the U.S. House and Senate. There are general Congressional directory files (many of them searchable), and the House and Senate's committee schedules are posted each week. This site even posts hearing cancellations. This is a good site to visit before heading for Capitol Hill, and a good place to check for your member of Congress's room number, telephone/fax numbers, picture, bio, and the names of senior staff members, too. If you don't know who your Congressperson is, you can perform a search using your ZIP code. There is a convenient form for sending e-mail messages to many members of the House and Senate, as well as tips for making your message effective.

Catalog of Federal Domestic Assistance (General Services Administration)
http://www.gsa.gov/fdac/
"The Catalog of Federal Domestic Assistance (CFDA) is a government-wide compendium of Federal programs, projects, services, and activi-

ties which provide assistance or benefits to the American public. It contains financial and non-financial assistance programs administered by departments and establishments of the Federal government." In short, it is the "Bible" for government grant seekers. Only recently has this information been available free of charge, and the fact that it is searchable makes it doubly attractive to all but those commercial providers who used to charge steeply for this level of access. Seeking funds for a domestic violence program? Our search on the term "domestic violence" yielded almost 100 hits. If you are seeking federal funds for your agency, there is no better place to start than at this site.

Council of State Governments
http://www.csg.org/
"The Council of State Governments is a national, nonpartisan organization that champions excellence and innovation in state government. Founded in 1933, CSG serves all three branches of government through leadership education, research and information services." Surf to this site, and the latest index of issue alerts flashes before your eyes like an electronic billboard at Times Square. You can find files of suggested state legislation, the full text of the organization's monthly publication *State Government News* (put online three months after the issue comes out to regular subscribers), issue alerts (for example, one was online about the tobacco company settlement with the states within five days of the deal being consummated), and press releases. Need to know the political composition of the state house for each state? It's all here, as well as a list of each House and Senate member, district number, and political affiliation.

The Department of Education
http://www.ed.gov/
Here you can find education-related news, funding opportunities, fact sheets on many issues and topics, and full-text newsletters and journals. The "pick 'o the month" chooses three Web sites to feature each month. The site also offers The Educational Resource Information Center (ERIC), a clearinghouse of information about education in the United States (*http://www.aspensys.com/eric/*).

The Department of Health and Human Services
http://www.os.dhhs.gov/
The HHS site is loaded with information, includ-

ing news, fact sheets, and Congressional testimony on health and human services issues; announcements of new HHS programs and initiatives; a link to Healthfinder (see separate review on page 183); and a search function. There is a wealth of information in the employee section—a directory of HHS and HHS agency employees, as well as listings of job openings and student internships in all HHS agencies. There are gateways (links) to related sites. Don't miss HHS on the Web!

Department of Labor

http://www.dol.gov

Right on the home page, you can click on the button "minimum wage" and see useful information about this issue, including a map of the United States showing which states have higher, the same, or lower minimum wage requirements than the federal law. Click on the state and get detailed information. There is a "What Employers Need to Know" file giving information about changes to the Fair Labor Standards Act enacted in 1996. There are plenty of files on the 1996 welfare reform law, which can be accessed from the home page by clicking on the "welfare to work" button. If you are an employer, this is a good site to browse periodically for information about new rules and regulations affecting the workplace.

The Federal Register Online via the Government Printing Office (GPO)

http://www.access.gpo.gov/su_docs/ aces/aces140.html

This site contains the entire *Federal Register*, which is the official federal government publication for agency and department rules and regulations. Here, you can search these databases for the particular document(s) you need, including information about federal grants. Before 1995, this service cost $375 to use. It is publicly available now at no cost. The *Federal Register* includes all published documents from federal agencies, including new regulations, administrative orders, requests for comments and (important for fund-raising purposes) Notices of Funding Availability (NOFAs). Every federal grant is released through a NOFA, which contains all pertinent information on the grant program such as program descriptions, eligibility criteria, submission deadlines, and descriptions on how to obtain application kits.

FedWorld

http://www.fedworld.gov/

FedWorld is a site administered by the National Technical Information Service Technology Administration, U.S. Department of Commerce. It is a shopping mall for government information, providing access to 15,000 files, more than 100 government agencies' databases, and even hourly updates of satellite photos of the east and west coasts of the U.S. You can search abstracts of government reports and order many by credit card. This is a good place to browse for studies, reports, and publications involving your niche.

The Library of Congress

http://lcweb.loc.gov/ and

Thomas

http://thomas.loc.gov/

The Library of Congress has a well-organized and extensive site directing you through the morass of federal government agencies and departments. "Thomas" is a specific project through which much of this is done. Below is a list of some of the things you can find in Thomas or access through Thomas and the Library of Congress:

a) *Bills in Congress.* You can look at the text and other information on bills currently receiving or expected to receive floor action in Congress (*http://thomas.loc.gov/home/hotweek.html*). Bills are typically available within 48 hours of their introduction. Virtually any other bills' and amendments' text and other information can be found here.

b) *The Congressional Record.* Access and follow debates and speeches, searchable by term and browsable by index in various ways.

c) *Committee Reports.* Most, though not all, committee reports are posted here.

d) *Historical Documents.* Find many documents from the Federalist Papers to the Bill of Rights, along with backgrounds and descriptions of them.

e) *The legislative process* and how bills are enacted into laws.

f) Search the U.S. Code and Public Laws (*http:/ /thorplus.lib.purdue.edu:8100/gpo/ GPOAccess.cgi*).

National Governors Association

http://www.nga.org

"As the only bipartisan organization of, by, and for the nation's Governors, NGA provides a forum for Governors to exchange views and experiences. NGA also provides assistance in solving state-focused problems, information on state innovations and practices, and a bipartisan forum for Governors to establish, influence, and implement policy on national issues." The site is colorful, animated, and provides good source material on public policy issues, including NGA position papers (more than 100 when we last checked), and a page devoted to welfare reform that includes statistics, studies, reports, and other valuable primary source material. When the NGA speaks on public policy issues, the White House and Congress listen. And if you engage in advocacy on public policy issues, so should you.

The Office of National Drug Control Policy

http://www.whitehousedrugpolicy.gov/
ONDCP's site features statistics, speeches, press releases, and other information on drug control policy. There is much useful information on prevention and education, including links to other sites, program descriptions, and information for parents. A kids and teens section features "Make-a-Zeen," an online magazine that encourages kids to contribute stories, art, and games. This section was "under construction" when we reviewed it—there was no actual content there yet, but it looked like a great resource with good potential.

U. S. Census Bureau

http://www.census.gov/
The U.S. population increases by one person every 12 seconds. How did we know? We watched the projection of the U.S. population increase by clicking on a population clock linked to the home page of the U.S. Census Bureau. There is a clock for the world population, as well. This searchable Web site is "user-friendly" and fun. In fact, there is a file accessed from the home page called "Just for Fun" that features the Census Bureau's Map Stats, an interactive site that presents statistical profiles for states, congressional districts, and counties as well as detailed maps for counties. Click on your state on a colorful map of the U.S., and link to a map of your state, divided by counties. Click on a county, and view a map that permits you to zoom in and identify thousands of important features. These maps may be downloaded as GIF files (suitable for Web pages). Being on this site is like visiting the Smithsonian— you don't know what to look at first. The page claims to be "your source for social, demographic, and economic information." And it is. There is a cornucopia of

information, including economic indicators, statistics relating to your client base, radio broadcasts, and videoclips. So much Web site and so little time! Is there useful material at the Census Bureau site? More than we can count!

U.S. Code

http://www.law.cornell.edu/uscode
This site is a service of the Legal Information Institute, a part of the Cornell Law School. This searchable database permits you to access the *U.S. Code*, the entire codified body of federal law that has been enacted up to the most recent printing of the Government Printing Office's CD-ROM (which is perhaps 18 months out-of-date at any one time). This site also provides guidance on finding current information (such as using the Library of Congress's Thomas database). Each of the 50 titles of the U.S. Code is available for searching, using a form that permits you to search by a particular section, a popular name, or by keyword. The Institute's site also hosts a page on recent and historic Supreme Court decisions, historical legal documents, and many other databases of interest to the legal community.

The U.S. House of Representatives Home Page

http://www.house.gov/
This colorful and functional home page links to pages that provide the schedule of bills to be considered each week (updated each session day), the current order of business on the House Floor (including a minute-by-minute account of each motion and other action), an annual schedule of dates when Congress is in session (great for planning those Washington lobby days!), holidays when there are no sessions, a target date for when Congress will adjourn, and files about the legislative process. There are plenty of related links on the home page, including links to leadership offices, the Library of Congress's Thomas, C-Span, and the Internet Law Library. You can even take a virtual guided tour of the U.S. Capitol from here. There are links to each of the House's 18 standing committees and the Joint Economic Committee. ***Note****: A new, companion site is available at: http://clerkweb.house.gov.*

The U.S. Senate Home Page

http://www.senate.gov/
The Senate's home page is more compact and better organized than its House counterpart, but has basically the same information. Click on the "Legislative Activities" button and view in-

formation about bills, the Senate's schedule, committee meetings and hearings, and related links. There are files concerning nominations and treaties (one difference between the House's and Senate's Constitutionally mandated duties). "Learning About the Senate" takes you to files about the Senate's history, a virtual tour of the Senate, and a glossary of Senate terms. There are lots of related links, and the entire site is searchable. There are individual pages for Senate Committees and Senate members.

U.S. Supreme Court Decisions from 1930-1975

http://www.fedworld.gov/supcourt
This site accesses the full text of 7,407 U.S. Supreme Court decisions from 1937 to 1975. Decisions are available as ASCII text files. The database can be searched by title or by full text search engine.

The White House

http://www.whitehouse.gov/
This site offers information about the President and Vice President and other resources that might be helpful to you, such as *The Interactive Citizens Handbook*, which contains a link to the Government Information Locator Service (GILS) and other pointers; *The White House Virtual Library*, which contains White House papers, audio versions of speeches, and executive orders; *Commonly Requested Services*, which offers quick information most frequently requested; and *The Briefing Room*, which provides updated daily information on what is happening at the White House, as well as a link to federal statistics.

HEALTH CARE

American Public Health Association

http://www.apha.org/
This organizational site has sections for Legislation and Advocacy; News and Publications; Science, Practice, and Policy; and Public Health and Resources. The legislation and advocacy page includes online copies of testimonies, action alerts, and an online "pledge" form to pledge to do advocacy for the organization's issues. The news and publications section has news releases, and information on the *American Journal of Public Health*. Science, Practice, and Policy includes information on fields of public health, including a mental health special interest group, which has its own site at *http://www.shepscenter.unc.edu/*

apha_mh/apha_mh.html. The Public Health and Resources section has links to other sites.

AMSO Managed Care Forum

http://www.amso.com/
This site, sponsored by a managed care company, is mainly about open discussion relevant to health care and managed care specifically. The main feature of this site is the discussion forums, where individuals can exchange thoughts on managed care, health care reform, cost-cutting, capitation and other issues. The site also organizes opinion polls related to these topics. In addition, the site organizes panels of experts on particular subjects, and there is a useful glossary of managed care terms.

Australian Institute of Health and Welfare

http://www.aihw.gov.au/
"Australia's national agency for health and welfare statistics and information." The site includes a full-text publication on welfare, statistical links for populations of Australia, New Zealand, Canada, and Sweden. Health links include: National Centre for Health Statistics (US); Agency for Health Care Policy and Research (US); Canadian Institute for Health Information; and the National Public Health Partnership.

Band-Aides and Blackboards

http://funrsc.fairfield.edu/~jfleitas/contents.html
Subtitled "When Chronic Illness...Or Some Other Medical Problem...Goes to School," this site is part of the doctoral dissertation of Joan Fleitas, a nursing doctoral candidate at Columbia University. Bright graphics and cute animations accompany personal stories and poetry written by chronically ill children, siblings, and others. There are three sections—kids, teens, and adults. An online story written and illustrated by kids is included, as are tips from experts. There is an informed consent form for parents of children who participate in the project.

Center for Eating Disorders at St. Joseph Medical Center

http://www.eating-disorders.com/
General information is presented, answering such questions as "What is an eating disorder?" and "Do you have an eating disorder?" Symptoms are listed. There are also message boards, which are frequented by people with eating disorders, and there is an "e-mail a doctor" feature. Links to related sites are also included.

Families USA

http://www.familiesusa.org

Families USA "advocates high-quality, affordable health and long–term care for all Americans." The site has plenty of articles and reports on Medicaid, Medicare, managed care, and consumer protection issues relating to health care. There are full reports online and press releases on Medicare, Medicaid, and Health Policy. The design is not particularly pleasing, but the information appears to be the best in the field. Managed care companies are likely to find the information hazardous to their health. There are hundreds of health care-related links, and these are well organized. If you are involved in health care issues, go right to the "Health Policy Links" file, and bookmark it immediately.

Healthfinder

http://www.healthfinder.gov

This U.S. government site started in April 1997 is "a gateway consumer health and human services information Web site." There are searchable links to online resources on every imaginable health care topic. Some examples of the types of links you will find here are libraries (public and medical), news (recent health-related press releases, for example), state health departments, online medical/health journals, online support groups, publications (medical dictionaries, for example), and more. One useful feature is the online guided tours, which are organized by topic and age group. There is too much here to list in a short review. Take a look and see for yourself!

HealthGate

http://www.healthgate.com/HealthGate/home.html

This online source for health, wellness, and biomedical information is operated by HealthGate Data Corporation and funded by advertising space at the site and membership fees. Services include free searches of Medline through the site (*http://www.healthgate.com/HealthGate/MEDLINE/search.shtml*) or nine other databases (at a cost of $14.95/month). Users of HealthGate can register for additional benefits and services. The basic membership is free and allows access to member–only areas and information. The extended membership requires a fee, but gives the user certain additional access and services, including AIDSDRUGS, AIDSLINE, AIDSTRIALS, BIOETHICSLINE, CANCERLIT, and HealthSTAR. HealthGate is also

home to several online magazines and includes a help desk, a user tips page, and a customer service page to assist registered users. One of its services includes the ability to order full-text articles from abstracts that are available online. There is also a Wellness Center (*http://www.healthgate.com/HealthGate/hic/index.html*), "an interactive health information service and community support group for people with chronic or acute health conditions."

The HMO Page

http://www.hmopage.org

Sponsored by Physicians Who Care, this is a wonderful site for those who wish managed care had never been born. Included is a page of HMO humor, the HMO "atrocity of the month," "The Managed Care Hall of Shame," news, legislation, a useful glossary, and almost anything else clinicians might want to know about managed care. In addition, there are patient complaints, physician complaints, links to pro-patient organizations, and a list of acronyms, which, in the alphabet soup world of today, might be very useful. Links to other pages and sites are primarily in one place and are very easy to read. There's not too much specifically mental health HMO information.

Make-A-Wish Foundation

http://www.wish.org/main.htm

The mission of the organization "is to ensure that wishes are granted to children in the United States with life-threatening medical conditions creating the probability the children will not survive beyond their 18th year. [Make-a-Wish accomplishes] this by chartering chapters and providing them with consistent policies, substantive resources, comprehensive training and wholehearted support." The site includes links to files headlined Make-A-Wish Story, Chapter Listing, What Is Make-A-Wish?, How Are Wishes Granted?, How To Donate, Myth Of Craig Shergold Wish (relating to an unauthorized Internet chain letter encouraging people to send business cards to a seriously ill boy), Potpourri Of Wishes, a Frequently-Asked Questions file, Our National Speakers Bureau, Major Make-A-Wish Sponsors, and News Center (organizational press releases).

MedSWIS Software

http://www.medswis.com/

Information on software for case managers and discharge planners in hospitals.

Something Fishy Eating Disorder Site
http://www.something-fishy.com/ed.htm
This site has extensive information on eating disorders, including definitions, signs, symptoms, dangers, and words from "victims." Some sections of the site are in Spanish. You can submit names for a memorial site or buy a CD to raise awareness of eating disorders. There is information on prevention and recovery, stress management, and how to volunteer to help with the site. A bulletin board and discussion list are also featured, and you can download a multi-media presentation designed for schools, doctors, friends, and family members to use.

HIGHER EDUCATION

CSWE Doctoral Student Funding Programs
http://www.cswe.org/MFP.htm
This site gives information on clinical fellowships for doctoral students who will be leaders in mental health and/or substance abuse.

CT (Cyber Towers) Distance Learning Center
http://cybertowers.com/selfhelp/dlc.shtml
This site is "an online resource for the public-at-large and licensed professionals wanting continuing education units. The Center is run completely online and offers courses from HTML basics to self-help type instruction." Course content is posted online (accessed with a student ID and password) and discussed in weekly one-to two-hour sessions in a chat room, although participation in the chat is not mandatory. During the rest of the week, students can access message boards in the Student Lounge, where they can post questions and get to know each other. Instructors also participate regularly in the discussion boards.

Directory of Social Work Faculty
http://www.primenet.com/kids/
This Web site serves as a directory for social work faculty from Alabama A&M University to University of Wisconsin at Milwaukee. Where available, the links provide e-mail connections to the faculty at each of the schools. This site is well organized and divided by state. The site provides access to Canadian, Australian, and British Universities. Information on school of social work rankings is also available.

Graduate Fellowships Newsletter
http://www.grad.nd.edu/gfn/
Stay informed about funding opportunities and other information relevant for graduate fellowships at this site managed by Notre Dame University.

iCollege: the Internet College Consortium
http://www.learnwell.org/~edu/icollege.shtml
This site focuses entirely on online courses, from college level to graduate school level programs. It currently does not include any offerings specifically related to social work, but it is expanding.

Online Study Abroad Directory
http://www.istc.umn.edu/osad/Default.html
This University of Minnesota site offers a search engine for study abroad programs and support sources. Undergraduate and graduate students can specify their interests in research opportunities, classroom, or internships for their area of study, and can select particular locations. The *International Study and Travel Center* (*http://www.istc.umn.edu/*), under which this is run, is organized by a student organization for the benefit of the public. It also includes information about visas and traveling abroad, discussions with people sharing their experiences, and work and volunteer opportunities abroad. The ISTC database has information on more than 200 funding sources and offers advice on other methods of funding such ventures.

Peterson's Education Center
http://www.petersons.com/
An option for researching schools of social work is to use the Peterson's online guide. Peterson's is searchable by terms, so you can find schools by the name of particular faculty, by geographic area, or by area of study. Peterson's also offers an online form for requesting information from the schools. After you fill out the site's "instant reply" form, Peterson's contacts the school's admissions office for you and directs it to send you application material. Peterson's Educational Center also offers a great deal of substance beyond this. Some of its features include a discussion board (*http://www.petersons.com/ugrad/discuss/wwwboard.html*) that appears to be very active in generating conversation among student applicants, a wide variety of related options for educational opportunities, such as summer learning programs (*http://www.petersons.com/features/soss.html*) and Learning "Adventure" programs (*http://www.petersons.com/adventures/*), resources for thinking about financing your education (*http:/*

/www.petersons.com/resources/finance.html), and career services (http://www.petersons.com/career/), from résumé help to job postings.

The Social Science Research Council

http://www.ssrc.org/

The Council provides fellowships and grants for pre-dissertation, dissertation, and postdoctoral studies.

The Student Guide to Financial Aid

http://www.ed.gov/prog_info/SFA/StudentGuide/

A resource from the Department of Education, this site gives the basics on obtaining financial aid. It also offers articles on job search, and enhanced features for registered users. There is no charge to register.

Student Services

http://www.studentservices.com

A database of scholarships, grants, fellowships, and loans. Type in your major and get back a list of resources. We got three listings for social work, but when we clicked on "more," we got a form to submit for more information on the company's services, including a no-obligation information packet from a lending institution for student loans.

Uniguide Academic Guide to the Internet

http://www.aldea.com/guides/ag/attframes2.html

This site, formerly funded by the National Science Foundation, and currently owned and administered by Aldea Communications, is geared especially toward the higher education community. Sites are listed and described in various academic categories, including social, behavioral, and economic sciences. One feature is a Community Commentary, where users of the guide can comment on the academic value of a listed site.

HOMELESSNESS/HOUSING

Habitat for Humanity International

http://www.habitat.org/

Habitat for Humanity International is a nonprofit, ecumenical Christian housing ministry dedicated to eliminating substandard housing and homelessness. Best known for former President Jimmy Carter's active participation (one file on the site tells the story of his involvement), the organization has an online store/catalog (orders are taken by an 800 number rather than online), a "news" site of organization press releases, and a searchable database of organizational affiliates. This site also solicits donations and provides information about volunteer opportunities. It is a pleasant, functional site, with additional versions in Spanish and French.

National Coalition for the Homeless

http://nch.ari.net/

Fact sheets on homelessness, legislative alerts, and links to other sites are a few features of this graphically pleasing site. Especially useful features include an online library that readers can search or browse and online directories of national, state, and local housing/homeless organizations and street newspapers. There is information about ordering NCH publications by mail.

North American Street Newspaper Association

http://www.speakeasy.org/nasna/

Information about the street newspaper movement and links to related sites.

Real Change Homeless Newspaper

http://www.speakeasy.org/realchange/

Includes articles from Seattle's homeless newspaper, *Real Change.* There is a street newspaper organizing manual, as well as links to other sites. An interesting and enlightening feature is Hobson's Choice, an online game about what it's like to be homeless. It took a long time for graphics to load on this site.

HUNGER

HungerWeb

http://www.hunger.brown.edu/Departments/World_Hunger_Program/

"The aim of this site is to help prevent and eradicate hunger by facilitating the free exchange of ideas and information regarding the causes of, and solutions to, hunger. It contains primary information, made available by the World Hunger Program—the prime sponsor of this site—and its partners, as well as links to other sites where information of relevance to hunger can be found." The World Hunger Program is part of the Watson Institute of International Studies at Brown University. The site is indexed, and has a file accessed from the home page introducing the issues of hunger and malnutrition. The pages are organized under the general headings of Research (institutions, research results, and major hunger-related data sources), Field Work (non-governmental organizations, UN agencies, situation updates, and reference materials), Advocacy and Policy (organizations and materials, upcoming legislation), and Education and Training (training materials for hunger education at all levels). Little information is provided on these pages other than links to organizations with pages that have valuable material. Some substantive material (particularly on international hunger issues) was available from the World Hunger Program Web site.

Results

http://www.action.org
An international citizen's lobby fighting hunger and poverty. Legislative briefings are available and include relevant calls to action.

INTERNET SEARCH ENGINES AND DIRECTORIES

AccuFind

http://www.nln.com/
AccuFind is a useful site if you need to use more than one search engine. AccuFind allows you to search with one engine and then instantly search with another without taking the time to go to the other's actual search site. It is a little tricky to use but, with practice, is very valuable for comprehensive searching.

Alta Vista

http://altavista.digital.com/
A popular search engine (not directory), Alta Vista features the ability to search either the Web or newsgroups separately. It gives you the option to decide how much information you want about each Web site it finds for you. A search in Alta Vista is likely to yield thousands of resources. It is best to narrow your search as much as possible when using this powerful search tool.

Catalist

http://www.lsoft.com/lists/listref.html
This is the official catalog of LSOFT LISTSERV mailing lists. A search on the term "social work" gave us 20 lists, ranging in size from 1 subscriber to 398.

Excite

http://www.excite.com/
Excite is both a directory and a search engine and gives options of searching the Web, the Excite directory only, Usenet newsgroups, and

Usenet classified. There is also a newstracker. In addition to its directory, Excite has organized a variety of "tours" based on particular topics. If you desire, you can organize your own tour connecting a set of sites related to a particular topic, and can submit it to Excite for inclusion in its tour directory. Excite also allows you to create a personalized page similar to Yahoo!'s. Excite's "Citynet" offers you an opportunity to find information on most metropolitan areas, and its "Reviews" section evaluates various sites for the quality of information they offer. The Excite search engine is fairly large, and it scores sites, orders them by confidence level (showing you the top ten sites), and provides a summary. A unique feature is that Excite gives a "more like this site" option, so you can expand your search beyond your original search terms to find other sites containing similar content.

InfoSeek

http://www.infoseek.com/
In addition to English, it also includes a directory in Spanish, French, German, and Japanese. InfoSeek features the ability to search by a phrase (e.g., entering a question rather than just the words). It also gives you a value rating or "score" for each page it finds (e.g., 38%) to tell you the "confidence level" that it matches your inquiry. Factors that affect the score include the frequency with which your term appears, and the proximity of it to the top of the page. The sites it finds are ordered according to these scores. InfoSeek has an enormous database. If your first search yields too many sites, you can refine your results by searching again (with a narrower focus) within the sites identified.

Infoseek also offers a unique service in the ability to perform "specialized searches" such as:

1. searching just for pictures or graphic images.
2. limiting your search to a word or phrase in a particular Web site only.
3. searching for pages with a link to a particular Web site (e.g., so that you can find out how many people have made links to your Web page).
4. searching only the URLs on the Web or the title lines.
5. NetClock: a search engine and directory of events happening on the Internet, such as audio broadcasts and celebrity discussions.

Liszt's Directory

http://www.liszt.com/

Liszt's Directory is a leading directory and search engine of mailing lists and newsgroups.

Lycos

http://www.lycos.com/

Like Yahoo, Lycos offers scores of useful services, including searching for pictures and sounds, and providing content such as news, sports, and financial information (and more than a dozen other categories, as well). This is one of the better places to begin surfing the Web.

Magellan

http://www.mckinley.com/

Magellan is run by Excite, but offers an even more expansive database. It features Web reviews, news, stock quotes, sports, weather, and other categories of information.

TILE.NET/Lists

http://tile.net/listserv/

Tile.net is an excellent search engine and is well-organized for finding appropriate mailing lists and newsgroups.

Yahoo! *http://www.yahoo.com/*

Yahoo! is both a search engine and a directory. If you are trying to find something on the Internet, Yahoo! provides a one-two punch, and automatically searches Alta Vista if a search of Yahoo! does not turn up much. With news, weather, sports, people finder, maps, and other services, this site is simply one of the best for finding information on the Internet.

MEN'S ISSUES

The Fatherhood Project

http://www.fatherhoodproject.org/

This site provides information on publications available from The Fatherhood Project, a national research and education program of the Families and Work Institute. There are also links to other useful sites on fatherhood.

The Men's Issues Page

http://www.vix.com/men/

As part of the World Wide Web Virtual Library, this page's mission is to "cover the several men's movements encyclopediacally." It provides a comprehensive reference list of men's movement books, periodicals, organizations, Web links, and other resources. It also addresses such topics as domestic violence, false accusations, men's health, fatherhood and fatherlessness, single fatherhood, men's friendships, romance, and sexual harassment.

Sexual Abuse of Males: Prevalence, Lasting Effects, and Resources

http://www.jimhopper.com/male-ab

This is one of the few sites we have found dealing with this topic. The author, a psychologist, offers this page as a way to help those looking for Web resources on the sexual abuse of boys, to inform men who were sexually abused as boys but who might look for this information in scholarly journals or books, and to help people understand how researchers come up with statistics on child sexual abuse.

MENTAL HEALTH

American Counseling Association

http://www.counseling.org/

ACA has more than 55,000 members who, along with anyone else, can benefit from this Web site's information. This information includes news of educational programs and workshops by state, date, and topic. Visitors can access resources from the ACA, keep apprised of the latest news and developments in the field, and can read the full text of selected articles from *Counseling Online* (*http://www.counseling.org/ctonline/*), a professional journal.

American Mental Health Alliance

http://www.mental-health-coop.com

This is the web site of the American Mental Health Alliance, a "growing national alliance of over 2,000 mental health professionals," which was developed as an alternative to managed care. There is useful information without being pushy about a truly ethical practice model for clinicians; the site also includes an excellent consumer-oriented article on choosing a therapist. However, there is too much to read and absorb on the screen without printing it out. The site is textually overwhelming, and when it prints out, the material doesn't always fit on the width of a typical 8½ x 11 page. Nevertheless, mental health clinicians ought to visit this page as part of any exploration of managed care alternatives.

American Mental Health Counselors Association

http://pie.org/amhca

This simple but functional site includes membership information for this organization of professionals with a master's in counseling or a closely related discipline. A section on legislative information was empty when we did this review. Membership and publication order forms are included on the site.

Bazelon Center for Mental Health Law

http://www.bazelon.org/

The Bazelon Center is "the leading national legal advocate for people with mental illness and mental retardation." This organization seeks reform in the areas of housing, health care, and support services. The Center's site features action alerts describing legislative updates and proposals. The site also contains a large volume of substantive information on advocacy in this area. It also contains resources and text of the Americans with Disabilities Act.

Behavior Online

http://www.behavior.net/index.html

This membership-based online community focuses on communication and planned discussions with professionals in mental health and the applied social and behavioral sciences. Most of the discussion forums are organized in the same format as a Usenet discussion group. The limitation of participation to professionals, however, makes it particularly useful in this regard. Behavior Online is also working to establish online classes in the near future.

The Bipolar Information Network

http://www.moodswing.org/index.shtml

This site links to online support groups, chats, and mailing lists relating to bipolar disorder. It also includes an FAQ about the illness, an online bulletin board, bookstore, a weekly chat, and information on how to contact advocacy and support groups.

The Bipolar Kids Page

http://www.geocities.com/EnchantedForest/ 1068/

This page consists of bipolar-related links for kids, families, and schools.

Dr. Bob's Psychopharmacology Tips

http://uhs.bsd.uchicago.edu/dr-bob/tips/ tips.html

This extensive site lists and describes psychotropic medications. It has a number of psychopharmacology tips posted by members of the Interpsych psycho-pharm discussion list run by

Ivan Goldberg, M.D., and information sent to the site developer, Robert Hsiung, M.D., University of Chicago. The site is intended as a resource, and comes with a disclaimer aimed at patients. There is an efficient search engine and a list of other psychopharmacology links. There's also a page of questions from patients about various medications, which the doctors answer. The information is useful, easy to find, and not too technical.

Dual Diagnosis Web Site

http://www.erols.com/ksciacca/

This site focuses on those with dual diagnoses involving mental illness, drug addiction, and/or alcoholism. Its interactive features include a bulletin board, chat room, mailing list, and guestbook. There are links to other related sites. A directory of dual diagnosis programs, "being upgraded," could not be found when we reviewed the site. Published by Sciacca Comprehensive Service Development for Mental Illness, Drug Addiction, and Alcoholism (MIDAA), the site also includes information on events, presentations, videos, and publications by Kathleen Sciacca, as well as an order form that can be printed out. There are some full-text articles written by Sciacca and other professionals.

Internet Depression Resources Page

http://earth.execpc.com/~corbeau/

This is an annotated listing, with links, of newsgroups, mailing lists, and Web pages related to depression. It has won several awards, including Grohol Best of Web MH, Starting Point Choice Award, Netpsych.com Cutting Edge Site, MHNet 4 stars, and Luckman Award 4 star.

Mental Health Net

http://www.cmhc.com/

This comprehensive mental health site is one of the most impressive we have seen. It includes an online magazine, *Perspectives*, and a humor page of mental health/psychology jokes. Readers can vote online on various poll questions, and can rate linked sites with a "thumbs up" or "thumbs down" vote. The site features more than 6,500 individual resources on disorders such as depression, anxiety, panic attacks, chronic fatigue syndrome, and substance abuse, as well as professional resources in psychology, psychiatry, and social work. This site offers a clinician's yellow pages that allows clinical social workers to register for referral purposes. Currently 600 people are registered. Rates are $40/year for an individual and $80/year for a group practice.

Mentalwellness.com—For Patients, Families, and Caregivers

http://www.mentalwellness.com

This site is a service of Janssen Pharmaceutica, Inc. It provides a few links to mental health sites, news stories from Reuters, a listing of mental health organizations and how to contact them, and a reference room with a not-so-extensive glossary of mental health terms. It also offers information about Janssen programs and services, as well as articles such as "What Do We Really Know About Schizophrenia?"

Milton's InterPsych Page

http://141.214.71.83/web/intpsych/

"InterPsych is a non-profit making, voluntary organization, established on the Internet with the aim of promoting international scholarly collaboration on inter-disciplinary research and intervention efforts in the field of psychopathology. The organization offers a variety of scholarly electronic conferences via e-mail, and real time conferences. Plans are underway for an electronically distributed journal." This site provides a listing of "scholarly electronic conferences" (mailing lists) and instructions for joining them, real-time conferences, and the Interpsych Newsletter (distributed by mailing list). The site appears not to have been updated in quite some time, so some of the information may not be current.

The Mining Company Mental Health Resources

http://mentalhealth.miningco.com

The Mining Company is a collection of comprehensive sites/online communities on virtually every subject. The Mental Health site has a little of everything—articles about mental illnesses, a mental health search function, links to professional and consumer sites, 24-hour chat with special events scheduled, a mental health bookstore, and more. This site is very comprehensive and informative—a real "goldmine."

Mood Disorders Page

http://avocado.pc.helsinki.fi/~janne/mood/mood.html

This site includes a comprehensive Depression FAQ originally developed by Cynthia Frazer for the newsgroup *alt.support.depression.*

National Coalition of Mental Health Professionals and Consumers, Inc.

http://www.execpc.com/~mastery/coalitionMain.html

This is the web site of the National Coalition of Mental Health Professionals and Consumers, Inc., a grassroots organization devoted to developing alternatives to managed care with the idea of eventually replacing it. The coalition is, "dedicated to fighting the negative impact of managed care on both clients and professionals, while advocating fair and reasonable health care reform." Pages include a legislative action site, a link to the editor of the coalition's newsletter, a lobby kit, a petition for legislators, and lists of regional chapters of the organization. The coalition has developed some creative ideas to replace managed care, many of which are set forth on the site. The site also provides a way of keeping up to date with the latest news on the struggle for health care reform, but the typeface used on the site is small and faint, making it difficult to read. It's far easier to read if you print it out. The last update of the site appears to be June 1997, although the material is still useful.

The National Mental Health Services Knowledge Exchange Network

http://www.mentalhealth.org/

The National Mental Health Services Knowledge Exchange Network (KEN) "provides information about mental health via toll-free telephone services, an electronic bulletin board, and publications. The National Center for Mental Health Services developed KEN for users of mental health services and their families, the general public, policy makers, providers, and the media." There is information on the site on prevention, treatment, and rehabilitation services for mental illness. Features include a calendar of events, statistical information on mental health, a publication list, and information on supported agencies and research centers. There are also online databases, including a mental health directory that contains more than 18,000 organizations and a consumer/survivor database. This site is a service of the U.S. Department of Health and Human Services, Substance Abuse and Mental Health Services Administration, Center for Mental Health Services.

Pendulum Resources—Pendulum Pages
http://www.pendulum.org
The Pendulum Pages contain many articles relating to bipolar disorder, as well as writings (poetry and essays) by "Pendulees." There is medication information, a support page with links to support resources, and a humor section. The site also features an online bookstore.

Psych Central
http://www.grohol.com/
This award-winning site, developed by John Grohol, Psy.D., provides extremely comprehensive annotated (and sometimes rated) links to mental health-related mailing lists, newsgroups, and Web sites, both for consumers and for professionals. The *Page One* section is an online magazine, with such articles as "Starting a New Online Support Group," "FAQ of Life," and "Distinctions Between Therapists' Degrees." Dr. Grohol hosts three weekly chats for discussion of mental health issues. You can also find book reviews and links to suicide-related resources here.

PsychScapes Worldwide Inc.
http://www.mental-health.com/
PsychScapes' strength is in its searchable databases of mental health conferences and workshops, therapists, products and services (several searches in this and the speakers' category yielded nothing, though), and speakers. Also includes career opportunities in mental health, previews of related publications, and news items.

The Schizophrenia Home Page
http://www.schizophrenia.com/
This site has extensive information for people with schizophrenia, family and friends, researchers and professionals, and students/writers/authors. There are full-text newsletters online and discussion areas/chat rooms on the site. Brian Chiko, whose brother John suffered from schizophrenia and committed suicide in 1995, started this "virtual nonprofit organization." A very good site.

Self-Help and Psychology Magazine Online
http://cybertowers.com/selfhelp/
While this site bills itself as an online magazine, resources such as its distance learning class, professional zone, and discussion zones make this also characteristic of other professional community sites.

U.S. National Institute of Mental Health
http://www.nimh.nih.gov
The Web site contains up–to–date information, including a reading room, with English and Spanish versions of documents containing specific information on mental health disorders. Conference information, both recent and from as long as 10 years ago, is available, as well as order forms for publications and research reports.

NON-PROFIT/ASSOCIATION MANAGEMENT

American Society of Association Executives (ASAE)
http://www.asaenet.org
ASAE, founded in 1920, is the professional association of more than 23,000 non-profit association executives and their suppliers of products and services. The home page is designed to encourage you to return again and again; it is updated each week with important, breaking news of concern to its membership. Its "CEO Center" is for members only, but click on the "Government Affairs" icon and you will find action alerts on issues of importance to associations. There is the usual information about publications and membership information, and a gateway to the association's members.

The Internet Nonprofit Center
http://www.nonprofits.org
This site has been available since 1994 and was initially sponsored by the American Institute of Philanthropy. It has spun off as an independent non-profit corporation. The home page boasts that it has "information on more nonprofits than any other site in the world!" This is not hyperbole. It is clearly one of the most comprehensive and aesthetically pleasing Internet Web sites for non-profits. The home page is divided into four sections:

Gallery of Organizations—features a non-profit locator to find almost any charity in the United States, a site for home pages of many non-profits, and information on how new non-profits can join.

Library—includes publications and data about non-profits and the non-profit sector compiled by third parties, and also includes files of ethical standards published by the National Charities Information Bureau and the New York Philanthropic Advisory Services organization.

Parlor—links to a site for live "chat," back issues of *Non-Profit News,* files on how to prepare World Wide Web pages, and how to find free or reduced space to post non-profit home pages.

Heliport—provides links to other Internet sites useful to non-profits.

Peter Drucker Foundation for Nonprofit Management

http://www.pfdf.org/
Founded in 1990 by Peter Drucker, *the* name in non-profit management, the site provides information about conferences, publications, awards bestowed by the Foundation, fellowships offered and, of course, information about how to purchase Drucker's best-selling non-profit management books and publications.

PERSONAL WEB PAGES

Christian Marcel Itin's Web Site

http://www.du.edu/~citin/welcome.html
Itin is an assistant professor at the University of Denver Graduate School of Social Work, and his major interest area is adventure-based practice. The site reflects this interest, including information and links related to the topic, as well as an adventure-based therapy chat room. When we reviewed the site, Itin was conducting a qualitative research project through use of an online survey on social work and adventure-based practice. Another feature of the site is a listing, with links, of social workers and others involved in this area of practice.

Deb Smyre's Home Page

http://www.primenet.com/~dsmyre/
This is a nicely done personal home page of an undergraduate social work student. Smyre focuses her site on the issues of adoption, diversity, genealogy, health, HIV, AIDS, social work, gardening, engineering (her husband's profession), and her family. Nice graphics.

The Social Worker

http://onlinemac.com/users/anthonyvg/
This is Anthony Gagliardo's page of social work and other links. Anthony is a social worker and computer consultant in Eugene, Oregon. The links on this site are not as comprehensive as some other sites, but there are some interesting categories—Oregon, Neurolinguistic Programming, Reference, Substance Abuse, Software,

Federal Government, Entertainment, Search, and Adolescent/Gang.

Marson and Associates

http://www2.nconline.com/marson/index.html
This is the site of Steve Marson, director of the social work program at the University of North Carolina at Pembroke. He includes on the site links related to aging, social work, legal issues, political issues, and personal favorites.

Michael Shernoff's Web Site

http://members.aol.com/therapysvc/index.html
Shernoff is an openly gay social worker with a private psychotherapy practice. His site features the full texts of numerous articles (published) he has written on such topics as AIDS/HIV, gay male lifestyles, and counseling/psychotherapy. There is a list of books he has edited or co-edited, as well as a list of links to gay/lesbian/HIV/AIDS sites. A gold mine of writings by this prolific and talented social worker/writer.

Pat McClendon's Clinical Social Work Home Page

http://www.ClinicalSocialWork.com
This site includes many articles McClendon and others have written relating to trauma. She has extensive social work links, information on trauma and dissociative/post-traumatic stress symptomatology, Kentucky resources and therapists (she's in Kentucky), treatment modalities, chronic fatigue syndrome, HTML/Web development, and more.

Tom Cleereman's Social Work Site

http://www.sparknet.net/~tjcleer/
Tom Cleereman is a social work student whose site features information on criminal thinking errors and defense mechanisms, social work jokes, a social services page with links to relevant articles, and links to social work sites. Cleereman also has a social work chat room on the site, which he has encouraged other sites to link to. He also created the Social Work Web Ring, which includes his own site and others, in December 1997.

PUBLICATIONS

The Advocate's Forum

http://www.chas.uchicago.edu/ssa/advocates_forum.html
This is an online version of *The Advocate's Fo-*

rum, a print journal that is managed and written by social work students at the University of Chicago School of Social Service Administration. At the time of this review, the site included the full text of articles from Volumes 1 (1994) to Volume 4, Number 2 (Spring 1998). Topics of articles range from welfare reform to surviving the working world after graduation.

Age and Aging
http://www.oup.co.uk/ageing/contents/
Age and Aging is an international journal relating to geriatric medicine and gerontology. The Web site provides searchable abstracts of articles from January 1996 onward. This page is an example of numerous similar journal sites published by Oxford Journals, such as the *British Journal of Social Work* and the *Journal of Refugee Studies*. Information on subscriptions and article submissions is also available.

Alcohol Alert
http://silk.nih.gov/silk/niaaa1/publication/alalerts.htm
This site provides full-text articles from a quarterly bulletin of the National Institute on Alcohol Abuse and Alcoholism. Each issue focuses on a single topic, such as college drinking, alcohol violence and aggression, and alcohol and tobacco.

American Medical Association (AMA) Journals
http://www.ama-assn.org/scipub.htm
This site is an index to AMA publications, including *JAMA, American Medical News*, and the *Archives of Family Medicine, General Psychiatry, Women's Health*, and others. In each case, the tendency is to provide abstracts and the current table of contents for each issue, along with subscription information for those interested in obtaining the printed version. However, in some cases, such as *JAMA*, there are online services (typically available at an additional cost) for accessing the full text of archived issues. In many other cases, however, the full text of selected articles is available for free online.

The American Prospect Online
http://epn.org/prospect.html
"A Journal for the Liberal Imagination," edited by Paul Starr and Robert Kuttner. It offers full-text articles, archived articles, and subscription information. This site touches on a variety of social justice issues from a liberal perspective.

American Psychological Association (APA) Journals
http://www.apa.org/journals/
The APA produces dozens of journals on topics such as mental health, research, and public policy, and the site is a guide to these, usually with tables of contents, abstracts of articles, and subscription information. Substantial information is reserved for member access only. The *APA Monitor Online* (*http://www.apa.org/monitor/*), however, is a full-text publication available at the site. Begun in March 1995, this publication offers a great deal of content on a wide variety of issues. It also provides a classified section for finding positions available by state. In addition to its Newsline and featured articles, each issue includes several regular departments, including a calendar of events, information about people in the field, and a judicial notebook.

Child and Adolescent Psychiatry
http://www.priory.co.uk/psychild.htm
Child and Adolescent Psychiatry Online is a journal adapted to the nature of Internet communication, information access, and learning. In this regard, it seeks to be a continuing education source, and to emphasize shared information, accepting contributions in a variety of forms (articles, stories, and examples) from practitioners worldwide and covering topics that fit within the broadest possible definition of child and adolescent psychiatry. Archived articles are organized by subject matter, such as Affective Disorders, Debates, Editorial, Epidemiology and Public Health Issues, Personality Issues, Substance Abuse, and Reader Surveys. Readers can respond and, although not every letter is published at the site, every one is considered for publication. These include substantive letters, as well as general comments and questions posed to others. This feature makes the site nicely interactive. Other features of the site include an online bookstore, a list of resources on the Web reviewed by the editors, and a notice board of events.

Child Welfare Review
http://www.childwelfare.com/kids/news.htm
This is "an electronic journal that brings together current papers on important topics in child welfare. Many of the articles are located at Web sites around the world. The links to the articles allow quick access to these papers." Also on the site are original articles, reports, policy studies, thought pieces, and book reviews from a variety of contrasting perspectives. The goal is to col-

lect the most important papers on child welfare subjects located on the Web into one place. Topics covered in this online publication are Child Abuse, Foster Care, Welfare Reform and Children, and Child Poverty and Inequality.

Counseling Online

http://www.counseling.org/ctonline/
This is a full-text online version of selected articles from this journal by the American Counseling Association. It contains current and archived articles relating to a wide variety of clinical social work and counseling issues and practices.

The Electronic Newsstand

http://www.enews.com/
"The Electronic Newsstand is the Web's premiere magazine site. Founded in 1993, it was also one of the first content-based sites on the Internet." With a colorful, animated, frame-utilizing home page, The Electronic Newsstand is the virtual home for more than 2,000 magazines. Most provide sample articles, and some provide their entire contents. You can usually find bargain subscription prices here and you can order them online using a credit card. This searchable site provides archives that can be searched as well. There are links to the home pages of many of the magazines featured. This is a good site to do research, or just browse (and there is no store clerk hovering over you annoyed that you are reading but not buying).

The Future of Children

http://www.futureofchildren.org/
This journal site, sponsored by the Center for the Future of Children, the David and Lucile Packard Foundation, makes available each volume online in full text, providing you have Acrobat Reader to read them. Recent issues have included: *The Juvenile Court*—Vol. 6, No. 3, Winter 1996; *Financing Child Care*—Vol. 6. No. 2, Summer/Fall 1996; *Special Education for Children with Disabilities*—Vol.6, No.1 Spring 1996; *Long-Term Outcomes of Early Childhood Programs*—Vol.5, No.3 Winter 1995; *Critical Issues for Children and Youth*—Vol.5, No.2 Summer/Fall 1995; and *Low Birth Weight*—Vol.5, No.1 Spring 1995

Idea Central

http://epn.org/idea/
This virtual magazine, created by Paul Starr and the Electronic Policy Network (see *http://epn.org/*), actually consists of four online magazines—the Health Policy Page (*http://epn.org/idea/health.html*), the Civic Participation Page (*http://epn.org/idea/civic.html*), the Economics and Politics Page (*http://epn.org/idea/economy.html*), and Welfare and Families (*http://epn.org/idea/welfare.html*).

Habit Smart

http://www.cts.com/~habtsmrt/
This site contains numerous and lengthy articles on the subject of addiction, a self-scoring alcohol check-up, and cognitive therapy pages. Also, a family page features online stories for kids and articles for parents. There is little in the way of graphics here—the site is heavy on information.

Journal of Social Work Practice

http://www.carfax.co.uk/jsw-ad.htm
Only subscription information is online—no full or abstracted articles.

Medical Matrix

http://www.medmatrix.org/index.asp
"Ranked, Peer-Reviewed, Annotated, Updated, Clinical Medicine Resources." This site is a premier Web site that includes access to not only full-text journals, but also to complete online textbooks, forums, patient education areas, news, and more on medicine.

NASW Press

http://www.naswpress.org/
The books, journals, and reference works of the NASW Press can be explored and purchased at this nicely designed and easy-to-navigate site. A section on 'Tools for Authors' provides everything an author needs for publishing in any of the NASW forums, from how to submit articles and books for publication to the policies and practices that apply and guide the publication process. The publicity pages section includes information about books currently being written and the dates they are scheduled to go to press.

The New Social Worker

http://www.socialworker.com
This is an online version of the print magazine for social work students and recent graduates. Besides providing the full text of some articles from each issue, the site includes tables of contents of past and current issues, and information on subscribing, writing for, and advertising in the magazine. There is an online career cen-

ter, including current job listings. You will also find links to other social work sites. Interactive features of this colorful site include a "Social Work Careers Chat" and an active message board focusing on social work careers.

NonProfit Times On-line

http://www.nptimes.com/
The online version of *NonProfit Times* includes the full text of lead articles in a newspaper style format. A "teamworks" section provides a discussion forum for topics in non-profit management and fund-raising.

Page One, by Psych Central

http://www.grohol.com/pageone.htm
This online article source welcomes contributions from the field, which are then posted at the site.

Perspectives

http://www.cmhc.com/perspectives/
This mental health online magazine is published every other month exclusively on the Web. No print or e-mail version of this electronic journal is available. Submissions are invited from professionals or laypeople.

Philanthropy Journal On-line

http://www.philanthropy-journal.org/
Philanthropy Journal is a non-profit newspaper for the non-profit sector. The entire site is searchable. There is a chat discussion area with frequent guest speakers, and the transcripts of their comments are posted. There is job information, a "National Headlines" icon that links to alerts and news of interest, a free e-mail newsletter called *Philanthropy Alert* with breaking news of interest to the non-profit sector, and lots of links. There is a link to a *Meta-Index of Nonprofit Organizations*, which provides one-stop shopping for non-profit links. The foundation section, for example, has links to 110 foundations and six regional associations of grantmakers, as well as 21 mailing lists. There are additional categories relating to government sources and media.

Psyche News International

http://www.cmhc.com/pni/
"*Psychnews International* is an electronic publication distributed monthly (except for combined August-September and December-January issues) devoted to issues in psychology, psychiatry and the social sciences." It is distributed via e-mail mailing list (send e-mail to listserv@listserv.nodak.edu, and in the body of

message, type SUBSCRIBE PSYCHNEWS YOURFIRSTNAME YOURLASTNAME). The publication is also available at the Web site.

Psychotherapy Finances

http://199.190.86.8/psyfin/pfintro.htm
This web site belongs to *Psychotherapy Finances*, the practice management newsletter. In addition to access to articles from the newsletter, this site offers you, if you're a clinician, the chance to list yourself and your practice (in 50 words or less) on the Web site. Then, visitors to the page can search by state or name, and perhaps you'll get a referral. We personally know of one clinician who did. This site boasts a broad array of useful practice management materials; in addition, free back issues are offered. There is helpful managed care information. However, the site is a little clumsy to navigate. Articles you can read on the Web site are from issues at least six months before we visited it for this review.

Social Research Update

http://www.soc.surrey.ac.uk/sru/Sru.html
This full-text journal, edited by Nigel Gilbert, has been published online since the March 1993 issue. The articles usually cover topics of general interest to the social researcher, although some are specific for the U.K.

Social Service Review

http://www.journals.uchicago.edu/SSR/
This site provides information about *Social Service Review*, a journal published by the University of Chicago Press. Included on the site at the time of this review are Tables of Contents beginning in 1996, and author and subject indexes for 1990-1995. Guidelines are provided for submission of manuscripts. Subscription rates, advertising rates, and reprint request information are also online. An online order form was "under construction" at the time of this review.

Who Cares

http://www.whocares.org
Who Cares, launched in 1993, is a national quarterly magazine devoted to community services and activism. Lycos awarded it one of its top 5% Web sites. It has a searchable resource directory database, a national calendar of events, workshops and services, full text of back issues and, of course, subscription information. (Note: As this book went to press, the *Who Cares* site

was undergoing a major revision. All the above information had been removed, and there was only contact information, with an announcement to watch for changes in the coming weeks.)

The Wounded Healer Journal

http://idealist.com/wounded_healer/
This electronic journal, maintained by social worker Linda Chapman, is an excellent resource for psychotherapists and survivors of abuse and trauma.

RACE/ETHNICITY

Asian American Resources

http://www.mit.edu:8001/afs/athena.mit.edu/ user/i/r/irie/www/aar.html
Asian American Resources is a Web site that offers a variety of services and references for Asian–Americans and anyone who is interested in learning about and becoming an active participant within the Asian–American communities. This site provides fast access to the latest calendar of events, clubs and organizations, and media resources, relating to art, bands, literature and magazines, music, theatre and video/film. This site includes an "AAR Guestbook," where you can leave your comments/messages and e-mail addresses for the Internet community visitors to this site. AAR also features ongoing forums for those interested.

The Black Information Network

http://www.bin.org/
This site lists organizations, businesses, and family and educational information, as well as events. It includes news, discussions, opinions, and employment information from participants and invites communication among participants.

Chicano Latino Net

http://latino.sscnet.ucla.edu
This is a free service for the Internet community, supported by UCLA, volunteers, and other organizations. The site is aimed at both those seeking Chicano/Latino resources and students and faculty who work or study in this area. The site includes a library of papers, articles, and other works and material, as well as online accessible databases of materials and people (some are still under development). There is a "Community Center" with information on culture, demographics, education, housing, social service resources, and more. There are also "centers" for employment, conferences, research, statis-tics, and classes. There is a "Student Center" listing documents, details of events, and organizations at various schools and universities.

Indian Education and Research Network

http://www.doe.ernet.in/
Project ERNET is a computer-networking project for 700 research and educational institutions in India. For 70,000 users, it provides e-mail, connection to the World Wide Web, and other Internet functions.

Maven—The Virtual Know-It-All

http://www.maven.co.il
An A-Z guide to Jewish resources online.

MSBET

http://www.msbet.com/home.html
A joint venture between the Black Entertainment Television Network and Microsoft. The site invites participation in chat forums, celebrations of black culture and history, and encourages the use of Internet technology in the African–American community. There is a Teen Summit online, as well as online information on the magazine *Emerge*.

National Indian Child Welfare Association

http://www.nicwa.org/
This organizational site includes information on membership (with a printable application), publications, conferences, and workshops. There are public policy updates, and information on the Indian Child Welfare Act of 1978 is included. You will also find links to Native American-related sites here.

Native American Resources

http://www.pitt.edu/~lmitten/indians.html
This site is the effort of Lisa Mitten, a mixed-blood Mohawk urban Indian who works as a librarian for the University of Pittsburgh. The site's goal is to link individual Native Americans, as well as to connect to online "solid" information about Native Americans. The site is organized into topical categories. One section links to information about particular Native American Nations and another to organizations, centers, and Tribal colleges. An events section describes pow-wows and festivals and sources for Indian music. There are links to about 20 Native American newspapers and journals. Individual artists, performers, and activists and links to sites about these topics are listed, as well as links to Native American businesses.

Universal Black Pages

http://www.gatech.edu/bgsa/blackpages.html/
The UBP site resides at the Georgia Institute of Technology but is not affiliated with the university. UBP is a Yahoo!-style directory of African American businesses, events, resources, writings, and educational material. It contains a complete listing of African Diaspora ("African Diaspora" refers to the forced scattering of Africans to the New World by means of the trans–Atlantic slave trade and colonization) related Web pages at a central site. UBP provides both resources and networking connections. It serves to encourage development of categories and topics that are not currently available. Suggestions to improve the UBP site are welcomed. There is also searchable information relating to art, history, music, resources, educational opportunities/activities, schools, and student organizations, among other topics.

RELIGION-SPONSORED

Catholic Charities USA

http://www.catholiccharitiesusa.org/
Catholic Charities USA is the largest private network of social service organizations in the United States. The section relating to Capitol Hill testimony and news releases is a good source for those interested in material relating to social services advocacy. New material has been added on the latest welfare reform law. A button labeled "Our Opinion" includes speeches and remarks by organization officials at various conferences and press conferences.

Catholic Relief Services

http://www.catholicrelief.org

Catholic Relief Services was founded in 1943 by the Catholic Bishops of the United States. "In over 80 countries throughout Africa, Asia, Europe and Latin America, Catholic Relief Services (CRS) serves the poor by providing emergency and long-term assistance based on need, not creed, race or nationality." When we visited, the Web site was under construction and was a single page, with a few links to outside organizations. The page gives information about the mission of the organization, how to contribute, and the history of the organization.

Christian Children's Fund

http://christianchildrensfund.org/
The Christian Children's Fund is one of the largest independent child care and development organizations. The site is simple, providing links to related organizations and to local affiliates.

Council of Jewish Federations

http://jon.cjfny.org/
The Council of Jewish Federations is the continental association of 189 Jewish Federations, the local community fund-raising and social service/education management organizations of the Jewish community. Included on the site is The North American Jewish Data Bank, established by the Council of Jewish Federations and the Center for Jewish Studies of the Graduate School and University Center of the City of New York. Its primary role is to act as the repository for computer-based population and survey data on Jewish communities in the United States and Canada. The "Other Jewish Websites" button is a link to hundreds of Jewish organizations around the world.

The Interfaith Working Group

http://www.libertynet.org/~iwg/
The mission of the Interfaith Working Group is to "inform the public of the diversity of religious opinion on social issues where it is not widely recognized by providing a voice and a forum for religious organizations, congregations and clergy in the Philadelphia area who support gay rights, reproductive freedom, and the separation of church and state." This site provides a gathering place for religious organizations and individuals committed to religious diversity. The site lists participating member organizations and individuals. Relevant interfaith and other events are listed, alerts are posted (helpful not only for showing your network what you're actually doing, but also good templates for others to use in preparing such letters for the first time), and an online record of organizational letters sent (*http://www.libertynet.org/~iwg/letters.html*). A nice feature of this site is its *Member Pulpit* (*http://www.libertynet.org/~iwg/forum.html*), which gives cyber-air time to members to discuss their views and experiences. The site includes a searchable list of progressive interfaith organizations, which helps advocates tap in to local like-minded individuals. There is also an e-mail list visitors can join to stay in touch.

RESEARCH—GENERAL

Acronyms

http://www.ucc.ie/cgi-bin/acronym
This award-winning site (Magellan 4-Star Site, and a top 5% award) boasts a searchable database of (as of this writing) almost 16,000 acronyms. This site also provides a convenient way to electronically submit new acronyms to the database. We submitted the Association of Committees of Reform Organizations Never Yielding to Mindlessness.

AT&T 1-800 information

http://www.tollfree.att.net
This is a searchable database of more than 150,000 toll free numbers for commercial businesses and organizations. But don't expect to find any of AT&T's national competitors here (we tried a search using the word "sprint" and "MCI" and came up empty). We found the "dead tree" paper version of this publication free on our doorstep, with a $24.95 cover price.

Bartlett's Book of Quotations

http://www.columbia.edu/acis/bartleby/bartlett/
This site is a part of Project Bartleby, administered by Columbia University. What makes it particularly useful is a searchable database of quotations, not just those available from Bartlett's, but from many other sources. For example, a search on the word "taxes" resulted in not just the well-known Ben Franklin quote of "but in this world, nothing is certain but death and taxes," but more than 30 additional matches. For speaking engagement preparation or spicing up the agency newsletter or legislative testimony, this is a useful and engaging site to explore. And you can quote us on that!

The Brookings Institution

http://www.brook.edu
The Brookings Institution, founded in 1916, is the United States' oldest think tank. Among the features of this searchable site are full-text policy papers (there were 15 when the site was reviewed), Congressional testimony, op-ed articles, conference notices, and information about the organization's publications. This is a useful site to browse (and perform a search) if you are preparing to give testimony on a current public policy issue.

CIA World Fact Book

http://www.odci.gov/cia/publications/pubs.html
This is a great place to start for researching countries you are planning to visit. This site is a treasure-trove of information about geography, climate, economy, and political stability. Among the files you can spy on this site are *The World Factbook 1996; The 1995 Factbook on Intelligence; Chiefs of State and Cabinet Members of Foreign Governments* (which appears to be updated each week); *Handbook of International Economic Statistics, 1996*; and *CIA Maps and Publications Released to the Public.* There is a searchable database for the site.

Database America

http://www.lookupUSA.com/
Among other useful free databases, this site includes a "reverse lookup" directory. You can find a name and address when all you have is a telephone number.

Encyclopaedia Britannica

http://www.eb.com/
A free trial offer provides seven consecutive days of free access to the 32-volume industry standard "plus thousands of newly added articles, graphics, and related Internet links." An FAQ file explains the offer. Unlike most online services, you do not have to worry that you will be charged in the event that you decide not to subscribe and forget to let them know. There is a subscription fee, which can be paid yearly or monthly.

The Gallup Organization

http://www.gallup.com/
This is a commercial site of the Gallup Organization, perhaps the best commercial polling service in the United States. It includes press releases about publicly available poll results, averaging about five such polls each month. This is a good site to browse when looking for general topics that are on the public's mind and for identifying public trends. The site also has online polls for visitors.

General Sources of Women's Legal and Public Information Policy

http://asa.ugl.lib.umich.edu:80/chdocs/womenpolicy/legpol.html
This guide was compiled by Lydia Potthoff and Tom Turner of the School of Information and Library Studies, University of Michigan, Ann

Arbor. *The Legal and Public Policy Information Guide* contains links to legal and public policy information from the United States Federal Government, the United Nations, several international organizations, and links to Internet resource guides. Although copyrighted in 1994, there are still working links to useful sites.

Internet Public Library

http://ipl.sils.umich.edu/

The Internet Public Library is the first public library of the Internet, founded in 1995 and run by real librarians. The IPL began in a graduate seminar in the School of Information and Library Studies at the University of Michigan. It has a budget of almost a half-million dollars, mostly from grants from the Mellon and Kellogg foundations. Its database, entitled *Stately Knowledge: Facts about the United States (http://www.ipl.org/youth/stateknow/)*, is billed by the site as "a fact-filled and fun-to-use resource for students, teachers, parents and anyone interested in finding out more details about the United States and Washington D.C." There are pages loaded with information for each state, and a page loaded with, for the most part, offbeat trivia. There are useful state-related links as well. The library maintains a collection of network-based ready reference works and responds to reference queries. And the best thing is, you don't get "shuushhed" for screaming "Cool Site!"

Project Gutenberg

http://www.promo.net/pg/

Project Gutenberg was started in 1971 with the goal of making available in ASCII format the complete text of books that are in the public domain, either as a result of copyrights having expired or having the rights donated by the works' creators. In addition to the usual classics one might expect, you can also find useful books about the Internet. Books may be searched by author or title. This Web site can be very useful to those who need to research important historical documents and books when the library is closed. Imagine how the inventor of the printing press would have reacted to seeing the World Wide Web!

Research-It!

http://www.itools.com/research-it/research-it.html

This site is like having your own research librarian 24-hours/day in your computer room, only this one knows how to conjugate French verbs and doesn't say "shhhhhh" when you talk. The site scrolls to forms that permit searches to find word meanings, spellings, and translations to and from almost two-dozen languages. There is a thesaurus, a quotation finder, a biographical dictionary, stock quotes, maps, a rhyming dictionary, acronym dictionary, a place to look up telephone numbers, and scores of other useful reference materials that individually can be found throughout the Internet but not, to our knowledge, at a single site. As one of the promotional lines on the site says about itself, why not "Give it a whirl!"

Switchboard

http://www.switchboard.com

This is one of the most useful sites on the Web and, not unexpectedly, has become one of the most linked-to sites. What can it do? Type in a name of a company, hit the search button, wait a few seconds, and the name, address, and telephone number of the company appear. Click on the map icon, and a color map of the company's location appears, which can be zoomed in or zoomed out. Trying to read the address of someone who scrawls illegibly? Type in as much data as you can read and let a computer do the rest. Why pay $100 or more for those CD-ROMs with telephone book data when you can have free access to (as we write this) 106 million residential listings and 11 million business listings? Our advice is to bookmark this site immediately!

The Quotations Page (Michael Moncur's Collection of Quotations)

http://www.starlingtech.com/quotes/

The site includes files on Quotes of the Day, Random Quotations, Quotes of the Week, Search for a Quotation (with a 1,500-quote database), Contribute a Quotation, Quotation Links, and an FAQ file.

UnCoverWeb

http://uncweb.carl.org/

UnCover is a database of article information taken from over 17,000 multidisciplinary journals. This database contains brief descriptive information for over 7,000,000 articles that have been published since Fall 1988. The articles found in any given search query can be ordered for purchase (if the publisher has given permission to UnCover for document delivery). There is even a one-hour delivery option.

University of Chicago's Department of Humanities Dictionaries

http://www.lib.uchicago.edu/LibInfo/Law/ dict.html

Included at this site are links to the *World Wide Legal Information Association Legal Dictionary, Oxford English Dictionary, English Language Dictionaries, Roget's Thesaurus of English Words and Phrases* (based on the text of the 1911 edition from Project Gutenberg), *Bartlett's Familiar Quotations* (based on the 9th edition, 1901), *Notable Citizens of Planet Earth* biographical dictionary containing information on more than 18,000 prominent people, and the *Dictionary of PC Hardware and Data Communications Terms*. Why buy the commercial CD-ROM of these texts when you can get them free for a click of the mouse at your bookmark?

World Time

http://www.stud.unit.no/USERBIN/steffent/ verdensur.pl

Find the correct time here for over 100 cities around the world. The time is updated every minute, and your page reloads automatically every five minutes.

ZIP Code Information

http://www.usps.gov/ncsc/lookups/ lookup_zip+4.html

Enter an address and find the ZIP code, Carrier Route, County, and other information.

RESEARCH—PROFESSIONAL

The Center for Health Administration Studies

http://www.chas.uchicago.edu/

This University of Chicago site offers certain data to the broader research community as well as to its internal researchers. For example, Chicago–area community health and demographic data are available here as are data collected over five years for the National Study of Internal Medicine Manpower. Some other completed projects are described and reports can be ordered. When we last reviewed this site, it had received a $20,000 grant from the Robert Wood Johnson Foundation to put health policy data online.

The Federal Information Exchange

http://nscp.fie.com/

Offers a free service in which registrants receive e-mail announcements of funding opportunities related to their specific areas of interest, and *Molis Scholarship Search* (*http://www.fie.com/ molis/scholar.htm*) provides a search engine for finding funding opportunities for minority students. Fedix and Molis are highly acclaimed research support services sponsored by several federal agencies.

Illinois Researcher Information Service (IRIS)

http://carousel.lis.uiuc.edu/~iris/iris_home.html

From the University of Illinois, this is an outstanding search service and site open to the larger research public. Individuals can subscribe and fill out a profile form detailing their areas of research interest and can specify how frequently they wish to have updated information on government grants, including the ability to specify for dissertation support.

The Jerome Levy Economics Institute of Bard College

http://epn.org/levy.html

Founded in 1986, the purpose of this non-profit, nonpartisan, independently funded research organization is to generate viable, effective public policy responses to important economic problems both within the United States and abroad. Contains reports and briefs on policy issues related to the institute.

Projects and Centers Affiliated with Columbia University School of Social Work *http:// www.columbia.edu/cu/ssw/projects/*

These projects include research, training, and activist projects such as *The Action Coalition for Social Justice* (*http://www.columbia.edu/ cu/ssw/acsj/*), which serves as a resource center and meeting place for those involved in activist activities in New York City; *Battered Women and Their Children* (*http:// www.columbia.edu/~rhm5/*), a research project that posts its reports, papers, and training material online; and *The Center for the Study of Social Work Practice* (*http:// www.columbia.edu/cu/csswp/*), which includes report summaries of a number of current and completed research projects and full text of its publication.

Regional Research Institute

http://www-adm.pdx.edu/user/rri/

Portland State University School of Social Work provides sites for a number of current research projects and programs. The Research and Training Center on Family Support and Children's Mental Health (*http://www-adm.pdx.edu/user/*

rri/rtc/default.htm) includes an online form for ordering documents from its National Clearing-house. Its publication, *Focal Point* (*http://www-adm.pdx.edu/user/rri/rtc/FP/WELCOME.HTM*), which is mailed to more than 25,000 people, is also available in full text online or can be ordered (free of charge) by completing an online form. Conference information and registration forms are available at the site. In addition, reports on completed research are published at the site.

Social Disadvantage Research Group (SDRG)
http://marx.apsoc.ox.ac.uk/sdrgdocs/
Based at the University of Oxford in England, this site lists current research projects, as well as provides abstracts of recent articles. Group members are listed by name, research interest, and e-mail link. There is news about SDRG and links to other poverty and social disadvantage research groups, most of which are in the United States.

Social Work Research Centre (Scotland)
http://www.stir.ac.uk/departments/humansciences/swrc/
This is a basic page describing the Center.

University of Melbourne Social Work Research Report
http://cwis.unimelb.edu.au/research.report/current/196.html
This site is used to simply list the research that is taking place at this university in areas of Aging, Alcohol and Drug Dependency, Child and Family Welfare, Community Services, Health Services, HIV/AIDS, Law and Social Work Education, and Profession. It also lists the works published and student theses.

SOCIAL JUSTICE/ACTIVISM

AFL-CIO's LaborWeb
http://www.aflcio.org/
The AFL-CIO represents "the interests of labor, organizing and advocacy on behalf of workers." Besides using the Web site to make numerous documents, policy statements, and news available, there is a "You Have a Voice" (*http://www.capweb.net/aflcio/*) section that allows visitors to send pre-composed letters to legislators. At this site, visitors can join the organization's National Issues Mobilization, which provides participants with a toll-free number to call their members of Congress and re-

ceive mailings and updates on national issues of interest to the AFL-CIO. Another online advocacy use by the AFL-CIO is the inclusion of a boycott listing of those businesses currently in dispute with the organization. Visitors can obtain more information about the particular dispute in each case. There is also a section on women's issues in the workforce, including a survey used to determine the conditions in the workplace for women.

American Civil Liberties Union
http://www.aclu.org
The ACLU is "a 275,000-member, nonprofit, non-partisan, public interest organization devoted to protecting basic civil liberties for all Americans." Within this colorful, meaty, and searchable site, the ACLU posts its organizational positions on everything relating to basic constitutional freedom, including church/state separation, death penalty, free speech, reproductive rights, racial harmony, workplace rights, student rights, voting rights, women's rights, gay and lesbian rights, and lots more. Additionally, you can e-mail your congressional representative or take a Free Exercise of Religion non-credit course via America Online (AOL). You can even become a card-carrying member of the organization online. This site has received almost every major Web site award, and deservedly so.

Amnesty International
http://www.amnesty.org/
Amnesty International "is concerned solely with the protection of human rights, regardless of either the ideology of the government or the beliefs of the victims." Its Web site is no-nonsense, easy to navigate and, while not particularly fancy, gets straight to the point of its mission. The site presents the visitor with three cases of specific human rights violations each month, and makes it easy for them to act — summarizing the facts of the cases, telling where and to whom to write, and also giving information on how to write a letter. It also includes descriptions of ongoing campaigns, and archives of press releases. The site includes a "Webzine" of Amnesty International, chock full of information concerning human rights. For example, a recent edition dealt with Ginetta Sagan, founder of the Aurora Foundation, which records abuses and helps families of "prisoners of conscience." There is also information on campaigns (such as urgent actions), programs/networks (involving rights for women, gays, and even those on

death row), and publications. Additionally, you can find out how to write a letter and help to save a life. Finally, there are opportunities concerning joining Amnesty USA. In essence, there is a ton of news, instructions, and other bits to help you sort out exactly what is what in the world of human rights. Online activity includes a place where visitors and members can find out how and what to write to named countries found to be committing human rights violations. Place your mouse over one of the page's buttons and an explanation appears telling what happens if you click there. Nice touch!

The Center on Budget and Policy Priorities
http://epn.org/cbpp.html
"A nonpartisan research organization and policy institute that conducts research and analysis on a range of government policies and programs, with an emphasis on those affecting low- and middle-income people." This site includes reports issued by the Center on the budget battle, welfare reform, living standards, and health policy.

The Center for Law and Social Policy (CLASP)
http://epn.org/clasp.html
"A national public interest law firm with expertise in both law and policy affecting the poor. Through education, policy research and advocacy, CLASP seeks to improve the economic conditions of low-income families with children and secure access for the poor to our civil justice system." When we visited, there were online CLASP documents on block grants, early implementation, child support, and state welfare waivers.

The Center for Public Integrity
http://essential.org/cpi/
This membership organization publishes a newsletter, "The Public i," online. A form for membership is included at the site (donations requested). Investigative studies are available in full text dating back to 1990. Several databases relating to campaign expenditures of political candidates are available for downloading.

Civic Practices Network
http://www.cpn.org/
This site organizes topic-based forums with documents and articles relating primarily to civic participation and community building. It seeks to be a "learning collaborative for civic renewal" comprised of community organizers, civic journalists, and youth activists. It is a collaborative of various kinds of organizations gathering around the theme of a new civic movement. The site's topic areas cover Community, Health, Youth and Education, Work and Empowerment, Families, Gender/Children, Community Networking, Religion, Journalism, and Environment. Within each of these are articles, stories, case studies, and training manuals and guides. These same documents can be found according to any particular state in the U.S., or by keyword searches for particular issues. You can also access information provided by specific member affiliates. Members and non-members are invited to share their own information to add to this growing archival resource.

Civix Database
http://ibert.org/
An excellent format can be found here for presenting budget data and federal budget education for all levels. High school students across the nation participate in the virtual congress. Budget information is from 1992, but is being updated.

Do Something
http://www.dosomething.org/
This site's mission is to "inspire young people to believe that change is possible and we train, fund and mobilize them to be leaders who measurably strengthen their communities." There are links to information about grants available through the organization, the National Kindness and Justice Challenge, and other projects. Complex graphics make the load time long for this site.

Economic Policy Institute
http://epn.org/epi.html
The Economic Policy Institute is "a nonprofit, nonpartisan think tank that seeks to broaden the public debate about strategies to achieve a prosperous and fair economy." The site includes complete text online of reports issued by the Institute. Articles and reports fall into the categories of economics and politics, living standards, and the battle of the budget. There is also a section called "reading between the lines," which seeks to clarify and correct articles published in the *New York Times*. Publications can also be ordered at cost.

The Electronic Activist

http://www.berkshire.net/~ifas/activist

The Electronic Activist is part of the Web site of the Institute for First Amendment Studies. Founded in 1984, IFAS is "a non-profit educational and research organization focusing solely on the activities of the radical Religious Right." This site is an e-mail address directory of members of Congress, state government officials, and media entities, categorized by state, in addition to a federal/national file. You can use its "Zipper" program to obtain the name of your member of Congress and Senators, and you can send an e-mail message to every member of the House and Senate (provided it is less than 5,000 bytes long). There is a searchable database, which can tell you about key votes in the House and Senate.

Fifty Facts About Poverty

http://garnet.berkeley.edu:3333/faststats/povertystats.html

A simple list of facts. There are actually *51* facts here.

HandsNet

http://www.handsnet.org

Founded in 1987, HandsNet links 5,000 public interest and human services organizations and individuals using the Internet to promote collaboration, advocacy, and information-sharing by the non-profit sector. The public pages are updated daily, and the members-only pages are considered to be the most valuable around for non-profits that engage in advocacy. The organization offers a free trial membership for 30 days. The subscription fee is much less for organizations that choose to access the service through the Internet site rather than through a separate dial-up service. The site's Action Alerts provide lots of government links, state-of-the-art information on current issues (most of which is provided by member organizations whose niche includes that particular public policy issue), capsule summaries, sources to find more information about the issue, sample advocacy letters, and information about new legislation. The pages are colorful with excellent graphics, but there is no sacrifice on substantive content. The *Weekly Digest* includes samples from hundreds of policy, program, and resource articles posted by members. The "Welfare Watch" button is a must-click for those interested in this hot issue, as it leads to information on the latest developments including public policy alerts, analyses, notices of new bills, rules and regulations, legislative studies and reports, new programs, *Federal Register* notices, funding information, and daily summaries of newspaper and wire services articles. The site also links to the Training and Resource Center, whose mission is to "provide leadership in helping human services organizations use new information technologies to embrace communication, information sharing and collaboration." The basic annual membership fee is $300, but there is plenty of useful material accessible to non-members.

League of Women Voters

http://www.lwv.org

The mission of the League of Women Voters, founded in 1920, is "to encourage the informed and active participation of citizens in government and to influence public policy through education and advocacy." There are the usual files on how to join, how to contribute, programs administered by the organization, and how to purchase league publications. The legislative priorities pages have up-to-date advocacy information on public policy issues. The "League Action Line" button links to a Legislative Action Center, which includes schedules for the House and Senate, Legislative Alerts, Congressional e-mail lists with automated forms for e-mailing members of Congress, and a guide to the 105th Congress with biographies, photos, committee assignments, and the names of key staff members. Among the key staff included are not only the top staff director and legislative assistant, but also the current appointments secretary. Put your ZIP code in an online form, and find out who represents you in Congress. There is also a first rate primer on tips and information about lobbying members of Congress, called "Tell It To Washington." Before you head for the Capitol, head here first!

Legislative Hotline Directory

http://www.piperinfo.com/state/hotline.html

Published by Government Research Service, this site lists hotlines in each state of the United States to call for legislative bill status.

National Association of Community Action Agencies (NACAA)

http://www.nacaa.org

This site has information on the association's conference and membership services, as well as a bulletin board addressing welfare issues.

The National Budget Simulation

http://socrates.berkeley.edu:3333/budget/budget.html

A project of the University of California at Berkeley's *Center for Community Economic Research* (*http://garnet.berkeley.edu:3333/.aboutccer.html*), this site features an online "game" in which students can adjust the budget for each federal agency. The results of the changes made by the student are analyzed by a program, giving the overall effect to the economy. The site also has links to information on the Federal budget.

PeaceAction of Washington (State)

http://www.scn.org/ip/peaceact/

Peace Action of Washington "is more than 13,000 dedicated individuals who work together in a grassroots effort to bring peace—internationally, in our communities, and in our own lives." This site is a good example of how a local affiliate of a large national organization is able to use the Internet to rally its members and provide them with easy access to information on key issues, and the means to act on it. It includes contact information for local members of Congress and links to their biographies and voting records.

Southern Poverty Law Center

http://www.splcenter.org

The SPLC is "a non-profit organization that combats hate, intolerance, and discrimination through education and litigation." The site includes information on legal action, the Klanwatch program, the magazine *Teaching Tolerance*, and the center itself. This site has some great links for teachers and others working with children in grades K-12.

Speak Out!

http://www.vida.com/speakout/home.html

This national non-profit speakers' and artists' registry lists people who speak and perform on social change issues, such as AIDS, gangs, prisons, safe sex, welfare, student activism, mental health, law and social justice, and others. Based in California, the organization is a good place to look for people to speak at a campus or organizational event. Also includes a list of upcoming speaking engagements.

SOCIAL WORK/GENERAL

Gary Holden's Web Resources for Social Workers (W3RSW)

http://pages.nyu.edu/~gh5/gh-w3-f.htm

This page should be at the top of every social worker's bookmarks list. This regularly updated site is an online update of several printed articles by Gary Holden, Gary Rosenberg, and Andrew Weissman. It consists of an extensive listing of more than 1,200 links to sites that are related in some way (more or less) to social work. Categories include government, indexes, journals/e-letters, measurement, net tools, newspapers, psychology, reference, search, social cognitive theory, social science, social work (general, client issues, ethnicity, and schools), telecommuting, universities, and virtual reality! Something for everyone at this site.

Michael McMurray's "List of Social Work Chat Rooms"

http://129.82.209.104/chatrooms.htm

A short list of links to social work sites that have chat rooms.

Michael McMurray's "Lists of Interest for Social Workers"

http://129.82.209.104/lists.htm

Similar to his Web resources page, this page lists mailing lists of interest to social workers, complete with "mailto" links for easy subscribing right from McMurray's site. It is updated weekly, but also has some outdated listings.

Michael McMurray's "The New Web Resources for Social Workers"

http://129.82.209.104/webstuff.htm

One of the first sites to provide an extensive listing of social work links, this site is maintained and updated weekly by Michael McMurray, BSSW, MSW, CAODAC. He has maintained the site since 1995, when he was an MSW student at Colorado State University. The site is divided into the following categories: personal Web pages, international sites, disabilities, addiction/substance abuse, mental health, domestic violence/child abuse, social services, veterans, political, social work schools, miscellaneous, adoption, cancer, and gerontology. Created using Microsoft® FrontPage 2.0, the site has some "cool" animated graphics, but many of the links are "dead."

The Settlement House: A Social Work Resource

http://www.users.csbsju.edu/~swrk/

This creative site is sponsored by the College of St. Benedict/St. John's University. An image map of a settlement house allows Net surfers to "visit" various rooms: the classroom (online course syllabi), the front hall (an introduction to the site), a reading room (links to other sites), the club room (information about the schools' social work clubs), an art gallery (biographies and pictures of Jane Addams and others), a community center (the student field manual and other resources for students), and the offices (how to contact faculty). A good example of how a little creativity can make an interesting Web site even more exciting!

"Shirley's List"

http://www.uindy.edu/~kml/resources/ socialwork/index.html

This site, largely created by Shirley Bigna, a librarian at the University of Indiana, contains reviews of and links to over 500 social work-related Web sites. Social workers at all practice levels should benefit from this site, developed as a resource for BSW instruction.

Social Work Access Network (SWAN)

http://www.sc.edu/swan/

"As evidenced by thousands of hits per month, SWAN has become the site of choice for professionals, educators, and students searching the web for resources related to social work. Many web surfers have enjoyed the information and the networking opportunities afforded by this web site. In response to their confidence, SWAN enters the third year of its existence with a revived commitment to quality and usefulness." There is a virtual community here where you can search for colleagues, and you can become a SWAN member yourself by simply filling out an online form. You will then be listed in the SWAN "virtual community," and other social workers with similar areas of interest (or maybe an old classmate/co-worker!) will be able to find you through this resource. There are numerous links to social work chat rooms (Web events), social work-related Web sites, schools of social work, publications, mailing lists, newsgroups, policy and government sites, social work organizations, and conferences. We found the format for listing conferences, including e-mail links and other vital information, especially useful. As of early January 1998, there were 833 SWAN

members listed, including 381 "field professionals," 122 faculty members, 286 students or recent graduates, 7 social work staff members, 18 information service personnel, and 19 "friends" of social work. A very nice format and simple graphics. Easy to navigate, and full of useful information. A major social work resource on the Web.

The Social Work Cafe

http://www.geocities.com/Heartland/4862/

The Social Work Cafe is an effort to create an international online directory of social workers and social work students. There are links to schools of social work, personal Web pages of social workers, and other sites of interest to social workers. You can fill out an online form to request that a link be added to your Web site or e-mail address. Nightly chats are held at this site, which is maintained by Tobi Shane, a social work student.

Social Work History Station

http://www.idbsu.edu/socwork/dhuff/XX.htm

The Social Work History Station takes you (in style) on a Web tour of the origins of the profession of social work. This project is sponsored by the Social Welfare Archives and Boise State University, and is a CSWE Millennium project. The train begins at the era of scientific philanthropy (1860-1900) and continues through the Settlement era, the Progressives, the Professionals, and Crises. Graphics and text combine in this online exhibit presentation. You can even hear a short audio clip of Jane Addams.

Social Work Online

http://www.geocities.com/Athens/9050/ socwork.html

Among other things offered at this site is its "Say Hi to a Social Worker" page that lists the personal Web sites of social workers around the world.

The Social Work Student Nexus

http://www.chas.uchicago.edu/ssa/swsn/

This collaborative site run by students is "a place for all student social workers and those interested in social work education." Based at the University of Chicago School of Social Service Administration, the site's goals include networking, education, advocacy, and social exchange. There are links to student social work organization sites, publications, and related sites. NexusCon, a yearly mailing list-based international discussion/conference on social work topics, is a part of the project.

The Social Worker Networker

http://www.accessone.com/~hammer/

This site is a collection of pages of links, including "Best of the Web" mental health resources, consumer resources, Internet search engines, professional resources, and a social service resource list. While the links are fairly comprehensive, some links are outdated, such as the NASW 1996 conference registration form link.

Your Social Work Advisor

http://www.socialworkadvisor.com/articles/

This site is brought to you by Jesus Reyes, the author of the *1997-98 Guide for Selecting and Applying to Master of Social Work Programs*. Includes articles of interest to MSW program applicants, as well as information about the book and an online order form. You can subscribe to a free monthly e-mail newsletter, *The Social netWorker*, with articles relating to issues in the social work profession.

SOCIAL WORK LICENSING/CREDENTIALS

American Association of State Social Work Boards (AASSWB)

http://www.aasswb.org

AASSWB is the professional association representing members of state social work licensing boards. Its site includes social work licensing requirements for each state and the District of Columbia, a directory of state social work licensing boards, and information about the exams and how to register. Four sample questions are provided from AASSWB's study guide. There is a listing of AASSWB board and committee members and an online newsletter, as well as a listing of social work conferences, social work links page, and an order form for AASSWB products, which can be printed out and mailed in. Links are provided to six state social work licensing boards that have their own Web sites—Arizona, California, New York, New Mexico, Missouri, and Oregon.

American Board of Examiners (ABE) in Clinical Social Work

http://www.abecsw.org/

This organization issues the Board Certified Diplomate (BCD) credential. The site features the ABE Code of Ethics, a directory of people with the BCD credential (requires registration to search) searchable by practice characteristics and focus of practice. An application for the BCD can be printed out (it's in 7 HTML documents). There is also a list of the Board of Directors, with names and cities listed only.

Association for Advanced Training in the Behavioral Sciences

http://www.aatbs.com/socialwork/

This site provides information about social work examination preparation materials available from this company. There is an online order form, as well as a page of links to mental health sites.

Social Work Examination Services

http://www.tiac.net/users/swes/

This publisher of licensing examination review guides for social workers maintains this commercial site, but it does more than just advertise SWES' services and products. The site includes general licensing information, a full list of state social work licensing boards, social work links, 15 sample exam questions, sample review notes, and articles about continuing education requirements and other licensing-related developments. Includes description of SWES' home study program and a schedule of SWES lectures (in New York and New England areas).

SOCIAL WORK ORGANIZATIONS

American Network of Home Health Care Social Workers, Inc.

http://www.homehealthsocialwork.org/

The organization's mission statement and conference information can be found here. There is a bulletin board, but it was empty when we visited. You can print out a membership form, as well as a form to order merchandise such as t-shirts, earrings, and a manual of handouts from a previous conference.

Association for the Advancement of Social Work With Groups

http://dominic.barry.edu/~kelly/aaswg/aaswg.html

Find out about this organization's projects, read the newsletter, and subscribe to the online mailing list from this site. You can also find sample groupwork syllabi and assignments, information on state chapters (with e-mail links), membership information, and some links to other sites.

Association of Baccalaureate Social Work Program Directors (BPD)

http://www.rit.edu/~694www/bpd.htm

This site is maintained by Professor Marshall Smith at Rochester Institute of Technology, chair of BPD's Committee on Information Technology and Social Work Education. One of the best and most comprehensive general social work sites around, it includes links to all schools of social work (BSW, MSW, and doctoral programs) that have Web pages or sites, and also links to numerous social work-related sites. In addition, information about the BPD itself is provided, including membership information, a list of board members and officers with contact information, full text of BPD's *Update* newsletter, information about the *Journal of Baccalaureate Social Work,* annual conference information, and call for papers.

Association for Community Organization and Social Administration (ACOSA)

http://www.bc.edu/bc_org/avp/gssw/acosa.htm

Here, you can access information about ACOSA membership, publications, and projects. Also includes links to online syllabi and other sites.

Association of Latino Social Work Educators

http://www.ollusa.edu/alswe/alswehome.htm

This site features the ALSWE mission and purpose, a roster of board members, a listing of Latino social work educators by state and university, and general information about the organization. The links to Latino and social work sites should prove helpful to anyone looking for more information on the Latino population. When we reviewed the site, the organization was holding a logo contest, which was announced online.

Association of Oncology Social Work (AOSW)

http://www.biostat.wisc.edu/aosw/aoswhello.html

This is a nice, simple site, easy to navigate with few graphics but a pleasant look. It includes AOSW's mission statement, board member listing, membership information, descriptions of special interest groups, conference information, and links to related sites.

British Association of Social Workers

http://www.basw.demon.co.uk/

Here you'll find the usual organizational infor-

mation, along with the full BASW Code of Ethics, a listing of publications available for sale, and links to other social work sites.

Canadian Association of Social Workers

http://www.intranet.ca/~casw-acts/info-e.htm

This site features a directory of board members and provincial associations (some of which have their own Web sites), conferences and other activities, publications, a "What's New" page, and a links page that leads to lots of Canadian social work sites.

Clinical Social Work Federation

http://www.cswf.org

The Clinical Social Work Federation (formerly National Federation of Societies for Clinical Social Work) site includes information on CSWF membership and services, legislative alerts, a clinical resources page, board member directory, and links to other sites. You can subscribe to the CSWF mailing list or participate in a members' chat from the site.

Council on Social Work Education

http://www.cswe.org/

CSWE is the body that accredits BSW and MSW programs. The site features sections on accreditation, conferences, governance, news, projects, programs and services, and publications. You will find an online directory of social work degree programs, a directory of CSWE staff, and a president's message. There is a links page, and an FAQ page was under construction when we reviewed the site.

International Federation of Social Workers

http://www.ifsw.org/

Find out how to get involved in cases in which IFSW is fighting human rights violations against social workers. Also, you will find the text of IFSW's social work ethics documents, as well as information on membership and the organization's international symposium.

Irish Association of Social Workers

http://www.iol.ie/~iasw

This association, like many others, has put its code of ethics online. You can also read editorials from past issues of *The Irish Social Worker.* There is a job listing page, although it was empty when we looked, as well as information on conferences and links to other sites.

Latino Social Workers Organization

http://www.whittier.cps.k12.il.us/Community/ PrOrg/LSWO.html

Besides providing information about the LSWO's mission and activities, this site features a job bank, call for papers, membership application, mentoring and networking opportunities, a newsletter, Latino links, conference information, and contact information for LSWO.

National Association of Social Workers (NASW)

http://www.socialworkers.org/

As one would expect from the nation's largest association of professional social workers, this is one of the most comprehensive social work sites around. Much of the site's focus is NASW programming and membership. You can shop for journals and books from the NASW Press (there is an online secure order form), search the NASW *Clinical Register* for a social worker, read NASW's advocacy alerts, and find social work news. A new feature is the addition of an online, searchable version of NASW's JobLink service (*http://www.socialworkers.org/ JOB.HTM*). When we visited, we found six jobs listed for Pennsylvania, and 28 jobs throughout the Northeast United States. The full text of the NASW *Code of Ethics* is available on the site, as well. Other features include links and contact information to all state NASW chapters, membership information, and a listing (with links) of upcoming conferences and calls for papers. The site is updated regularly, so bookmark it and check back often. NASW Chapters with their own sites are as follows:

NASW California Chapter

http://naswca.org/

NASW Illinois Chapter

http://www.mtco.com/~rlongmsw/ilsw.htm

NASW Kentucky Chapter

http://members.aol.com/NASWKY/index.html

NASW Nevada Chapter

http://members.aol.com/NASWNV

NASW New Jersey Chapter

http://www.stockton.edu/~falkd/nasw.htm

NASW New Mexico Chapter

http://www.naswnm.org/

NASW New York City Chapter

http://www.naswnyc.org/

NASW New York State Chapter

http://www.naswnys.org

NASW North Carolina Chapter

http://members.aol.com/naswnc

NASW Oklahoma Chapter

http://www.ionet.net/~naswok/

NASW Oregon Chapter

http://www.home.earthlink.net/~nasw/

NASW Texas Chapter

http://www.naswtx.org/

NASW West Virginia Chapter

http://members.aol.com/naswwv/naswwv.html

National Committee for Educating Students to Influence State Policy and Legislation

http://www.statepolicy.org

This site is maintained by a committee that was formed at the March 1997 annual program meeting of the Council on Social Work Education (CSWE), with the mission "to assist faculty and students in learning to influence effectively the formation, implementation, and evaluation of state level policy and legislation." The site includes sample student projects that can be used in social policy courses. It also includes assignments from a course at Virginia Commonwealth University, "Social Welfare Policy, Community Planning, and Organizational Practice II." It includes welfare reform links and a social policy bibliography. With continued development, this site should prove valuable to both faculty and students of social policy.

National Network of Social Work Managers

http://www.uncg.edu/swk/nnswm.htm

This site contains information on membership and a printable application, a board member list with phone numbers and e-mail links, and conference information. It consists of one long page with no graphics, and some links are outdated.

National Organization of Forensic Social Workers

http://www.nofsw.org/

The NOFSW site provides a good source of general information about this practice specialty. We also found a link to detailed information about NOFSW's annual conference, and information on how to contact the organization.

Newfoundland and Labrador Association of Social Workers

http://www3.nf.sympatico.ca/nlasw/index.html
This site focuses on social work in a specific region of Canada. There is a jobs page with links to job-related sites, a social work links page, a listing (by name only) of Registered Social Workers (RSWs) in the region, and information on how to lodge a complaint against an RSW.

School Social Work Association of America

http://members.aol.com/SSWAAWeb/SSWAA1.htm
The SSWAA site provides general information about the association and a printable membership application. The *SSWAA Bell* newsletter is online in full text, and there are links to other school social work sites and individual members/board members. The site is a good resource for school social workers, but it is very difficult to read, using a dark red background and various typefaces in different colors.

Society for Social Work Leadership in Health Care

http://www.sswahc.org/
Formerly the Society for Social Work Administrators in Health Care, this is the professional association for hospital social work directors and social work administrators/leaders in other health care settings. The site tells about the organization, lists its board of directors, and provides job listings. There is an active bulletin board on the site, as well as committee and chapter news, advocacy information, links, and other useful information.

SUBSTANCE ABUSE

Join Together On-line

http://www.jointogether.org/
Join Together On-line is "a national resource center and meeting place for communities working to reduce substance abuse (illicit drugs, excessive alcohol, and tobacco) and gun violence." This is a comprehensive, professionally designed, colorful, and informative site, with plenty of useful information, advocacy tips, electronic discussion lists, funding sources, and more. Join Together uses its site in just about all of the major ways an advocacy organization can. It is interactive, encouraging all communities and organizations serving their communities to share their stories (both successes and failures) with

others. One unique online advocacy effort is Faces of Addiction, co-sponsored by Join Together and cable television's HBO, and funded by the Robert Wood Johnson Foundation. This public education site provides background information leading into a televised program on the topic of drug abuse. Using multimedia, the site complements substantive information with personal accounts of the effects of drugs, tobacco, alcohol, and their impact on family violence, workplace success, health, and safety. Links to organizations and online resources for getting help are provided.

Kickbutt.org

http://www.kickbutt.org/
The purpose of this organization is "to learn all about the dangers and health risks of tobacco, about the sneaky tactics the tobacco industry uses to peddle their stuff, and how you can act through government to make our country a safer and healthier place." In addition to providing relevant facts and strategy resources for activism, this site includes a section for smoking out specific policy makers to urge them to vote in favor of legislation designed to curb tobacco use. You must be a member of kickbutt.org to take advantage of the site but, according to its Webmaster, "Registration is free, easy, and confidential."

National Association of Alcoholism and Drug Abuse Counselors

http://www.naadac.org
The organization's ethical standards, position statements, and advocacy updates are posted here. Also, there is an application for liability insurance and a good collection of links to other sites.

Substance Abuse and Mental Health Services Administration (SAMHSA)

http://www.samhsa.gov/
SAMHSA, an agency within the Department of Health and Human Services, offers information from each of its three centers, the Center for Mental Health Services (CMHS), the Center for Substance Abuse Prevention (CSAP), and the Center for Substance Abuse Treatment. CMHS supports the National Mental Health Services Knowledge Exchange Network (KEN) *(http://www.mentalhealth.org/)* which is a user-friendly gateway to mental health services information, agencies, and clearinghouses from across the country. KEN also features a bulletin board ser-

vice available 24 hours/day through a toll-free number. In addition, Community Mental Health Services Block Grant applications, certifications, and applicable legislation are available here online. CSAP operates, in conjunction with other agencies, Prevline (*http://www.health.org/*) The National Clearinghouse for Alcohol and Drug Information (NCADI), the largest repository of substance abuse treatment and prevention information in the country. This serves as the central national resource for current information on all aspects of substance abuse. Within Prevline, anyone can review the latest research and statistics, find resources needed, order publications, obtain information about events, and search any of a number of databases, including Medline, Smoking, and ETOH, the most comprehensive online resource covering alcohol-related biomedical and behavioral research. Prevline also features private and public forums for discussion of substance abuse and mental health issues. CSAP features an interactive forum and resource service on treatment, called the Treatment Improvement Exchange (TIE). Here one can find documents, resources, and state information, and can participate in roundtable discussions.

SUPPORT/SELF-HELP

Support-Group.com
http://www.support-group.com/
If you work directly with clients in any way, don't miss this site. Support-group.com "allows people with health, personal, and relationship issues to come together and share their experiences" through Internet Relay Chat, bulletin boards, and other online support systems. The site provides links to online support groups on virtually every illness or issue imaginable. There is a list of chat groups and more than 175 bulletin boards. A professional links section has a social work page, which was under construction when we looked at it. Some chat groups are facilitated. Great site!

Tell-a-Group
http://www-personal.umich.edu/~bertcher/
Retired University of Michigan social work professor Harvey Bertcher has posted on this site the full text of his newsletters on how to run a telephone support group. This is a nice (and free!) resource for anyone who wants to start such a group.

TECHNOLOGY

Center for On-Line Addiction
http://netaddiction.com
This is the site of Dr. Kimberly S. Young, assistant professor of psychology at the University of Pittsburgh at Bradford. Young has done extensive, pioneering research on Internet addiction. The site includes the full text of some of her research on Internet addiction, as well as information on training for professionals on the topic, and treatment options for those she considers addicted to the Internet.

Computers in Teaching Initiative Centre for Human Services
http://www.soton.ac.uk/~chst/
Run by the Department of Social Work Studies of the University of Southampton in the UK, this site offers software directories and information. Software is not available online, but can be ordered by e-mail. Updated information on conferences and workshops is available. There are some articles from the Centre's journal and newsletter online, and there is a request for submission form. The Department also runs a mailing list and is interactive to the extent that it welcomes people to seek advice or to ask questions on computer uses in social work. Information can be found at the site on projects involving computerized modules for social work students and nurses.

Computer Use in Social Services Network
http://www.uta.edu/cussn/cussn.html
"The Computer Use in Social Services Network (CUSSN) is an informal association of professionals interested in exchanging information and experiences on using computers in the human services. It has been in existence since 1981." Dick Schoech manages CUSSN at the University of Texas at Austin. "Cuss-net," as it is called, is an outstanding resource for those who use computers in social services or who want to learn more about computer applications to social service delivery. Computer use in this context includes Internet uses, but is focused more on software applications for such activities as case management, financial accounting, billing and fund-raising, data analysis, and education and training. There is a section for downloading software from the site to your hard drive. Some are "freeware" (no cost), while other applications are either limited use demonstrations of the real

product, or "shareware" (you are asked to pay only if you use it). In some cases, software programs are offered for either Macs or IBMs. There is information about the journal *Computers in Human Services*, where many of these applications are reviewed. For joining a sustained dialogue on computers in human services, there is a mailing list. The site also humanizes and demystifies computers through personal stories and humor, and tries to envision the future of human services through a section on fictitious futures, imagining what human services will look like in the year 2025.

Computer Uses in Social Work

http://lrs.ed.uiuc.edu/students/b-choksi/cswfin.html

This site contains an article on how to use computers in social work. It covers uses of computers as solitary tools, as well as for networking, databases, and diagnosing.

New Technology in the Human Services

http://www.soton.ac.uk/~chst/nths/

This site is an online quarterly journal devoted to the "dissemination of information about the application of information and information technology in the human services." All the articles, policy and practice reports, book and software reviews, news items, and announcements have been carefully selected through blind peer review. This site also offers two free electronic services (New Technology in the Human Services' own software directory and SWBIB indexing and abstracting service in both English and Dutch). There is information on subscriptions and article contributions, and how to get a free trial issue.

The Psychology of Cyberspace

http://www1.rider.edu/~suler/psycyber/psycyber.html

This copyrighted "hypertext book" was created in 1996 by John Suler, Ph.D., of the Department of Psychology of Rider University. Dr. Suler invites anyone to "contribute ideas and resources to this ongoing site." His intention is to develop a "conceptual framework for understanding the various psychological components of cyberspace and how people react to and behave within it." His hope is that the site will evolve into a research and informational community. Of particular interest is Suler's study of "The Palace," a client/server program that creates a highly visual, spatial, and auditory chat environment.

The site covers topics not often seen on the web: "Transference to Cyberspace," "Identity Management," "Deviant Behavior," "Cyberspatial Relationships," "Group Dynamics," research, romance online, and a host of other intriguing ideas for clinicians and their clients to explore. A surfer could spend hours here and still want to stay. Talk about obsession!

Psychotechnology

http://www.psychotechnology.com

This site, provided by Dr. Jeri Fink, a clinical social worker, offers lively text, excellent graphics, and animation to help present a new behavioral paradigm. This is Dr. Fink's "investigation into the partnership between two powerful forces: psychology and technology. Here you will find the voices, ideas, resources, and links to an entirely new study in human behavior . . . [as] we plunge into the next millennium, seeking to understand what happens when people live, love, work, and play in an electronic environment." The exploration of "The Virtual Ego" as a conglomeration of Freud, computers, cyberspace and some serious research provides cyberfood for thought.

Technology Use in Social Work

http://www.ssc.msu.edu/~sw/comput.html

This site is a simple list of Internet resources for computer uses in social work. It includes a bibliography with abstracts of articles and books on the subject. Information is available on distance learning, gender and computers, and software applications.

VETERANS/MILITARY

Disabled American Veterans (DAV)

http://dav.org/

Go to this site to find information about DAV, how to join, and how you can help disabled veterans. The full text of *DAV Magazine* is online, and veterans can join the Vets Connection discussion forum. There is also information on programs available through DAV, such as help with claims for benefits, and transportation to VA hospitals and clinics.

National Military Family Association (NMFA)

http://www.nmfa.org/

"The National Military Family Association is the only national organization dedicated to identifying and resolving issues of concern to military families." On this site, you'll find FAQs about

NMFA, a What's New section, information on issues of concern to military families, and information on joining NMFA. There are legislative updates and newsletter "shorts" online, including articles on projects the organization is working on.

Sgt. Mom's—The Internet Site for Military Families

http://www.sgtmoms.com

This is simply a great site for any family with a member in any branch of the U.S. military (past, present, future, and reserve). There are links to the official sites of the Army, Air Force, Navy, Marines, National Guard, and Coast Guard. Sgt. Mom's "tank taxi" takes you to information on virtually any topic you could possibly think of related to military family life. The "mail room" has resources for finding a military person's e-mail address, lost persons, sending an e-mail postcard, and other goodies. The award-winning site has sections for kids, parenting, family support, relocation, moving tips, baby names, military links, people finder, and lots more. There is also a jukebox that will play music in the background. Run by a full-time mom and military spouse.

Veterans Affairs

http://www.va.gov/

This site contains most of the usual suspects—information about the agency, its organizational structure, its programs, news updates and press releases, relevant data on veterans and expenditures, and job opportunities. In addition to these, those wanting to understand their benefits and confirm the level of benefits that they are due can use the site. Benefits forms are available here. The site can be used to find answers to some of the questions frequently asked of VA staff, such as medical issues and cemetery information. If the information sought cannot be found online, a variety of helpful resources will assist in finding the right office or individual to call or write. There are useful resources for the professional, including clinical practice guidelines and activities. Finally, and perhaps most interesting, is the VA's use of the site for sharing innovations among VA clinicians.

Vietnam Veterans Home Page

http://www.vietvet.org/

Includes "a visit to Vietnam," "Remembrance" (stories, poems, pictures, search aids for the Wall in Washington, D.C., a glossary of terms, and more), links to veterans' organizations and support groups, and "the post exchange" (books and other items for sale).

VIOLENCE

Abuse-Excuse Home Page

http://www.abuse-excuse.com/

This site provides information for adults falsely accused of child abuse. It includes information on child protection laws, "Tong's Tips" for the falsely accused, links, and contact information for various organizations and lawyers. This site was developed by Dean Tong, a "victim and survivor of false incest charges" and author of several books on the topic.

Family Violence Prevention Fund

http://www.fvpf.org/fund/

The Family Violence Prevention Fund is "a national non-profit organization that focuses on domestic violence education, prevention and public policy reform." Those advocates interested in domestic violence issues can sign up here on an e-mail list to receive news, or read news or statistical information about family violence, as well as personal stories from victims, people who have taken action against domestic violence, and children and family members exposed to violent domestic relationships. The organization uses its site to promote its public education campaign and its slogan: "There's No Excuse for Domestic Violence." It does this through advertising shirts and bumper stickers and by posting quotes from its celebrity sponsor, actor Danny Glover, online. There is a wealth of training and educational information for people in a variety of settings. Another creative use of the Web site is to provide a celebrity watch that details stories of family violence committed by celebrities, juxtaposed by ways other celebrities are fighting or increasing awareness of domestic violence. The site also features a quiz to test your knowledge of domestic violence facts. The What You Can Do page gives information on how to talk with victims of domestic violence, educate others, and keep informed about domestic violence. Also, the FVP collects information from its site through an online survey, which it uses to learn about visitors and their concerns, the level of their involvement, and how useful they find the information provided by the organization.

Forensics Page

http://www.sunlink.net/~browning/forensic.htm

This page links to various resources on child abuse and forensics.

Minnesota Higher Education Center Against Violence and Abuse

http://www.umn.edu/mincava/

An electronic clearinghouse on issues of violence and abuse, the site welcomes submissions of information by disk or by e-mail. Brochures and newsletters are published online, and long articles may be downloaded from the site. In addition, there are articles and scholarly papers by various authors, course syllabi, and reports. Associated information includes a gallery (or tour) of children's art and a collection of poetry and prose. Updated information includes news of job positions and events (mostly in Minnesota, but also nationally or internationally).

Muslims Against Family Violence

http://www.mpac.org/mafv/

This site presents articles about domestic violence in the Muslim community, a Frequently Asked Questions page, and links to resources in the San Francisco Bay Area.

The Nonviolence Web

http://www.nonviolence.org/

This site has a discussion board, issue pages on things like peace and taxes, links to other sites with descriptions of those sites, and a fund-raising appeal for the Nonviolence Web.

SafetyNet Domestic Violence Resources

http://www.cybergrrl.com/dv.html

This site contains the *Domestic Violence Handbook* online, and a bibliography of other reading materials. Submissions are welcome. It includes a number of statistics on domestic violence (both in the U.S. and U.K.) and lists some organizations, projects, and programs dealing with this issue.

SESAME (Survivors of Educator Sexual Abuse and Misconduct Emerge)

http://home.earthlink.net/~jaye/index.html

Features stories written by survivors of abuse by teachers. Also contains links to other sexual abuse sites.

The Sexual Assault Information Page

http://www.cs.utk.edu/~bartley/saInfoPage.html

This site serves as a directory to numerous articles and papers online about the topic of sexual assault. The site is also interactive, and allows people to sign up for an online newsletter for sharing and obtaining information on this topic.

Students Against Violence Everywhere

http://www.s-a-v-e.com/

Includes how to start a SAVE club, lesson plans for teachers, and an online newsletter. There is a discussion board, but nothing was posted in it when we reviewed the site. The site is a good idea, but needs further development.

VOLUNTEERISM

Action Without Borders

http://www.idealist.org/

This is a nicely done site helpful for connecting to volunteer opportunities, events, internships, and more. It provides access to worldwide volunteer opportunities, linking to more than 10,000 organizational Web sites. Organizations with or without their own Web sites can participate in this site. The site organizes events online, provides tools for non-profits, and provides a job search resource.

Corporation for National Service

http://www.cns.gov/

"The Corporation for National Service is a public-private-nonprofit partnership that oversees and evaluates three national service initiatives: AmeriCorps (a "domestic Peace Corps" with 25,000 members engaged in a year of service in return for an educational scholarship), National Senior Service Corps (with a half-million older Americans serving as Foster Grandparents, Senior Companions, and RSVP volunteers), and Learn and Serve America (which provides models and resources for teachers integrating service projects into the classroom curriculum of more than 750,000 students from kindergarten through college)." The site has information about grant awards and grant availability from the Corporation, news affecting its programs, press releases, and the online version of *National Service News* (which is also available automatically in your e-mail by subscribing to its mailing list). You can apply online for an AmeriCorps position. Click on "Resources" and find useful publications relating to citizen service, and links to related organizations, including state, national, and community service commissions, and general non-profit organizations/resources. This is an attractive site and a must-visit place for those interested in citizen service issues.

Impact Online

http://www.impactonline.org/

Impact Online's mission is to "facilitate and increase community involvement. Using technology, Impact Online has become a vehicle for turning good intentions into action." This collaborative organization seeks to complement existing services and build on community resources to get more people involved. Individuals can be members and can detail the skills they offer to agencies or organizations. Members can also share stories, articles and other information at this site. Finally, Impact Online offers a chat room for members to hold real-time discussions with colleagues. You can, for example, use this site as a meeting place (although a public one). This searchable site is flashy and the winner of many prestigious awards. And, in our opinion, there is as much steak as sizzle. The site has information about its program on Virtual Volunteering, which targets the development of volunteer activities that can be completed over the Internet. This is an idea that can really catch on, and by the time you read this, this program may be "virtually" everywhere.

Peace Corps

http://www.peacecorps.gov/

The Peace Corps site details the history and current work of this organization. Designed especially for those interested in volunteering, it details the work being done by 6,500 volunteers in 90 countries. Overviews, maps, political, economic, and other information for each country is available online, as well as contact information for the Peace Corps representatives there. Those visitors with specific skills can find out where they are most needed. Essays by and interviews with current and former Peace Corps volunteers help newcomers understand the rewards and challenges participation offers. For those interested in joining, the site includes an online application form as well as an order form for the packet of application materials. The global lesson plans, published entirely online, should be very useful to educators.

ServeNet

http://www.servenet.org/

A main function of this extensive and well-designed site is to enable potential volunteers to enter their ZIP code and find volunteer opportunities in their area. Organizations seeking volunteers can use this site to post volunteer positions available. Other resources here include extensive news items relating to national service, calendars, and discussion areas. The site features Youth Services America, a multi-organizational collaborative aiming to build healthier communities and to foster youth service. A "Source" section provides job opportunities and a database of volunteer–driven organizations in the U.S.

Volunteer Web

http://www.epicbc.com/volunteer/

This site allows would-be volunteers to post their interests and skills online for agencies to review and contact those with necessary skills. There is a discussion board, serving as an Internet version of a Usenet group on the topic of volunteerism. Organizations also can post their Web sites and volunteer opportunities here.

WOMEN

Cybergrrl

http://www.cybergrrl.com/

Community areas of this Web site are restricted to registered members only. Other resources and activities, such as shared stories and book reviews, are open to all. The site has several "Guides to Life," including college, social, love, family, and career. Visitors can submit their own stories for posting on the site.

Femina Resources for Women and Girls

http://www.femina.com/

A directory of Web resources for women and girls. It includes a search engine and topical organization including: art, business and finance, culture and diversity, education (women's studies, resources), family and motherhood (pregnancy, birth, parenting, family resources), feminism (activism, women's issues), girls, health and wellbeing, lesbians and bisexuals, organizations, politics (issues and actions), publications, religion and spirituality, resources, and women's writing.

The Feminist Majority

http://www.feminist.org

The Feminist Majority's mission is to work "in a variety of ways toward social, economic, and political justice and equity for women." This site is a well-rounded model for advocacy by a diverse group. Eleanor Smeal and Peg Yorkin founded the organization in 1987. Today, some 150,000 concerned women and men who firmly believe that women deserve political, economic, and social equality have joined The Feminist Majority. The site is a good example of a lot of information assembled in a very user-friendly fashion, making it easy for advocates to get current and archival information and to act on their interests. It contains a list of action steps people can take to help the cause, including options for joining feminist student and faculty networks, and the ability to submit information to an events calendar and share viewpoints in an ongoing census of public opinion on feminism. It has a collection of women's issues mailing lists; job banks; a site for posting research questions and answers; and a page to help advocates find and contact their members of Congress by entering their state of residence, names of members, or ZIP code.

National Abortion and Reproductive Rights Action League (NARAL)

http://www.naral.org

NARAL's mission is to promote "reproductive freedom and dignity for women and their families." Its site is another well-organized and focused site with a great deal of content online. In terms of online advocacy, there are some particularly nice touches. One is the ability to test legislators. One section asks how you would have voted on recent legislation and then presents how your legislators actually voted. Another feature is a clickable map listing all NARAL state affiliates and providing e-mail links, as well as the state status on reproductive rights and sex education. Third, there is a wonderfully comprehensive media contact list providing e-mail and Web links to the national TV networks (and all of their state affiliates online), the national news magazines, and a link to another site where you can search for your local newspapers and magazines. Another section includes shared stories of the site's visitors' experiences relating to the difficult choices involved in abortions.

Women Leaders On-line (WLO) Women Organizing for Change

http://www.wlo.org/

The purpose of WLO is "to build a powerful network of one million women and men to improve women's lives." This site was the first and largest women's advocacy group created on the Internet. The award-winning site is a wealth of women's information, with interactive e-mail lists, a feminist faxnet, lots of alerts, and various newsletters, feature stories, and even a humor page (with a unique and interesting "Family Values Flow Chart" that is a hyper-linked poignant joke/political statement). The site contains a lot of information and ways to get involved—both important for building an online movement.

Appendix A

State Home Pages on the World Wide Web

Alabama
http://alaweb.asc.edu

Alaska
http://www.state.ak.us

Arizona
http://www.state.az.us

Arkansas
http://www.state.ar.us

California
http://www.state.ca.us

Colorado
http://www.state.co.us

Connecticut
http://www.state.ct.us

Delaware
http://www.state.de.us

District of Columbia
http://www.dchomepage.net/
dcmain

Florida
http://www.state.fl.us

Georgia
http://www.state.ga.us

Hawaii
http://www.state.hi.us

Idaho
http://www.state.id.us

Illinois
http://www.state.il.us

Indiana
http://www.state.in.us

Iowa
http://www.state.ia.us

Kansas
http://www.state.ks.us

Kentucky
http://www.state.ky.us

Louisiana
http://www.state.la.us

Maine
http://www.state.me.us

Maryland
http://www.state.md.us

Massachusetts
http://www.state.ma.us

Michigan
http://www.migov.state.mi.us/

Minnesota
http://www.state.mn.us

Mississippi
http://www.state.ms.us

Missouri
http://www.state.mo.us

Montana
http://www.state.mt.us

Nebraska
http://www.state.ne.us

Nevada
http://www.state.nv.us

New Hampshire
http://www.state.nh.us

New Jersey
http://www.state.nj.us

New Mexico
http://www.state.nm.us

New York
http://www.state.ny.us

North Carolina
http://www.state.nc.us

North Dakota
http://www.state.nd.us

Ohio
http://www.state.oh.us

Oklahoma
http://www.state.ok.us

Oregon
http://www.state.or.us

Pennsylvania
http://www.state.pa.us

Rhode Island
http://www.state.ri.us

South Carolina
http://www.state.sc.us

South Dakota
http://www.state.sd.us

Tennessee
http://www.state.tn.us

Texas
http://www.state.tx.us

Utah
http://www.state.ut.us

Vermont
http://www.state.vt.us

Virginia
http://www.state.va.us

Washington
http://www.state.wa.us

West Virginia
http://www.state.wv.us

Wisconsin
http://www.state.wi.us

Wyoming
http://www.state.wy.us

MY INTERNET BOOKMARKS

Use this page to list "favorite" Web sites and their URLs.

TITLE OF SITE

BPD
CSWE
Gary Holden's Web Sites For Social Workers
NASW
The New Social Worker
SWAN

URL

http://www.rit.edu/~694www/bpd.htm
http://www.cswe.org
http://pages.nyu.edu/~gh5/gh-w3-f.htm
http://www.socialworkers.org
http://www.socialworker.com
http://www.sc.edu/swan/

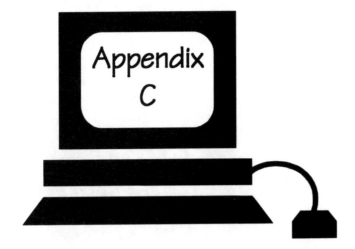

MY INTERNET PROJECTS

PROJECT	GOAL DATE	COMPLETED
Obtain Internet account	_____	_____
Send an e-mail message to a colleague	_____	_____
Join a professional e-mail mailing list	_____	_____
Find 5 Web sites I can use in my work	_____	_____
Find 3 ways to use the Internet with clients	_____	_____
Participate in an online social work chat	_____	_____

Create a Web site for:

myself	_____	_____
my agency	_____	_____

Additional projects:

_____	_____	_____
_____	_____	_____
_____	_____	_____
_____	_____	_____
_____	_____	_____
_____	_____	_____

Glossary

404—The error message that appears when you click on a hypertext link and the URL referenced by the link does not exist.

AltaVista—A popular and free search engine on the World Wide Web.

ASCII file—A file that contains only letters, numbers, and standard punctuation symbols from the American Standard Code for Information Exchange character set, and is the standard for the exchange of information between computer programs that may otherwise be incompatible. ASCII files do not contain formatting codes (such as those indicating that text is bold or italicized).

Binary file—A file consisting of characters other than those from the ASCII character set, including all word processing, sound, video, graphics, and compressed files.

BitNet—An acronym for Because It's Time Network, BitNet, operated by the Center for Research and Education Networking, is a network linking thousands of research and educational institutions. Its best-known application is Internet mailing lists.

Baud rate—The number of bits of information that can be transmitted through a modem, usually equal to about half the BPS (bits per second) rate.

Bit—A binary (consisting of two possibilities, 0 and 1) code that is the basic unit for the transfer of data in a computer.

Bookmark—A feature of a Web browser that saves a Web site's address in a log. It permits you to return to that Web page by clicking on "bookmark" or other icon (such as "favorite places") the first time you access the page, and then return to that page by accessing the bookmark rather than having to remember and retype that page's Web address.

BBS (Bulletin Board System)—A dial-in computer host, usually community-based, that permits you to log in and view information, and download or upload files.

Browser—A computer program that permits access to the World Wide Web by reading and interpreting HTML files. A browser may be text-only (such as Lynx), or graphical (such as Netscape Navigator or Microsoft® Internet Explorer).

Byte—A basic measurement of computer storage, using a binary system. A megabyte is 1,048,576 bytes, and each byte contains a unique 8-bit string of information, which is associated with a number, letter, or symbol.

Chat—A telecommunications system that permits two or more people to use their keyboards to communicate in real time and engage in "conversations." The chatters view on their monitors what each types in.

Commercial Service Provider—A commercial company (such as AOL, CompuServe, or Microsoft® Network) that provides an Internet connection as well as online content (such as forums, chat, news, and other information and files) that is accessible only to its subscribers.

Counter—A software program that tracks the number of accesses or hits to a web page.

Cyberspace—The virtual space in which electronic communication by computer takes place, including the physical and metaphysical residence of e-mail, Web sites, and other Internet communication modalities.

Domain name—The part of the Internet address that identifies the specific organization being communicated with and converts the numerical Internet Protocol addresses into names with letters, which can be more easily remembered.

E-mail (electronic mail)—Messages that arrive on your computer from other computers through the telephone lines via a data connection from the Internet or an Intranet or other network.

Emoticon—A drawing made by using characters from the ASCII character set, depicting emotion or body language that would otherwise not be able to be conveyed solely by conventional text-based electronic communication.

Encryption—Disguising messages for security purposes by using cryptography "keys" that permit only the sender and receiver to decode them. Those without the correct keys see only gobbledygook.

FAQ (Frequently Asked Questions)—A file of questions and answers found in Usenet News Groups, web pages, and other Internet-related documents that is prepared to assist new participants. May be pronounced "fack" or "F-A-Q."

File—A set of computer-generated information, such as a document, database, or Web page, that is identified by a unique name and is created, transferred, copied, or downloaded/uploaded as a distinct unit. Files are stored on hard disks or other storage media, and are organized by using directories and subdirectories.

Flame—An electronic message that contains abusive, denigrating, threatening, or inciting language, and is often directed to those deemed by the sender(s) to have violated the informal rules of Internet conduct.

Freenet—A type of Bulletin Board Service (BBS) that provides free (usually), community-based information and downloadable files, and inexpensive or free access to the Internet and e-mail.

Freeware—Software programs that are available free for public use.

FTP (File Transfer Protocol)—A standard for exchanging files over the Internet that requires log-in and use of a password (although many FTP sites permit "anonymous" or "guest" to serve as the password).

GIF (Graphic Image File)—The most popular format for graphics files on the World Wide Web. The file extension *.gif* is used for these files.

Gopher—A text-only, menu-based system developed at the University of Minnesota that helps find files, programs, and other resources on the Internet. Gopher servers are being replaced by the World Wide Web, which is graphical and more "user-friendly."

Graphical User Interface (GUI)—Software that utilizes windows, icons, menus, buttons, and other graphics-related devices.

Hardware—The physical components of your computer and its peripheral equipment, including the disks (although the coded instructions on the disk are *software*).

Hit—A count each time someone visits a Web page. The term also refers to the number of matches a search engine accesses in response to a search term.

Home page—The World Wide Web page that is intended as the entry point to an entire Web site of an identifiable person or group (it may also be the *only* page on a one-page site). It usually includes introductory and identifying information, as well as links to the rest of the site's pages. It also refers to the page that appears on your browser when you first open the browser.

Host—The computer that makes its files and data available to other computers and is directly connected to the Internet. An Internet host is the computer that serves as the intermediary from the Internet to the consumer end-user.

HTML (Hyper Text Markup Language)—The programming language for World Wide Web pages, which consists of coded tag pairs using symbols from the ASCII character set, formatting documents for the World Wide Web.

Hyperlink—A part of a Web page that is coded so that when a viewer clicks on it, he/she is taken to another Web page, and can navigate back and forth between these pages. Viewers see the hyperlink as text or a graphic that is bold, underlined, or a different color, and that, depending on the browser, indicates it is a link by a change in the icon that appears when the pointing device's cursor is on it.

Internet—The system in which millions of computers worldwide are linked for the purpose of electronic mail, mailing lists, newsgroups, and the World Wide Web.

Internet Relay Chat (IRC)—An online version of citizens band radio that permits real time communication over the Internet.

Internet Service Provider (ISP)—A business that makes the Internet accessible to consumers via a dial-up service to a local number for a monthly fee.

IP address—The numerical address that is unique to a computer and forms the basis of its domain name, which is converted from the IP address.

ISDN (Integrated Services Digital Network)—A type of telecommunications cable that permits data transfer at several times the speed of conventional modems.

JAVA—A programming language that supports animations and other sophisticated special effects on World Wide Web pages.

JPEG—A format for World Wide Web page graphics. The file extension *.jpg* is used for these files.

Keyword—A word used by an online service that serves as a gateway to files, chat, newsgroups, news, and other Internet content related to that word. It also refers to a word searched by search engines to find Internet files and pages.

Link—A reference to a file or Web page placed in an HTML file that, when clicked on using an Internet browser, takes the viewer directly to that Web page or file. (See also hyperlink.)

Listserv®—Commercially developed mailing list software that permits the management of e-mail mailing lists.

Lurk—To observe postings in mailing lists, newsgroups, or chat discussions without actively participating. Lurking is recommended before active participation.

Lycos—A popular, free search engine on the Internet.

Mailing lists—A system that permits Internet users to subscribe to an e-mail discussion group that is topical, and to post a message that will be automatically sent to all other subscribers of that list. The software that manages these lists is usually either Listserv® or MajorDomo.

MajorDomo—A freeware mailing list management program manager that uses the UNIX operating system.

Megabyte—A measure of computer data storage equal to 1,048,576 bytes.

Modem—A communications hardware device that transmits computer data over telephone lines by converting the computer's digital signals to analog, and the telephone's analog signals to digital.

MOO—MUD Object Oriented. A variation of MUD (see below).

MUD—Multi-User Dungeon (or Multi-User Dimension). An online simulated environment, in which one can interact with other users in real time. The first MUDs were simulations of the game Dungeons and Dragons, but they are now used for other purposes, such as education. Usually text-based, although some MUDs use virtual reality settings and 3-D.

MUSH—An online real-time interactive virtual environment. A variation of MUD. MUSH was not originally an acronym for anything, but some have dubbed it "Multi-User Shared Hallucination." Mostly text-based.

Netiquette—Internet etiquette, a set of unwritten (for the most part) rules that have developed in the Internet culture and serve as rules of conduct.

Newbie—An inexperienced Internet user who is not familiar with netiquette or FAQ files, and who often annoys experienced users, all of whom were once newbies.

Online—Being connected through the telephone lines to another computer.

Protocol—A set of technical standards that permits two different types of computer systems to interconnect, usually in a way that is transparent to the end user.

Public domain—Intellectual property (such as software, books, clip art) that is not copyrighted, and can be freely copied and distributed without paying royalties to the creator.

RAM (Random Access Memory)—The computer's primary working memory. The more you have, the more programs you can have running simultaneously.

Real Time—Communication between or among Internet users that occurs simultaneously, such as through chat, as contrasted to the exchange of e-mail.

Search engine—A computer program that searches a database (which may contain millions of World Wide Web pages) or the World Wide Web itself and that is accessed by filling out an online form with a word or phrase to be searched, and parameters relating to the format of the answer you desire.

Server—A computer that that makes services available on a network.

Shareware—Computer programs that are made available free-of-charge on a trial basis, with an address to send a fee if the user likes it or wishes to purchase upgrades or additional software.

Signature file—A footer automatically attached to an e-mail message, providing identifying information about the sender and, in some cases, artwork and inspirational messages or favorite quotations.

Snail mail—Communications sent via the U.S. Postal Service.

Software—The machine-language component of computer programs, which provides the instructions to the computer needed to drive applications such as word processing, database, spreadsheets, Web browsers, desktop publishing, and others.

Spam—Large numbers of inappropriate or otherwise undesirable e-mail messages, including bulk commercial messages (also called "junk e-mail"). When used as a verb, refers to the process of generating hundreds or thousands of such messages to a violator of netiquette as a form of punishment, or to sending bulk junk e-mail.

Surf—To navigate through the World Wide Web by following interesting links.

Telnet—A protocol that permits computers to access a remote computer using telephone lines, such as a Mainframe or those used on BBSs.

UNIX—A computer operating system used by many mainframe computers (because it was provided free by Bell Laboratories to hundreds of large institutions when the Internet was in its infancy), and thus continues to be in wide use, despite its reputation for not being "user friendly."

URL (uniform resource locator)—A unique address on the Internet.

Virus—A computer program, designed as a prank or sabotage, that modifies or destroys the victim's computer capabilities. A virus is uploaded to the victim's computer by deception.

Webmaster—The individual who designs or administers a Web site.

Web page—An individual file/document at a Web site, which has a unique address and appears when you click on the hypertext link coded with that address or when you type the address into your browser.

Web site—A collection of related and linked Web pages that is developed by one entity. Typically, a Web site has a home page that directs readers to other pages within the site using hyperlinks.

World Wide Web—A feature of the Internet that uses files containing hypertext links, which permit the viewer to navigate among potentially millions of computer hosts by clicking on the part of the computer screen that shows those links.

Yahoo!—A popular Internet search engine and directory.

ADDITIONAL
READING
RESOURCES

Here are some suggestions for further reading. Also, check out Smartbooks.com *(http://www.smartbooks.com)* or an online bookstore, such as Amazon.com *(http://www.amazon.com)*, for an up-to-date and comprehensive list of available books. Consider yourself warned—this field changes quickly, and books about the Internet quickly become outdated or obsolete. Books published within the last year are likely to be the most current and accurate.

ARTICLES

Kirk, Elizabeth E. (1996). Evaluating Information Found on the Internet. Available online at *http://milton.mse.jhu.edu:8001/research/education/net.html.*

Marson, Stephen M. (1997). A Selective History of Internet Technology and Social Work, *Computers in Human Services*, Vol. 14, Number 2, p. 35.

Summers, Edward H. (1998). Gateways to Social Work/Welfare on the Net, *College and Research Library News*, Vol. 59, Number 3. Also available online at *http://www.ala.org/acrl/resmar98.html.*

BOOKS

Broadhurst, Judith A. (1995). *The Woman's Guide to Online Services*. New York: McGraw-Hill.

Clark, David. (1996). *Student Guide to the Internet (Second Edition)*. Indianapolis, IN: Que.

Crumlish, Christian. (1995). *A Guided Tour of the Internet*. Alameda, CA: Sybex.

Glister, Paul. (1995). *The New Internet Navigator*. New York: John Wiley & Sons, Inc.

Glossbrenner, Alfred and Emily. (1994). *Internet Slick Tricks*. New York: Random House.

Grobman, Gary, and Grant, Gary. (1998). *The Non-Profit Internet Handbook*. Harrisburg, PA: White Hat Communications.

Grohol, John M. (1997). *The Insider's Guide to Mental Health Resources Online*. New York: Guilford Press.

Hahn, Harley & Stout, Rick. (1994). *The Internet Complete Reference*. Berkeley, CA: Osborne McGraw-Hill.

Haskin, David. (1997). *Microsoft Internet Explorer Tour Guide*. Research Triangle Park, North Carolina: Ventana Communications Group, Inc.

Johnson, Eugenia, and McFadden, Kathleen. (1997). *Seniornet's Official Guide to the Web*. Indianapolis, IN: MacMillan Computer Publishing.

Kane, Pamela. (1994). *The Hitchhiker's Guide to the Electronic Highway*. New York: MIS Press.

Kardas, Edward P. (1995). *Using the Internet for Social Science Research and Practice*. Belmont, CA: Wadsworth Publishing Company.

Kehoe, Brendan P. (1992). *Zen and the Art of the Internet: A Beginners Guide* (2nd ed.). Englewood Cliffs, NJ: PTR Prentice Hall.

Kennedy, Angus J. (1996). *The Internet & World Wide Web. The Rough Guide 2.0*. London, England: Rough Guides, Ltd.

LaBruzza, Anthony L. (1997). *The Essential Internet: A Guide for Psychotherapists and Other Mental Health Professionals*. Northvale, NJ: Jason Aronson.

Lambert, Steve and Howe, Walt. (1993). *Internet Basics*. New York: Random House.

LaQuey, Tracy with Jeanne C. Ryer; foreword by Al Gore. (1993). *The Internet Companion: A Beginner's Guide to Global Networking*. Reading, MA: Addison-Wesley.

Motan, Amanda M. (1997). *Cyberhound's Guide to Associations and Nonprofit Organizations on the Internet*. Detroit, MI: Gale Research.

Miller, Michael. (1995). *Easy Internet*. Indianapolis, IN: Que.

Pack, Ellen. (1997). *Women's Wire Web Directory*. Indianapolis, IN: Que.

Papert, Seymour. (1996). *The Connected Family: Bridging the Digital General Gap*. Marietta, GA: Longstreet Press.

Polly, Jean Amour. (1997). *Internet Kids and Family Yellow Pages, Second Edition*. Berkeley, CA: Osborne/McGraw-Hill.

Rankin, Bob. (1995). *Dr. Bob's Painless Guide to the Internet*. San Francisco, CA: No Starch Press.

Rosenfeld, Louis, Janes, Joseph, and Kolk, Martha Vander. (Eds.). (1995). *The Internet Compendium: Subject Guides to Social Sciences, Business and Law Resources*. New York: Neal-Schuman Publishers.

Stout, Rick. (1996). *The World Wide Web Complete Reference*. Berkeley, CA: Osborne McGraw-Hill.

Wiggins, Richard. (1994). *The Internet for Everyone: A Guide for Users and Providers*. New York: McGraw-Hill.

Young, Kimberly S. (1998). *Caught in the Net*. New York: John Wiley and Sons.

Zeff, Robbin L. (1996). *The Nonprofit Guide to the Internet*. New York: John Wiley and Sons.

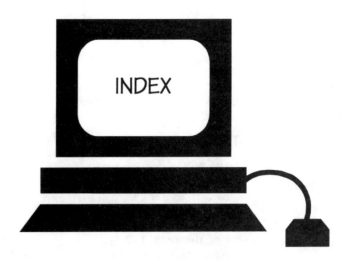

INDEX

*NOTE: Index entries in **bold** indicate glossary entries.*

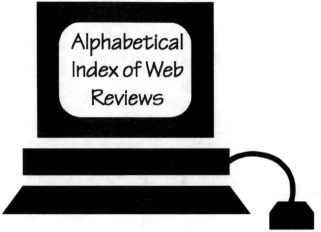

Alphabetical
Index of Web
Reviews

ABOUT THE AUTHORS

Gary B. Grant is Associate Dean for External Affairs at the University of Chicago School of Social Service Administration. He received his B.A. in history from the University of Chicago in 1987 and his J.D. from Illinois Institute of Technology, Chicago-Kent College of Law in 1994. He has been involved in many innovative projects at SSA that involve social work students and alumni in using the Internet, and he teaches professional development classes there on "Uses of the Internet in Social Work." In his spare time, Gary serves as a Vice-President with the Hyde Park/ Kenwood Community Conference, where he heads a project to build an Internet gateway to the community and to promote uses of the Internet for non-profit organizations and businesses. The co-author with Gary Grobman of *THE NON-PROFIT INTERNET HANDBOOK*, he lives in Chicago with his wife Kerry and their daughter, Alyann.

Linda May Grobman, ACSW, LSW, is editor and publisher of *THE NEW SOCIAL WORKER*, the national magazine for social work students and recent graduates, and editor of the book *DAYS IN THE LIVES OF SOCIAL WORKERS*. She received her B. M. (Music Therapy) from the University of Georgia in 1977 and her MSW from UGA in 1982. Linda has been a social worker in mental health and medical settings, and is a former staff member of the Pennsylvania and Georgia Chapters of the National Association of Social Workers. Linda uses the Internet daily to connect with other social workers around the world, and she has presented workshops on Internet use at national, state, and local gatherings of social workers.

ABOUT THE CONTRIBUTORS

John Aravosis is the founder of Wired Strategies, a strategic Internet consulting firm based in Washington, DC. He is the former online lobbyist at the Children's Defense Fund, and can be reached at: john@wiredstrategies.com.

Carolyn Biondi is a graduate of the University of Chicago School of Social Service Administration, and is employed by the Sinai Family Health Centers as a grants manager. She uses the Internet every day to assist her in project planning, fund-raising, and prospect research. A newlywed, she lives in Evanston, IL.

Robert Canon, Ph.D, is Systems Analyst at the University of Texas at Austin, School of Social Work.

Gary Grobman is the co-author with Gary Grant of *The Non-Profit Internet Handbook*. He also wrote *The Pennsylvania Non-Profit Handbook* and *The Non-Profit Handbook National Edition*. Before devoting himself full time to writing and publishing, he was executive director of a statewide non-profit organization for 13 years.

David Grotke, CSW(R), is a graduate of the University of Chicago School of Social Service Administration. Now retired and living in New York State, he has worked in mental health and child protective services settings.

Jennifer Luna-Idunate, MSSW, is Coordinator of the Career Development and Resource Center, University of Texas at Austin, School of Social Work.

Sheila Peck, LCSW, is a practice consultant, lecturer, writer, and computer buff who practices psychotherapy in Island Park, NY. She was co-founder of the Center for Women and Achievement, where she helped professionals build their businesses. She offers seminars and consultation in public relations and practice-building. She is also public relations chair for the New York State Clinical Social Work Society, heads Media Watch for the Clinical Social Work Federation, and edits several newsletters. She has presented a number of seminars on "Clinicians, Computers, and Cyberspace." She can be reached at sheila2688@aol.com.

Steve Roller is a graduate of the University of Chicago School of Social Service Administration with an A.M. in Social Administration. He is the manager of the Grant Development Unit of the Chicago Housing Authority's Grant Administration Department, and assists in the design and management of his employer's Web site.

Anna Senkevitch is the co-developer of the Alumni Internet Training Program and editor of the manual, The Online Social Worker, for the University of Chicago School of Social Service Administration, where she also is a doctoral student.

Tobi Ann Shane received her BSSW from Loyola University Chicago. In 1997, she became the Webmaster of the Social Work Café and a founding member of the Social Work Student Nexus. She has conducted corporate and college Internet seminars. While pursuing graduate studies at the University of Chicago School of Social Administration, Tobi will work as development assistant to the Dean of External Affairs.

Robert Tell is a graduate of the University of Chicago School of Social Service Administration with an A.M. in social work. He works for the Counseling Center of Lake View in Chicago, and is the creator of Rob's Page of Social Work at http://www.enteract.com/~ratell/socwork.html.

Also from White Hat Communications...

Spend a day with 41 professional social workers, each in a different setting. Take a look at the ups and downs and ins and outs of their real-life days in the "trenches" of social work practice.

Days in the Lives of Social Workers

41 Professionals Tell "Real-Life" Stories from Social Work Practice

Edited by Linda May Grobman

This book is the ultimate guide to social work careers. Whether you are a social work student, an experienced professional wishing to make a change in career direction, or just thinking about going into the field, you will learn valuable lessons from the experiences described in *DAYS IN THE LIVES OF SOCIAL WORKERS*.

Edited by Linda May Grobman, ACSW, LSW
Founder, publisher, and editor of *THE NEW SOCIAL WORKER*.

ISBN: 0-9653653-8-7   Library of Congress Cat. Number 96-61105   1996   Price: $14.95   266 pages
Shipping/Handling: add $2.00/first book, $.75/each additional book in U.S.
Canadian orders: add $4.00/book
Other orders outside the U.S.: add $8.00/book
If ordering from Pennsylvania, add 6% sales tax.

Please send ___ copies of *DAYS IN THE LIVES OF SOCIAL WORKERS*.
❑Enclosed is a check for $_____ made payable to "White Hat Communications."
Please charge my: ❑ MasterCard   ❑ VISA

Card # _____
Expiration Date _____
Name as it appears on card _____
Signature _____

NAME _____
ADDRESS _____
ADDRESS _____
CITY/STATE/ZIP _____
TELEPHONE NUMBER _____

Send order form and payment to: WHITE HAT COMMUNICATIONS
P.O. Box 5390, Harrisburg, PA 17110-0390
Telephone or fax orders (Mastercard or Visa): 717-238-3787
Online orders: http://www.socialworker.com

Table of Contents